Douglas Brooke Wheelton Sladen

A Century of Australian Song

Douglas Brooke Wheelton Sladen
A Century of Australian Song
ISBN/EAN: 9783337019624

Printed in Europe, USA, Canada, Australia, Japan

Cover: Foto ©Thomas Meinert / pixelio.de

More available books at **www.hansebooks.com**

FIFTY YEARS'

BIOGRAPHICAL REMINISCENCES.

VOLUME I.

FIFTY YEARS'

BIOGRAPHICAL REMINISCENCES.

BY

LORD WILLIAM PITT LENNOX.

IN TWO VOLUMES.

VOL. I.

LONDON:
HURST AND BLACKETT, PUBLISHERS,
SUCCESSORS TO HENRY COLBURN,
13, GREAT MARLBOROUGH STREET.
1863.
The right of Translation is reserved.

LONDON :
PRINTED BY MACDONALD AND TUGWELL, BLENHEIM HOUSE.

CONTENTS

OF

THE FIRST VOLUME.

CHAPTER I.

Memorable Year—My Father—His Duel with the Duke of York—The Great Event—My Godfather—The Right Honourable William Pitt—My Cousin Charles James Fox—Political Patronage—State of Political Parties—Pitt's Retirement—The Addington Administration—Mr. Pitt's Return to Office—His Death—The Grenville Administration—Demise of Mr. Fox, and Dissolution of "All the Talents"—Duke of Portland's Ministry—Death of Charles, third Duke of Richmond—His Character—My Father appointed Lord Lieutenant of Ireland—Goodwood—A Fox Hunt in 1739 1

CHAPTER II.

Duelling—The Pic-Nics—A Dinner at the Neapolitan Club—Scandals—Satirists and Caricaturists—Fashionable Entertainments—Sporting Events—The Barrymore Family—Colonel George Hanger—The Duchess of Gordon and her Beautiful Daughters—The Duchess of Devonshire—Mrs. Fitzherbert and her Serenader—The Prince and Princess of Wales—The Rival Courts at Carlton Palace and Blackheath—Fashion in Dress—Beau Brummell — Romeo Coates — Theatres and Operas — Fashionable Songs 33

CHAPTER III.

My Early Education—Westminster School—Its Distinguished Scholars—Very Old Westminsters—Travelling to Ireland—Holidays at the Phœnix Park, Dublin—My Pantomime—Revelries at the Castle—My Introduction to Sir Arthur Wellesley—Bet of the Lord Lieutenant with Sir Edward Crofton—Return to Goodwood—The Mansion and Estate—The Kennel—Tom Grant—Hunting at Stoke—Racing at Goodwood—Richmond House—Whitehall—Rival Beauties—Female Admirers of Mr. Pitt and Mr. Fox—Poetical Description of the Fair Foxites—Their Loss to Society 83

CHAPTER IV.

Thoughts of a Profession—Building Castles—Life of a Westminster Boy—Fagging—My School Contemporaries—The Margravine of Anspach—Dublin Society—Lady Morgan's Statements—Miss Owenson, the Wild Irish Girl—Marchioness of Abercorn—Dr. Morgan—He is Knighted by my Father, and Marries Miss Owenson—Dr. Cary, the Head Master of Westminster School—Results of going out of Bounds—I am Betrayed—My Tutor—Fellow Pupils—Theatre at Newbury—" Hamlet" Interrupted 111

CHAPTER V.

The Duke of Wellington—My First Letter from his Grace—My First Interview—Am appointed to join the Embassy at Paris as Attaché—Journey from England with the Duke—On board the *Griffon*—The Duke at Bergen-op-Zoom—Entertainments at Brussels—Presentation of the Order of the Bath to the Prince of Orange—The Duke and the Newspapers—Inspection of Fortresses—Mistaken for a Great Man—Journey to Paris—State Reception of the Duke of Wellington by Louis XVIII.—Fête of St. Louis—French Plays—My French Master, M. Galley 131

CHAPTER VI.

France in 1815—Comte d'Orsay—The late Duke of Cambridge—Distribution and Consecration of the Colours of the National Guard in the Champ de Mars—The Approach of Napoleon—

Meet of the Royal Hounds at Grosbois and Rambouillet—The Duke's turn-out as a Huntsman in the Style of the French Court—St. Germain-en-Laye—Taking French Leave of my French Master—The Chateau of Chantilly—A Day's Hunting at Versailles—I accidentally Lame one of the Duke's Horses—Talma in " Oreste"—The Duke's Kindness of Manner—French Stag-Hunting with Royal Sportsmen—The Duc de Berri—The Duc d'Angouleme—The Duc de Grammont—Versailles—Madame Grassini 157

CHAPTER VII.

Parisian Enjoyments—Proposed Congress—The Duke of Wellington takes leave of Louis XVIII.—Journey to Vienna—Society in the Austrian Capital—Distinguished Personages—Grand Tournament—The Imperial Palace—Royal Families of Austria, Prussia, and Russia—Court Ball—Death of Prince d'Arenberg—Introduction to the King of Rome—Lord Stewart's Fox-Hounds—Prince Eugene Beauharnois—Frederick von Gentz—Viscount Castlereagh—Prince Talleyrand—Interruption of the Congress—Isaby's Picture of the Congress of Vienna—English Quizzing 187

CHAPTER VIII.

Napoleon's Progress in France—The Empress Marie Louise and her Son at Schönbrun—Arrangements of the Allies—The Duke of Wellington leaves Vienna—Arrival at Brussels—I Join General Maitland's Staff—Riding a Cossack Horse—My Accident—Letters from the Duke of Wellington and Lord Saltoun—Preparations of Wellington—Napoleon's Advance—French Romantic Accounts of Waterloo—M. Thiers—The Duchess of Richmond's Ball at Brussels—Appearance of the Duke there—A Trap laid for the French Emperor—Victor Hugo's Romance of Waterloo—Visit to the Battle-field during the French Attack—General Alava—Lord Hay—Scene at Brussels—The Duke after the Battle 221

CHAPTER IX.

March of the English Army into France—Attack on Peronne—Letter of the Marshal Prince of Eckmuhl and General Davoust—Duke of Wellington's and Prince Blücher's Replies—My Visit to the Field of Battle—I accompany Colonel Hunter Blair to Paris—The Duke's General Order—The Dutch-Belgian Troops—A Visit to an Abandoned Village—French Sentries—Quarters in the Bois de Boulogne—Wellington and Napoleon 259

CHAPTER X.

Bourbonists and Bonapartists—The Allied Armies Enter Paris—The Duke of Wellington and the Assassin Cantillon—French Jokes—The English in France—Walter Scott—Catalani—Banquets by the King of France in Honour of the Duke—French Cookery—Celebrated Restaurateurs—The Parisian Theatres—The Horse-dealer Hunted—English Sports at Neuilly—Marshal Ney—Sir Charles and Lady Morgan in Paris—The Marquis de la Fayette—Mrs. Patterson and Jerome Bonaparte—The Baltimore Beauty in France—Her Love of Scandal—She Slanders the Duke of Wellington—Madame Grassini's Opinions of Napoleon and Wellington—Thomas Moore at Paris—The Irish Physician—The Fudge Family—Kenney, the Dramatist—Thomas Holcroft and his French Ward—A Nervous Man 279

CHAPTER XI.

My Mission to the " Hague"—Mistaken for a Russian General—Flemish Account—Interview with the King of Holland—Awkward Results of getting a Speech by Heart—A State Dinner at the Palace—Return to Paris—" Les Anglaises pour Rire"—Neglect of Duty—The Duke's Reprimand—A Dreadful Bore—The Duke's Kindness—His General Order—M. de Lavalette and Sir Robert Wilson—The English Army Retires from Paris—Newspaper Attacks on the Duke—His Visit to the Hague—Valenciennes—The Duke's Patronage of Field Sports—Colonel Felton Hervey—Negligence of the Duke's Staff—Regulation Uniform—Visit of the Dukes of Kent and Cambridge—Review on the Plains of Denain—Garrison Races—Joe Kelly—The Duke's State Coachman—Foxhounds 317

CHAPTER I.

MEMORABLE YEAR—MY FATHER—HIS DUEL WITH THE DUKE OF YORK—THE GREAT EVENT—MY GODFATHER—THE RIGHT HONOURABLE WILLIAM PITT—MY COUSIN CHARLES JAMES FOX—POLITICAL PATRONAGE—STATE OF POLITICAL PARTIES—PITT'S RETIREMENT—THE ADDINGTON ADMINISTRATION—MR. PITT'S RETURN TO OFFICE—HIS DEATH—THE GRENVILLE ADMINISTRATION—DEMISE OF MR. FOX, AND DISSOLUTION OF "ALL THE TALENTS"—DUKE OF PORTLAND'S MINISTRY——DEATH OF CHARLES, THIRD DUKE OF RICHMOND—HIS CHARACTER—MY FATHER APPOINTED LORD LIEUTENANT OF IRELAND—GOODWOOD—A FOX-HUNT IN 1739.

CHAPTER I.

THE year 1799 was remarkable for many memorable events, foreign and domestic. Among the former may be mentioned the capture of Gaza and Jaffa, by General Buonaparte, against whom, or rather against the Government by whom he was employed, in the month of April, Great Britain, Austria, part of the German Empire, Naples, Portugal, Russia, Turkey, and the States of Barbary, formed a second coalition. The French Plenipotentiaries, Bonnière, Roberjest, and Jean Derby, were attacked by assassins on their departure from Radstadt, and the first two died of their wounds. On the 4th of May, Seringapatam was taken by storm by the British force, and Tippoo Saib fell in the conflict; and on the 17th, Moreau was defeated by Suwarrow, near Alexandria. In July, Mantua surrendered, by capitulation, to the Allies, after a blockade of two months, and a bombardment of four days. In August, the French were defeated by the Austro-Russians at Novi, with the loss of ten thousand men, and Joubert, their commander; Surinam surrendered to the British; Sir Ralph Abercrombie landed at the Helder, Buonaparte left the army in Egypt to General Kleber, and embarked for France; Pope Louis VI. died, aged eighty-two; and the Dutch fleet in the Texel struck their flag to Admiral Mitchell. Before the end of the year the Duke of York landed in Holland, and shortly afterwards took Alkmaer; a new constitution for France was decreed in Paris, Buonaparte as First Consul, Cambacères the second, and Le Brun the third. Washington died in America, and the First Consul wrote his celebrated letter to George III.

At home a proposition was laid before Parliament for the union with Ireland; a tax upon income received the Royal assent; the Earl of Thanet and Mr. Robert Ferguson were found guilty of a charge of riot and assault at Maidstone, at the conclusion of the trial of Arthur O'Connor, for high treason; and the Earl was sentenced to be imprisoned one year, and pay a fine of £1,000, while the commoner was let off for the same amount of imprisonment, and a fine of £100. In June, the King reviewed 12,000 of the Volunteers in Hyde Park, and, owing to the inclemency of the weather, many of them—so the chronicler of the time records—caught cold and died. Parliament was prorogued on the 12th July, and on the same day printing-presses were licenced in England, in order to suppress the seditious temper of the times.

On the 24th of September, Parliament re-assembled; and in December it was announced that the Unredeemed National Debt of Great Britain amounted to £392,612,323, what was then considered an alarming sum: it has since reached three times this amount. Important, however, as were these events, one that ought to be considered of far deeper interest to "the courteous reader" I have yet to chronicle, and to one at least of the parties most nearly concerned it was really of vital importance. It was made known to the public, among the births that were announced in the daily newspapers, in the closing month of the year, in the following form :—

"*Lady Charlotte Lennox of a son.*"

This important event, of which I may consider myself the hero, took place at Winestead, the birth-place of another great man—if I say a great man, I do not think the reader will consider that I have done much violence to my modesty, for he was Andrew Marvell, as favourably known in history as in literature. His father was rector of the parish, and removed to Hull in Andrew's infancy, which has led some writers to describe him as a native of that port. The patriot is as well known as the poet, therefore I need say little about him; but of his charming verses I remember a few lines, which I now, with far more climbing experience than the writer, wish I had borne in mind:

> "Climb at court for me that will—
> Tottering favour's pinnacle;
> All I seek is to lie still,
> Settled in some secret nest,
> In calm leisure let me rest,
> And far off the public stage,
> Pass away my silent age.
> Thus when, without noise, unknown,
>   I have lived out all my span,
>   I shall die without a groan,
>   An old, honest, countryman."

To show how impossible it was for me to realise the poet's wish, I must acquaint the reader with circumstances that had a particular influence on my destiny. A few years before my birth, party feeling ran very high; and when the head of my family, alarmed by the excesses of the French Revolution, left the political friends with whom he had acted, and joined the young minister, William Pitt, in his strenuous endeavour to save the nation from the ruin which he thought republican doctrines were preparing for it, the outcry of the opposition against him was very violent.

The Duke of Richmond was a whig of the old school. He carried his party predilections into the hunting-field, by having the colours of the Goodwood hunt, those which his kinsman Fox had popularised in his familiar blue coat and buff waistcoat. The Duke's change of sentiments was fiercely resented by the Foxites—particularly by the Prince of Wales and his brother the Duke of York—and their hostility was exasperated by the support he gave Pitt in the stringent clauses of the Regency Bill. Such animosity became so venomous, that all the Lennox family were involved in the odium which the political adherents of the Heir-apparent chose to cast upon them.

In a fashionable club, mostly supported by officers of the army, known as "Daubigny's," this feeling was demonstrated in a most offensive manner, and the observations that were made, as it was said, in the presence of a member of the family, who held a commission in the Guards, were reported to the Duke of York, the Colonel of his regiment. The latter, who was as bitter against the Duke of Richmond as the most intemperate of the Foxites, replied that Colonel Lennox had listened to language which no officer or gentleman ought to have tolerated—adding, in a significant manner, "The Lennoxes don't fight." His Royal Highness was making an unfair allusion to the result of a challenge which the Duke of Richmond had received from a peer to whom his grace had made an offensive remark during a debate in the House of

Lords, to which I shall refer more at length in a subsequent page.

During an inspection of the regiment of the Coldstream Guards, in the parade in St. James's Park, in the spring of 1789, one of the captains was observed to leave his position, walk up to the commanding-officer, and, in a firm voice, demand an explanation of certain words of an offensive nature which His Royal Highness had been heard to utter in reference to him. The officers within hearing were filled with consternation, and the Duke of York was evidently taken by surprise. He contented himself with ordering the offender back to his post. His Royal Highness, however, knew that he had completely placed himself in the wrong, and that after so public a display of spirit by the person he had insulted, one course only was left to him. After the parade, when in the Orderly Room at the Horse Guards, he sent for the young Captain, and, in the presence of his brother-officers, thus addressed him:

"I desire to derive no protection from my rank as a Prince, or my station as commanding officer. When not on duty I wear a brown coat, and shall be ready, as a private gentleman, to give you satisfaction."

It should be borne in mind that the social status of the two presented not quite so strong a contrast as their military positions. The Captain, who was a

Lieutenant-Colonel in the army, was heir to a dukedom, and his ancestor had worn the English crown not much more than a hundred years before. The offence which the second son of George the Third had committed would have placed him on a level with any private gentleman, had it been directed against him, and had he resolved to resent it. This was so perfectly understood, that there was no difficulty in obtaining seconds for either party; and when they were selected, an apology or a duel became an imperative necessity. The former not being forthcoming, a meeting was arranged to take place at Wimbledon. Pistols were the weapons employed, and one was handed to each of the combatants, who were to fire together at the usual signal. When this was given, the Lieutenant-Colonel fired, and the ball was so near taking a fatal direction, that it grazed one of His Royal Highness's side curls. The Duke refused to fire. The seconds then adjudged that satisfaction had been given, and took their principals off the ground.

The affair created a profound sensation in society, but was very far, indeed, from having an injurious influence on the prospects of the young officer, who, in so unprecedentedly bold a manner, had stood up in defence of his own honour. The Duke of York was unpopular at Court, for the obnoxious part he had taken in supporting the Prince of Wales during the unseemly struggle the latter, in conjunction with his great political advisers, Fox and Sheridan, had been carrying on against Pitt, to wrest from their afflicted sovereign and father the royal authority. Completely to their discomfiture, the King recovered from his malady, and a public thanksgiving was manifested, under circumstances of extraordinary solemnity, at St. Paul's, on the 23rd of April.

The Duke of York's opponent was not only received, wherever he presented himself, with the most cordial demonstrations, but was honoured with an invitation to a State Ball, given at St. James's Palace, where all the loyal members of the Court rivalled each other in the warmth of their reception. This so annoyed the Prince of Wales, that he displayed his displeasure in a manner that was equally an affront to the Queen's guests as to the individual he wished to humiliate. In the country-dance in which they were engaged, his Royal Highness openly passed by the Colonel and his fair partner, without allowing them to join in the figure. This exhibition of pique, however, produced no effect. The young Lieutenant-Colonel became a favourite at Court. His success in the *beau-monde* had already been established by his carrying off from all competitors the *belle* of the season. That gallant officer was my father.

The howl of rage with which the Foxites assailed him, when they learned how he had vindicated his own honour, and that of his family, may be learned from the pages of "The Rolliad." One of the writers of that farrago of indecent libels, attacked Queen Charlotte in these lines :—

> "And thou, too, Lennox! worthy of thy name!
> Thou heir to Richmond, and to Richmond's fame!
> On equal terms when Brunswick deigned to grace
> The spurious offspring of the Stuart race.
> When thy rash arm designed her favourite dead,
> The Christian triumphed, and the mother fled:
> No rage indignant shook her pious frame,
> No partial doating swayed the saint-like dame;
> But spurned and scorned where Honour's sons resort,
> Her friendship soothed thee in thy monarch's court."

The penultimate line is a gross exaggeration of the "madness of many for the gain of few," which actuated those who chose to be influenced by party feeling in their conduct towards my father. The officers of his regiment were induced to hold a kind of Committee of Inquiry into his proceedings, and, as if afraid of committing themselves, they came to the conclusion that Colonel Lennox had conducted himself with perfect propriety up to the period of the challenge—the contingency that had been forced upon him, his avoiding which would have entailed on him the slanders that had assailed his uncle. The insinuations respecting the Queen's want of maternal solicitude are equally gratuitous. They arose out of Colonel Lennox's appearance at the Court Ball—the invitation to which he had received before the duel.

The "little stranger" was the fourth, Colonel and Lady Charlotte Lennox had welcomed, of a progeny of seven sons and seven daughters, all of whom survived to claim "honourable mention" in the Peerage, and most of them became connected by marriage with other families of equal historical importance.

I do not know how long a time elapsed before I became conscious of the advantages I possessed; but that they should not be overlooked, I was christened William Pitt, after the illustrious statesman who did me the honour to stand my godfather—to mark his esteem for my parents. I was still more intimately connected with the leader of the other great political party—the father of Charles James Fox, having married the sister of my father's uncle—Charles, third Duke of Richmond; we were therefore kinsmen.

The times to which I am referring were the good old times of family influence, when there existed a rivalry among a few members of the Peerage for political influence, which they endeavoured to strengthen by matrimonial alliances. By putting a little pressure occasionally on the Minister, they continued to obtain whatever patronage they required for themselves, for the cadet branches of their several houses, and for their dependents. By such means they generally managed to have several members in the House of Commons, and a considerable *clientèle* in the subordinate "public" offices—as well as a fair supply of brothers and cousins in the Treasury, the War Office, and other lucrative appointments at home and abroad.

Some were not above receiving salaries without doing duty; for sinecures might then be had for the asking—some accepted pensions without having performed any service, for such liberal rewards were obtainable, and why should they not accept them? But great as may have been the resources of the Government in this way, they did not satisfy the extraordinary demands that were made upon them.

The cry of the horse-leech was heard in Downing Street during the whole of business hours—it even followed the head of the existing administration wherever he sought to enjoy an hour of relaxation from official duties. His principal supporters were importuned by crowds of expectants, who helped to maintain their importance, and, yielding to the moral pressure, they besieged their powerful friend with incessant cries of "Give! give!"

It was during this session that Pitt made his last show of attachment to the liberal principles he had so warmly advocated while out of power, by bringing forward a bill for a reform in Parliament; but it was so inefficient a measure, that it was only ridiculed by the opposition; and as he did not use his own parliamentary influence to support it, it was clear he never intended that it should pass. He was ever after a resolute opponent of parliamentary reform, in whatever shape it was presented. In other matters the young premier met with several slight crosses and disagreements. The foreign policy of his ministry was an object of incessant attack to the liberal opposition; and a plan of national fortifications, brought forward by the Duke of Richmond, who had deserted his old colleagues to take office as Master-General of the Ordnance, was an object of great ridicule. After several animated debates, in which more was said of the Duke of Richmond's apostacy than of his fortifications, and which showed how much party spirit entered into the profession of patriotism, on a division, the numbers on both sides of the question were equal, and the Government scheme was thrown out by the casting vote of the speaker. This was the subject of several caricatures and squibs, in which the unceremonious extinction of the fortifications by the speaker is made a subject of no little mirth. In a print by Gillray, published in the year following, the Duke of Richmond is made to swallow his own fortifications by another individual, apparently intended to represent Lord Shelburne. It was designated, "A bitter dose."*

At no time did the fever of party politics rage higher than about the beginning of the present century, when the Pittites and Foxites, as the partizans of the distinguished leaders of the two great parties into which society was then divided, allowed themselves to be called, were so bitterly antagonistic, as often, not only to lose sight of justice, but of common sense. Mr. Pitt, however continued to carry with him the bulk of the property and intelligence of the country; but the war in which England had been engaged against republican France had so affected its resources, that peace was beginning to be desired, particularly by the mercantile community.

Mr. Addington, who was personally liked by the king for his agreeable manners, when Speaker of the House of Commons, was directed by his Majesty to form an administration, on the resignation of Mr. Pitt, and his ministry entered office in July 1801. Preliminaries of peace were signed between the representatives of France and England, on the first of the following October. This "Peace of Amiens," as it was called, though popular at first, soon lost ground in public opinion, and the disgraced minister, as he

* T. Wright's "England under the House of Hanover," chap. ii. vol. i.

had been considered, began to make it very clear to his friends in Parliament and elsewhere that he had parted with none of his real influence. Mr. Addington seemed to think otherwise, and from his elevated position fancied he was master of the situation.

The intentions of the ruler of France became obvious, and war was again declared early in the year 1803. Buonaparte had long been projecting an invasion of England, and now made preparations for it on a grand scale. This heightened the war fever throughout the country, and to a corresponding degree lessened the influence of the peace administration. The First Consul was proclaimed Emperor of France on the first of May, and Mr. Addington and his supporters took their leave of Downing Street on the 12th, the king having been forced to have recourse to his old minister. Mr. Pitt became Premier.

His further career of office unfortunately was not long. He died on the 23rd of January, 1806.

Lord Grenville, a statesman of high reputation, was selected to form a new Cabinet, in conjunction with Mr. Fox, to whom the King had long been violently opposed; and Mr. Addington, lately created Viscount Sidmouth, to whom his Majesty was still exceedingly partial—opposing influences that were expected to neutralize each other, and "make things pleasant," like the lemon and sugar in a bowl of punch. They became Secretary of State for Foreign Affairs, and Lord Privy Seal. Equal care was taken to fill the other offices in the ministry; indeed, it was boasted that the country had been exhausted of its administrative capacity, and that Lord Grenville had secured "All the Talents." However careful had been the selection, no such pains could ensure duration. Mr. Fox died on the 13th of the following September, and the Grenville ministry in the spring of the following year.

The Duke of Portland was now fixed upon to take the helm of affairs—or rather Mr. Perceval, for, although the one was appointed First Lord of the Treasury, and the other Chancellor of the Exchequer, the latter was the real premier. The ministry formed under their auspices, and though coming after "All the Talents," was not deficient in capacity. Among its eminent men were George Canning, Foreign Secretary; Viscount Castlereagh, Colonial Secretary; Lord Eldon, Lord Chancellor; with Sir Arthur Wellesley, as Chief Secretary for Ireland. There was one other appointment, in which I was far more nearly interested, and to this I will presently refer.

When I was about seven years old, an event occurred, which from its results necessarily made a great impression on my mind. This was the death of

Charles, third Duke of Richmond. His grace had not only established for himself a reputation for high administrative talents, particularly while filling the important post of Master-General of the Ordnance, but acquired a large share of popularity by the known liberality of his political opinions, when such opinions were rarely heard from the lips of persons holding so exalted a social position. To him have been attributed the ideas of Universal Suffrage and of Annual Parliaments; but he has a better claim to that of Parliamentary Reform, of which he was an earnest advocate.

It was at Old Richmond House, about the beginning of May, in the year 1782, that the first meeting of the friends of Parliamentary Reform took place, and Mr. Pitt brought forward the subject in the House of Commons a few days later.* When the horrors of the French Revolution were being enacted, like other sensible men, the Duke thought it prudent to modify his opinions. This brought on him a fierce attack in the House of Lords, from that red-hot politician, Lord Lauderdale. A double challenge rose out of this, after a spirited reply from the Duke. Lord Lauderdale sent him a challenge, and General Arnold challenged his lordship. In the first case the seconds elicited a peaceful arrangement; in the other, a meeting took

* Lord Stanhope's Life of Pitt, vol. i., p. 73.

place—Lord Hawke attending as the General's second, and Mr. Fox acting for the Earl. The former fired, and missed; and as Lord Lauderdale refused to fire, the seconds, as usual, considered that satisfaction had been given, and the affair ended.

There is a still more important suggestion of the Duke's to be noticed, which originated as much in his patriotism as in his military knowledge. This was a plan he proposed for fortifying the principal ports. It was debated in the House of Commons, and negatived solely by the casting vote of the Speaker, as has already been related.

The Duke had acquired the highest honours attainable by an English officer, for he had been raised to the dignity of Field-Marshal, and was Colonel of the Royal Regiment of Horse Guards—Blues.

By his marriage with Mary, eldest daughter and co-heiress of Charles Bruce Earl of Aylesbury, by Caroline, daughter of John, Duke of Argyle, the Duke may be said to have formed a connecting link between the contemporaries of Pitt and Walpole. Of the former he was a stanch supporter and steadfast friend. They were devoted to each other, as much by mutual admiration for the noble qualities of mind and heart they were known to possess, as by identity of views on all subjects of national interest.

In private, the Duke bore as high a character as in

public life. He was a kind landlord, and a popular Lord-Lieutenant of the county in which his principal estate lay. Not merely his tenants, but his tradesmen had equal reason to be gratified by his attention to their interests. Indeed, there was a standing notice at Chichester, directing all persons in the neighbourhood with whom his steward might have dealings, to send in their accounts for examination and settlement, without delay—or they would forfeit his support.

A remarkable proof of his foresight and honesty of purpose exists in a letter the Duke wrote to Mr. Pitt, from Goodwood, on the 24th of November, 1790, expressing his opinion of the impolicy of calling Mr. William Grenville to the House of Peers. It required more than ordinary courage to tell the minister :—

"I believe this country will not be satisfied to see you two younger brothers take the lead of the two houses of Parliament, and by yourselves you rule the country. With your abilities, which, without a compliment, are very transcending, you may take that lead in the House of Commons; but Mr. Grenville, whose parts, however solid and useful, are certainly not upon a level with yours, cannot, as I conceive, succeed in taking the lead in the House of Lords, where something of higher rank, and more fortune and dignity, are required; and I do apprehend that both of you, being in such situations, so nearly related with Lord Chatham at the Admiralty, will be thought engrossing too much in one family."

The whole is an earnest remonstrance against the ambitious designs of Mr. Pitt's relatives, which subsequent events proved was not uncalled for. Lord Grenville, when elevated to the highest position in the state, could only maintain it by aid of the personal popularity of Fox; and Lord Chatham, when appointed to a high military command in the expedition against Walcheren, made a display of incapacity which the country neither forgot nor forgave.

The Duke's memory ought to be held in especial respect by artists, for the impulse he gave to the study of the Fine Arts in this country, by throwing open his gallery in Old Richmond House, to all students who chose to avail themselves of its fine collection of casts from the antique. This was before the establishment of the Royal Academy; and most of the founders of the English school of painting owed their proficiency to the studies thus liberally permitted them. His Grace was a liberal patron of the meritorious artists of his time, whose works may still be found at Goodwood.

Political hostility to the Duke of Richmond elicited the following, among a score of similar attacks to be found in the pages of "The Rolliad."

" The triple honours that adorn his head,
A three-fold influence on his virtue shed;
As Gallia's prince, behold him proud and vain;
Thrifty and close as Caledonia's thane;
In Richmond's duke we trace our own John Bull,
Of schemes enamoured, and of schemes—the gull."

This malicious reference to honours the Duke inherited, must pass for what it is worth. It is entitled to as much attention as the insinuations of the same writers, as to the Duke's deficiency in courage and liberality. The sole cause of the prominence with which his Grace figures in that scurrilous publication, existed in the cordial support he gave to Mr. Pitt.

My paternal grandfather, Lord George Lennox, had died in the year 1805. He had been a General in the British Army. His eldest son, Colonel, by this time Lieutenant-General Lennox, and one of the members for Sussex, succeeded to the Ducal dignity and estates. The popularity my father's predecessor had possessed in the county, rendered the position of the new lord of Goodwood rather a trying one; but by maintaining the old Duke's arrangements as closely as possible, he continued to acquire a fair share of public favour.

Goodwood was one of the noblest residences in a county rich in fine mansions and estates, and I and my brothers, when transferred to it, were not too young to be insensible to its remarkable attractions.

Field sports had been encouraged there from time immemorial, and its hunting establishment enjoyed a wide celebrity.

The following account of a remarkable fox-chace with the Duke of Richmond's hounds, more than a hundred and twenty years ago, is copied from an old vellum manuscript, and may not be uninteresting to our readers, while upon the subject of Goodwood:—

"*A full and important account of the remarkable Chase of Charleton, on Friday the* 26*th day of January,* 1739.

" It has been long a matter of controversy in the hunting world, as to what particular country, or act of man, the superiority of power belonged. Prejudice and partiality have had the greatest share in their disputes, and every society have their proper champion to assert their pre-eminence, and bring home the trophies to their own country. Even Richmond Park has its Dymoke. But on Friday, the 26th of January, 1739, there was a decisive engagement on the plains of Sussex, which, after an hour's struggle, has settled all future debates, and given the brush to the gentlemen of Charleton.

" Present in the morning, the Duke and Duchess of Richmond, Duke of St. Alban's, Lord Viscount Harcourt, Lord Henry Beauclerk, Lord Ossulston, Sir

Henry Liddell, Brigadier Henry Hawley, Ralph Jennison, Esq., master of his Majesty's buckhounds; Edward Pancefoot, Esq., William Fangwill, Esq., Colonel Philip Honeywood, Richard Biddolph, Esq., Messrs. St. Paul, Johnson, and Freeman; Mr. Johnson of Chichester; Tom Johnson, huntsman; Billy Ives, yeoman, pricker to his Majesty's hounds; David Briggs, Nim Jones, whippers-in.

"At a quarter before eight in the morning, the fox was found in East Dean Wood, and run an hour in that cover, then in the forest up to Puntice Coppice, through Herring Dean to the Marlows, up to Coney Coppice, back through the Marlows to the forest Westgate; over the fields to Nightingale bottom, to Cobden's of Drought, up his Pine Pitt Hanger (there his Grace of St. Alban's got a fall), through my Lady Lukener's bottoms, and missed the earth; through West Dean forests, to the corner of Collar Down, where Lord Harcourt blew his first horse; crossed the Hacking Place Down, the length of Coney Coppice, through the Marlows to Herring Dean, into the forest, and Puntice's Coppice, East Dean Wood, the lower Teagles, crossed by Cocking Course, down between Graffham and Woolavington, through Mr. Orm's park and paddock, over the heath to Fielder's furzes, to the Hurland's, Selham, Amersham, through Totham furzes, over Totham heath, almost to Cowdray Park, there turned to the lime-kiln at the end of Cocking Causeway, through Cocking Park and furzes, there crossed the road, and up the hill between Bepton and Cocking. Here the unfortunate Lord Harcourt's second horse felt the effects of long legs, and a sudden steep; the best thing belonging to him was his saddle, which my lord had secured; but by bleeding, contrary to the act of Parliament, he recovered, and, with some difficulty, was got home.

"Here Mr. Faugwill's humanity claims your regard, who kindly sympathised with my lord in his misfortunes, and had not power to go beyond him at the bottom of Cocking Warren.

"The hounds turned to the left across the road, to the barn, near Herring Dean, then took the side hills to the north gate of the forest (here Mr. Hawley thought it prudent to change his horse for a true blue, which stayed upon the hills, Billy Ives likewise to a horse of Sir Harry Liddell's), went through the forest, and ran the foil to Binderton (here Lord Harry Beauclerk sunk), away to Hag's bushes, to the Valdoe, through Goodwood Park (here the Duke of Richmond chose to send three lame horses back to Charleton, and took 'Saucy Face' and 'Sir William,' that were very luckily at Goodwood); from thence, at a distance, Lord Harry was seen driving his horse before him to Charleton.

"The hounds went out at the upper end of the park, up to Stretington Road, by Sally Coppice (where his Grace the Duke of Richmond got a sumerset), through Halnaker Park, over the hill to Sebbige Farm (here the master of the staghounds, Colonel Honeywood, Tom Johnson, and Nim Jones, were thoroughly satisfied), up Long Down, through Eastham Common field, and Kemp's High Wood (here Billy Ives tired his second horse, and took 'Sir William,' by which the Duke of St. Alban's had no great-coat, so returned to Charleton from Kemp's High Wood).

"The hounds broke away through the Gumworth Warren, Kemp's Ruff Piece, over Slindon Down, to Madhurst Parsonage (where Billy came in with them), over Poor Down, up to Madhurst, then down to Haughton Forest (where his Grace of Richmond and Messrs. Hawley and Pancefoot came in, the latter to little purpose, for beyond the Ruell Hill, neither he nor his horse 'Tinker' cared to go); left Shewood on the right hand, crossed Offam Hill to Southwood, from thence to South Stoke to the wall of Arundel River, where the glorious twenty-three hounds put an end to the campaign, and killed the old bitch fox ten minutes before six. Billy Ives, his Grace of Richmond, and Henry Hawley, were the only persons in at the death, to the immortal honour of seventeen stone.

" The glorious twenty-three hounds :—

" *Old hounds.*—Pompey, Doxy, Taker, Jenny, Peggy, Dido, Alnarck, Ringwood, Lawless, Cruel, Veny, Edmund, Walent, Cryer, Traveller.

" *Young hounds.*—Buxom, Ruby, Rifle, Bloomer, Lady, Crowners, Rummers, ..." [Here the name is obliterated in the manuscript.]

Poor Tom Johnson, who died four years after this memorable run, is buried at Singleton, about five miles north of Chichester; his epitaph runs as follows :—

"NEAR THIS PLACE LIES INTERRED
THOMAS JOHNSON,
WHO DEPARTED THIS LIFE AT CHARLETON,
DECEMBER 20TH, 1744.

" From his early inclination to fox-hounds, he soon became an experienced huntsman. His knowledge in his profession, wherein he had no superior, and hardly an equal, joined to his honesty in every other particular, recommended him to the service, and gained him the approbation of several of the nobility and gentry; among those, were the Lord Conway, Earl of Cardigan, the Lord Gower, the Duke of Marlborough, and the Honourable Mr. Spencer. The last master whom he served, and in whose service he died, was Charles, Duke of Richmond, Lennox and Aubigny, who erected this monument to a good and faithful servant, as a reward to the deceased, and an incitement to the living.

" ' Go and do thou likewise.' Luke x. 37.

" Here Johnson lies. What huntsman can deny
Old Honest Tom the tribute of a sigh?
Deaf is that ear which caught the opening sound!
Dumb is that tongue which cheered the hills around!
Unpleasant truth! Death hunts us from our birth
In view; and men, like foxes, take to earth."

My great-uncle had served the State in several high and responsible posts, and after my father had become head of the family, this, for him, was probably as good a claim for official employment as either his influence or ability. The known personal friendship of Mr. Pitt, too, may also have been urged in his favour, upon his surviving colleagues. Whether these circumstances operated singly or collectively, certain it is that, in the year 1807, on the formation of the Duke of Portland's administration, the Duke of Richmond was appointed to fill the onerous duties of Lord Lieutenant of Ireland, as a successor to the Duke of Bedford.

The union of the island with Great Britain had scarcely been accomplished, though several years had passed since the measure which Lord Castlereagh had, with unusual difficulty, succeeded in making the law of the land, and the country was in a transition state —the discontented far from reconciled to the change, and those who had profited most by it not quite satisfied that they had got all that they ought to have received. The mass of the Roman Catholic population had not entirely recovered from the violent ferment the abortive revolution which preceded the legislative Union had plunged them, and regarded the loss of their Parliament as a wrong which they were bound to appeal against on the first opportunity.

Emmett's foolish attempt at insurrection showed the highly dangerous character of their disaffection. It demanded, therefore, unusual discretion in the Viceroy to keep such untranquil elements quiet. This, however, was a matter of the very greatest difficulty. The Grenville Ministry had absolutely promised Catholic Emancipation, and as their successors had taken office on the understanding that no such measure was to be sanctioned, the state of hostility which existed among Catholics of all ranks in Ireland can scarcely be conceived. "No Popery!" was the shibboleth of the supporters of Mr. Perceval, and however such a cry might answer in England, in the sister island it could only produce a degree of rage and animosity that threatened a repetition of the horrors of the revolution of 1798. For the Papists at once endeavoured to effect a reconciliation with the Protestants, with the object of making one more effort for independence.

In truth, the prospect of the country was most alarming. The Grenville party may have exaggerated the dangerous condition of this portion of the United Kingdom, to serve their own purposes—still the case was very bad.

Few men who had just succeeded to the enviable position then held by the Duke of Richmond, would have felt inclined to surrender the delights of Goodwood for such a hornet's nest as the Viceroyship of Ireland then appeared. The letters of Sir Arthur Wellesley, lately published by the Duke of Wellington, give a forcible exposition of the dangers and difficulties by which the Lord Lieutenant was surrounded.

Lord Temple, writing to his father the Marquis of Buckingham, in August,* pourtrays a most gloomy picture of the state of society in the island. Such, however, was the wisdom displayed by the Duke of Richmond in this hazardous employment, that Mr. Thomas Grenville, in September, 1809,† states the impression that the Duke was likely to be called upon, aided by Lord Sidmouth and the Marquis Wellesley, to strengthen the Perceval administration, when the Ministers' negotiation with Lords Grenville and Grey proved abortive. That his Grace had established a claim for an unusual mark of royal favour, may be gathered from the statement of another Grenville communication, dated a few months later,‡ wherein the Garter and the post of Commander-in-Chief in Ireland, are named as his probable rewards.

* " Court and Cabinets of George III." Vol. iii. p. 235.
† Ibid. 378. ‡ Ibid. 429.

CHAPTER II.

DUELLING—THE PIC-NICS—A DINNER AT THE NEAPOLITAN CLUB—SCANDALS—SATIRISTS AND CARICATURISTS—FASHIONABLE ENTERTAINMENTS—SPORTING EVENTS—THE BARRYMORE FAMILY—COLONEL GEORGE HANGER—THE DUCHESS OF GORDON AND HER BEAUTIFUL DAUGHTERS—THE DUCHESS OF DEVONSHIRE—MRS. FITZHERBERT AND HER SERENADER—THE PRINCE AND PRINCESS OF WALES—THE RIVAL COURTS AT CARLTON PALACE AND BLACKHEATH—FASHION IN DRESS—BEAU BRUMMELL—ROMEO COATES—THEATRES AND OPERAS—FASHIONABLE SONGS.

CHAPTER II.

Conspicuous among the social characteristics of the upper ranks in England, about the commencement of the present century, was their tendency towards duelling. When every gentleman wore a sword, he was expected to be skilful in its use. This impression found profitable occupation for a considerable number of fencing masters, whose rooms, or schools, became the rendezvous of young men of fashion. Some of these professors taught equitation—indeed, received pupils into their houses to perfect them in manly accomplishments. Prominent among them was the elder Angelo, to whom, and to his son and successor, Henry, a large proportion of the rising generation of the nobility owed their gracefulness of deportment, their seat on horseback, and their skill with the small sword. There were other masters of high reputation, all foreigners; they also opened similar schools in different parts of the metropolis, and sometimes tested their skill against each other, or against any new adventurer who professed superiority in the use of the favourite weapon. Such contests of skill were sure to attract attention, and as the buttons of the foils were usually coloured, the "decided hits" were made too evident to admit of dispute.

Contests much more frequently arose among the pupils than among the masters. The readiness of the appeal, and the conviction of being able to maintain it successfully, was a fruitful source of quarrels, some of which were decided on the spot and in the hour in which they occurred—others were conducted with the usual forms of the duel. The use of the pistol, however, was beginning to supersede the small sword, as a final resort—and generally with more fatal consequences. Where there existed a similar amount of skill in the antagonists, *carte* and *tierce* might proceed without much danger to either, and every gentleman was expected to know how to defend himself; but with fire-arms, the greater the skill the greater the danger, and where a flesh-wound was the result of one contest, a ball through the heart was the consequence of the other.

Frequently, quarrels would arise out of trivial causes, and were sure to be taken up by some " d—— good-natured friends," who acted as seconds, and the death of one or both the principals became almost a matter of course. Two dogs met in the park, snarled and fought. Their owners took an interest in the conflict, which shortly occasioned a feeling of hostility between themselves. They were Colonel Montgomery, a gentleman moving in the highest circles, and Captain Macnamara, of the Royal Navy. A meeting took place at Chalk Farm, where the Colonel was killed, and the Captain severely wounded.

In the following year, 1804, Thomas Pitt, second Lord Camelford, was killed near Holland House, Kensington, by Captain Best. The former held a commission in the Royal Navy, and was nearly related to the Pitt and Grenville families, which gave this homicide unusual prominence; but he had more than once evinced a violence of temper that made such a termination of his career not entirely unexpected. His opponent had the reputation of a fatal marksman.

The occurrence of this nature that created the most sensation was brought about by the folly of the sufferer. Viscount Falkland, who had long been a celebrity in the world of fashion, as the associate of Lord Barrymore, and other gay spirits of the age, chose to affix a nickname to Mr. Powell, a Devonshire gentleman, against which the latter had protested without avail. A challenge was the consequence, and Lord Falkland was killed.

Another conflict, which occurred in 1809, arose from totally different causes, and excited no less attention. This was the duel between Captain Cadogan and Lord Paget, which originated in the seduction by his lordship of Lady Wellesley, a sister of Captain Cadogan's wife.

Duels not unfrequently rose out of political differences—such was the meeting, in May 1807, between Sir Francis Burdett and Mr. Paul; the result was harmless—but Mr. Paul committed suicide in the following year. The more important one between Lord Castlereagh and Mr. Canning, occurred in September 1809, at Putney Heath. Mr. Canning was slightly wounded. Such encounters had long been far more common in Ireland, but the fatal termination of the one in which Captain Boyd was shot by Major Campbell, brought the affair under the attention of the Civil authorities; and, on a legal investigation, the "malice aforethought" became so clearly established, that the Major was found guilty of murder, and executed at Armagh, on the 12th of August 1808. This example did not deter duelists in either island, but the premeditated destruction of a person drawn into a quarrel became a much rarer occurrence—in England at least—and the gentleman who had "killed his man" ceased to be regarded as an individual who had established a reputation for courage.

It happened occasionally that these affairs of honour terminated without bloodshed; and, as a remarkable case, we may instance a meeting in 1802, between the Right Hon. G. Ogle and Bernard Coyle, Esq., in which eight shots were exchanged, without any effect.

While this mischievous spirit of antagonism was nurtured by fencing-schools and shooting-galleries, a feeling of good-fellowship was fostered by clubs and convivial meetings. The variety of the former was, at this time, almost infinite, and many were ridiculous from their affectation of singularity. They were organized not only to satisfy the desires of all classes, but their tempers; and in more than one some of the Royal Princes were pretty sure of being found. Order and sobriety did not form a rule in such society—indeed, the reputation of being a four, a five, even a six-bottle man, led to the most extravagant excesses.

Among the clubs the most fashionable went by the name of the "Pic-nics." They assembled for a supper, to which all were forced to contribute by lot. A bag containing tickets inscribed with the names of certain edibles and drinkables, was passed round, and each took a chance in this strange lottery. Individuals of both sexes belonged to it, and had to forward within a given time whatever they had drawn—a haunch of venison or a Welsh-rabbit, ortolans or oysters, pigeon-pie or lobster-salad—in short, anything the *maître d'hôtel* chose to put down in the proper bill of fare for the occasion. A good deal of amusement was occasioned by the difficulty of procuring, or of sending the required comestible—but wherever the supper was to come off, there the delicacy must appear. The young ladies however youthful, and the elderly gentlemen however aged, frequently had to use extraordinary exertions to fulfil their obligations.

The idea is said to have originated with the Lady Albina Buckinghamshire—a *belle esprit* of that day; but it had long been in familiar usage in good society in France. Colonel Greville, well-known in the fashionable circles, assisted her ladyship in naturalizing it in this country; and the first meetings of the club were held at Le Texier's public rooms in Leicester Square. They were also given at the Pantheon in Oxford Street.

Such reunions were not solely devoted to the material pleasures of eating and drinking—amateur concerts and amateur plays were occasionally got up by the members; but the club did not prosper. It elicited lampoons innumerable, and the squibs of the wits, or would-be-wits, were shortly accompanied by ludicrous attacks from the caricaturists. The honorary secretary, Colonel Greville, became embarrassed in his pecuniary circumstances. His handsome person was withdrawn to a distant part of the globe, where he had obtained an appointment, and the ladies, whom his winning manners had drawn together, abandoned the Pic-nics; shortly afterwards the club was dissolved.

There was a very fashionable club called "The Neapolitan"—possibly because there was nothing in it resembling the natives of the kingdom of the Two Sicilies, except perhaps a kind of volcanic characteristic in some of the more fiery spirits who had enrolled themselves among its members. They held their banquets at the Thatched House Tavern—a house that has long ceased to be thatched—they were considered to be not less *recherché* in viands and wines than select in guests; nevertheless, it occasionally happened that an amusing fellow found admission there without any questions being asked as to his social position or antecedents—conviviality being as much regarded as epicureanism.

I remember having heard a description of a dinner given by them in the summer of 1806, in which the Duke of Sussex presided, when the elder brother of his Royal Highness, the Prince of Wales, was a guest. The club also entertained Sheridan, Thomas Moore, Lord Archibald Hamilton, Sir Sidney Smith, Sir John Douglas, Sir John MacPherson, Colonel Doyle, Captain Halliday, Honourable Mr. Anstruther, and Messrs. Mercer and Angelo. Among the members present, the President was supported by Brummell and Beckford, the Marquis of Headfort, Sir William Worseley, Sir William Hillery, Mr. Egerton, Colonel Phillips, Rev. Mr. Manby, and Messrs. Baker, Bagwell, Magra, and John Smith—the majority small stars in the London hemisphere, that have long ceased to twinkle.

The King of the Dandies, however, and the author of "Vathek," then ranked as social planets, and have left traces of their shining path that deserve recognition. The first was an autocrat in dress, the other in taste. The Prince of Wales would scarcely dare to wear a coat that had not been approved of by his exquisite friend, and would gladly have taken the opinion of his connoisseur acquaintance before making any purchase in works of art. The collections the latter had formed at Fonthill and in London, had, by their public sale a few years before, displayed the extent of his devotion to the arts of luxury—and he was now engaged in making much more extensive collections of similar rare objects, to redecorate Fonthill Abbey.

Sir Sidney Smith and Captain, afterwards Admiral, Halliday, were men of a totally different stamp, but were as joyous and earnest in their good fellowship as such gallant spirits usually are on similar occasions. Anacreon Moore contributed to an equal extent to the enjoyments of the evening. There was plenty of singing after the repast—in which he distinguished himself by the performance of some of those exquisitely tender lyrics, to which no one could do such justice as himself—a striking contrast to which was a Gaelic war-song by Sir John MacPherson, with all the emphasis that prodigious muscular action and a very powerful voice could give it.

The Royal Princes kept up the entertainment with the warmest cordiality till the small hours; but previous to the departure of the Heir Apparent, a dwarf, who was not three feet in height, was introduced on the table among the dessert, dressed in a full court suit. He was in years a man, but sat for some time on the knee of the Prince, regaling himself with ices and cake like a petted child.

Popular reading was limited in extent, and rarely of first-rate excellence. The Metropolitan circulating libraries were few and dear. One or two that have survived to our own day—such as Hookham's and Booth's—gave their subscribers the cream of the current literature, but the bulk of the reading was at best but milk and water. Pamphlets and squibs of temporary interest, and novels and travels of no interest at all. Melodramatic romance had extraordinary influence in the productions of Maturin, Mrs. Radcliffe, Lewis, and Clara Reeve—the sentimental was represented by Miss Burney and Fanny Holcroft. Godwin had taken a higher flight, in "Caleb Williams," and maintained his reputation in "St. Leon" and "Fleetwood." Holcroft also came forward as a novelist, but with less success. An especial favourite was Miss Edgeworth, whose "Essay on Irish Bulls," "Moral Tales," and "Belinda," greatly assisted by "Castle Rackrent," placed her at the head of her female contemporaries.

In poetry, Moore had established a name, and Byron was trying to do so. This was evident in his "English Bards and Scotch Reviewers," rather than in his "Hours of Idleness." Wordsworth had brought out a couple of volumes of poems, and his "Yarrow Unvisited," with but moderate success. Coleridge, with higher and more varied resources, had still only a limited circle of admirers, compared with the increasing crowd that delighted in the more showy attractions of "The Lay of the Last Minstrel," "Marmion," and "The Lady of the Lake," of Walter Scott, then known as a poet only. Shelley was commencing his poetical crusade against established opinions, as declared in "Queen Mab."

The newspapers of the period were very different from similar publications of the present day. For instance, the *Times*, at the commencement of the century, bore no resemblance to the leading journal for the year 1863. The information or amusement its scanty columns contained was administered in infinitesimal doses, compared with the abundance of both now supplied in its broadsheet and supplements. In those days there was no Special Correspondent at the seat of war, or wherever—even at the further extremity of the globe if necessary—anything of great public interest happens to be going on. Magazine and Review reading was equally deficient and unattractive, and popular literature at a very low ebb— Tom Paine and Cobbett carrying on a successful contest, in public favour, against Hannah More and Mrs. Trimmer.

This deficiency of intelligence gave increased zest to news of a criminal character, and any event of remarkable enormity was sure of a long sensational career in every town-house or country-house in the kingdom. The abduction of Mrs. Lee—a natural daughter of Lord Despencer, possessed of considerable wealth and personal attractions—by two brothers of the name of Gordon, one a clergyman, created great excitement. She was forcibly carried off from her house in Bolton Row, Piccadilly. Her resistance was very feeble—indeed, it was proved at the trial which ensued, that soon after her captors had got possession of her person, she cast out of the carriage window "*a charm*" she had always carried about her against the seductions of pleasure. The incident is a curious illustration of the manners, morals, and intelligence of ladies belonging to the *Beau Monde*. The action Mrs. Lee brought against the Gordons for abduction could not be sustained, her own evidence proving that she was a consenting party; and the trial was stopped by the presiding judge. It came on at Oxford, in March 1804.

Among "affairs of gallantry," as they were considered, was the action brought by the Rev. Mr. Massey, in the following September, against the Marquis of Headfort, when the former obtained, as damages, the large sum of £10,000. In 1808 Lord Elgin obtained the same honorarium from Mr. Ferguson, and Lord Boringdon the same sum from Sir Arthur Paget. In the following year the penalty was doubled—the offender being Lord Paget—the lady so highly priced being the wife of the Hon. H. Wellesley.

A singular case of the same nature was made public a few days later. During Bartholomew Fair, a young gentleman was, by what was called a court of *pied-poudre*, sentenced to pay a penalty of seventy shillings, for taking an actress from Richardson's show, to the detriment of the manager; and a further penalty of one hundred shillings, for having so done to the detriment of her husband, she being a married woman.

An inquiry into the conduct of the Princess of Wales, in 1809, was a fruitful source of scandalous gossip. Her Royal Highness had, for several years, conducted herself in such a manner as to excite the apprehensions of her friends, and the suspicions of her enemies. It is believed that she took a perverse pleasure in deceiving both. Her conduct was not only thoughtless, but singularly unladylike. No act of criminality could be proved against her. The subsequent publication of Lord Malmesbury's and Lady Charlotte Bury's Diaries, have proved that there was ample cause for such an investigation, though it produced no beneficial effect.

But the much more scandalous inquiry was that which took place in the year 1809, into the conduct of the Duke of York. It was alleged that His Royal Highness, while Commander-in-Chief, had permitted Commissions in the British Army to be sold or given away by a notorious courtezan, Mary Ann Clarke; and it was proved in evidence that, among other disreputable recipients, her footman did, through her influence, obtain such a distinction for himself. The exposure created great excitement throughout the country, and the Duke was obliged to resign the direction of affairs at the Horse Guards. It subsequently transpired that the woman had induced Colonel Wardle to bring the affair before Parliament, with the hope of getting money, either from the Opposition or from the Government.

Rival satirists put themselves forward to abuse the two great political parties. The authors of "The Rolliad" had attacked the members of administration a few years before. They did not spare the head of the Lennox family, as I have already shown. Of the Duke of Richmond they further wrote:

> "Whether thou goest where summer heats prevail,
> To enjoy the freshness of thy kitchen's gale,
> Where, unpolluted by luxurious heat,
> Its large expanse affords a cool retreat."

This was not aimed at my father, whose hospitality was lavish, but on his predecessor, who had the reputation of maintaining a frugal board. His kitchen, however, whether in town or country, bore no resemblance to the cool solitude described by the poet.

Writers, even less scrupulous, followed their example—such as "Anthony Pasquin," and "Peter Pindar"—but their personalities were repaid with interest when Canning and his friends started "The

Anti-Jacobin Review." The wit of their attacks on the most prominent leaders of the Opposition, more especially on the advocates and promoters of the new philosophical and political opinions imported from revolutionary France, there was no withstanding.

Art was also invoked to increase the strife, and when the battle of parties was not sufficiently ludicrous at the booksellers', it was sure of having justice done it in the shop-windows of the caricaturists. Better taste and better feelings now prevail, so that it would be impossible to reconcile public opinion to the pictorial libels upon Pitt and Fox, and their friends, male and female, that were constantly being exhibited in the principal thoroughfares, for the gratification of gaping crowds. Gilray and Rowlandson were the favourite artists employed in such work, and coarse and rough was the fun they delineated. Two or three of the most amusing specimens of the latter humorist were in the Fine Art Gallery of the International Exhibition, and the visitors, whose attention was drawn to his French and English reviews, will not soon forget their drollery.

The talent has not been confined to professional artists—it was possessed in an eminent degree by the Marquis Townshend, Sir Henry Bunbury, and the Countess of Burlington, who enjoyed a wide celebrity in fashionable circles in the last century; and at

Mr. Humphreys' familiar temple of the arts in St. James's Street, they were as much in request as the doublures of Gilray. The latter resemble the illustrations that have lately appeared as novelties, with the title of " Shadows." For instance, in one of the most successful, the bust of Fox is made to produce a shadowy representation of Satan—that of the Duke of Bedford resembles a jockey—that of Sir Francis Burdett a well-known character in the " Beggar's Opera "—while " Silenus " is the double of the Duke of Norfolk.

Such works, coarse and vulgar as their style may now be considered, formed the chief source of entertainment of an artistic description known to the majority of respectable people. A society called "The Dilettante" made strenuous exertions to diffuse a classical taste, and the annual exhibitions of the Royal Academy of Arts in Somerset House generally contained some fine productions; but the caricature shops in the early years of the present century, produced a more popular entertainment.

When the singularly clever conceptions of George Cruikshank displaced Rowlandson and Gilray, the favourite exhibition maintained its influence and attraction. H. B's refined satire appealed to a more educated community. But the publication of "Punch" put an end to caricature shops. A visit to the collections of Leech and Cruikshank would show not only the wonderful resources of these unrivalled humorists, but their great advance upon the caricaturists of half a century back.

Fêtes were often given by the nobility on a grand scale, that brought together large assemblies of the aristocracy. Those arranged under the auspices of members of the Royal family were also very magnificent. On the 14th of July, 1801, Queen Charlotte gave one at Frogmore Gardens, to six hundred of the nobility and gentry, invited by tickets. It was on this occasion that Ducrow, subsequently so celebrated for his equestrian performances, entertained a distinguished company by balancing three coachwheels upon his chin, as well as a ladder to which two chairs were affixed with a child in each. These exhibitions, which were then as attractive as frying omelettes on a tight rope is now, were concluded by a ball given in a thatched barn by the Princess Elizabeth.

The "house-warming" of the King, on the 28th of February, 1805, on his return to Windsor Castle, after his recovery from his malady, was a much more splendid affair, though not more than four hundred guests were invited. The floor of the ball-room was painted for the occasion, and a banquet provided that cost £5,000. On the next morning, the Queen gave a breakfast at Frogmore to two hundred persons of distinction.

The Marquis of Buckingham, on the 15th of August, of the same year, entertained the Prince of Wales at Stowe, when four hundred of the nobility and gentry, including the Duke of Bedford, Lord Grenville, and Mr. Fox, were invited to meet His Royal Highness.

But the great year of feasting was the jubilee year 1809, when His Majesty had attained the fiftieth year of his reign. His loyal subjects rivalled each other in the magnificence of their entertainments, in honour of this—with one exception—unexampled event in English history.

Sporting events attracted a large amount of public attention, especially when of an unusual character. Such was a race run on the York Course on the last day of the races, August 25th, 1804. Colonel Thornton backed his wife for a thousand guineas to ride his chesnut horse Vingarillo a four mile heat against Mr. Flint's brown horse Thornville. The match attracted a very large concourse of spectators, including a liberal proportion of the patrons of the turf. The lady did all she could to win, but came in second. The race was run in nine minutes, fifty-nine seconds.

The arrangement was, that Mrs. Thornton should

ride her weight against Mr. Flint's. The lady's dress was a leopard-coloured body, with blue sleeves, the rest buff, and blue cap. Mr. Flint rode in white.

No less than 200,000 gs. were pending upon this match. Mrs. Thornton, dissatisfied with the result, addressed a letter to the *York Herald*, censuring her opponent for want of courtesy, and ended by challenging him to ride the same match—his horse Thornville against any of three he might select which Mrs. Thornton would hunt that year.

At the August meeting of the following year, Mrs. Thornton's two matches came off—one for four hogsheads of Coti Roti, 2,000 gs., h. ft., and 600 gs. PP. (which latter the lady stood herself). Colonel Thornton, Mr. Mills *alias* Clausum Frigit, ridden by Mrs. Thornton, walked over. The second, Colonel Thornton's Louisa by Pegasus out of Nelly, 9st. 6lb., rode by Mrs. Thornton, beat Mr. Bromford's Allegro by Pegasus, out of Allegranti's dam, 13st. 6lb., ridden by Buckle, the celebrated jockey, two miles, 500 gs. Rather a good afternoon's work—£2,205, and four hogsheads of Coti Roti.

In July, 1809, occurred the famous pedestrian feat of Captain Barclay, who had backed himself, to the extent of £16,000, to walk one mile every hour for a thousand successive hours. He performed his task within the given time, at Newmarket. In the year 1802, for a bet of £5,000, he had walked ninety miles in twenty-one and a half successive hours, on the road between York and Hull. He completed this task with one hour seven minutes and fifteen seconds to spare.

Pedestrianism has been much cultivated since then, both in running and walking, and the recent exploits of the North American Indian, known as "Deerfoot," have given a fresh impulse to it. In four mile and ten mile races, several of my countrymen have gained great distinction, and more than once have wrested victory from their fleet-footed opponent. A much higher phase of this useful accomplishment has been exhibited by tourists both abroad and at home, who have habituated themselves to taking very long journeys, combining a maximum of distance with a minimum of fatigue.

Climbing must be looked upon as a branch of the same art, and those dilettante tramps the Alpine Club, deserve to be regarded as the *elite* of pedestrianism.

A great patron of the turf was Lord Barrymore, about one of the wildest spirits then to be met with among the most reckless of the votaries of pleasure found in the metropolis, or anywhere else. Ireland contributed a large per centage of the sowers of wild oats, who made London their field of operations. His lordship, moreover, belonged to a family possessed of a celebrity for such cultivation—indeed, in the last generation, thus employing both sexes.

By the death of the sixth Earl, his progeny were consigned to a long and not undistinguished minority, the last years of which were spent in London society, where each succeeded in establishing for him, or herself, a "local habitation and a name"; but for particular reasons it was connected with distinct districts within the liberties of the city. One of this hopeful lot had been incarcerated, probably among the debtors—and was, in consequence, known as "Newgate;" the next was lame to some extent, and was christened "Cripplegate;" their sister, who was notorious for a too free use of the vulgar tongue, was ungallantly called "Billingsgate." There was another brother, said to have been educated for the Church, whose discourse so abounded in reference to a place not to be mentioned to ears polite, that he received the equally characteristic appellation of "Hellgate."

The elder, Richard, succeeded to the earldom, and by the time he had arrived at years of discretion, had become a most indiscreet member of the Peerage. It is impossible to do justice to his extravagance, his freaks, and his follies. Rich as modern society may be thought to be in the follies of fashion, they would shrink into commonplace vagaries compared with the excesses of his career. He began early—when a boy at Eton he is said to have gone to the spring meeting at Newmarket, where he betted a thousand on Rockingham. The horse won. He received his wager in pounds, when he demanded guineas—his lordship being already too knowing to be done out of fifty pounds.

He subsequently made a bet with the Duke of Bedford for £5,000, on the result of an election—which he also won, and doubtless took equal care of the odd shillings. His speculations in this way were, however, far too numerous for me to chronicle.

His lordship was so great a patron of the Prize Ring, that he occasionally got up fights near a little country house of his at Wargrave, near Reading. He frequently entertained pugilists at his table, and betted largely on them. One Tom Cooper he took into his service. This man not only wore his livery and waited on his guests at table, but attended his master in his most hazardous escapades, for the purpose of interposing in his behalf should Lord Barrymore get himself into a scrape. On one occasion, when a frolic was designed to come off at Vauxhall, Cooper was sent disguised as a clergyman. His vulgar cockney tongue betrayed him—he was identified, and the temporary representative of the Church militant was violently expelled the Gardens.

Lord Barrymore's end was sudden and unexpected. As a captain in a militia regiment, his lordship was marching with his company, guarding some French prisoners on the road between Folkestone and Dover, when a musket, in the hands of one of his men, accidentally went off, killing the commander.

His younger brother, Henry ("Cripplegate"), succeeded to the title—Augustus ("Hellgate") having previously "shuffled off this mortal coil;" and it is only justice to say, that the eighth earl was acknowledged to be a fit successor to the seventh. Fortunately he proved the last of such Mohicans: but his career extended to the year 1824. The name of Barrymore continued to appear in the public papers for some time afterwards, though the earldom was extinct—a female constantly coming before the magistrates to answer for most unladylike misdemeanors, who took the title of Lady Barrymore—one of a very large number of the sex who had quite as good a claim to it. She was a "Billingsgate," indeed, but not the original one, who, having married a French nobleman, had become Countess Melfort.

Conspicuous among the Barrymore circle was Colonel George Hanger, afterwards Lord Coleraine, an Irishman also, and qualified in every way to pair off with either of the brothers I have described. He had been an equerry of the Prince of Wales; and, like the Barrymores, the companion of His Royal Highness in many a wild frolic. He also died in 1824, and was the last of his race. He was present with the Prince at a prize fight, which excited so much animadversion against his Royal Highness, that the Prince caused a notice to be published in the newspapers, that he would not be present at any similar exhibition.

Among the ladies who attracted most attention in the world of fashion, I ought to place in the front rank my grandmother, so long celebrated as "the beautiful Duchess of Gordon." As Miss Maxwell, she had been a reigning toast in her youth, "the cynosure of neighbouring eyes" wherever she appeared; but when she passed with her charms across the Tweed, her attractions were found to be not less generally acknowledged. Alexander, fourth Duke of Gordon, carried off the prize from numerous competitors. The Duchess's celebrated portrait, lovely as it is, conveys but a faint idea of the influence she exercised for a quarter of a century on the circle in which she moved. Her personal graces she transmitted, apparently with no loss to herself, to her daughters, five in number, who became severally the *belles* of their season; indeed, for many years after the single blessedness of their career had terminated, when they appeared together at the opera, or theatre, in the same box with their mother, which was frequently the case, their extraordinary attractiveness became the source of universal admiration. All made excellent marriages. The eldest, Charlotte (my mother), became Duchess of Richmond; the next, Madelina, Lady Sinclair, on Sir Robert's death she married Mr. Fysche Palmer; the third, Susan, the Duchess of Manchester; the fourth, Louisa, the Marchioness Cornwallis; and the youngest, Georgiana, the Duchess of Bedford. As my aunts and grandmother were frequent visitors at Richmond House, when in town—or at Goodwood, when in the country—and were very affectionate towards their grandson and nephew, I think I may be permitted to claim a more intimate acquaintance with this family of beauties than any one else can boast of.

One of the most lovely women of her time was Georgiana, Duchess of Devonshire; but at this period her charms were fading under the influence of time. There is no doubt that her smiles did as much for her kinsman, Charles Fox, among his Westminster constituents, as the popular orator's professions; for, as is well known, her Grace personally canvassed the electors in his favour, and found few able to resist her fascination. The request of the coal-heaver to be permitted to light his pipe at her eyes, was one of many public evidences that transpired of the brilliance of her glances. Her mind corresponded with the beauty of her person. She possessed considerable literary talent, and published a poem on Mount St. Gothard, which was translated into French and Italian. She made Devonshire House the headquarters of rank and fashion in the Whig interest. Equally gay and alluring were Chatsworth and Chiswick, when the town season had concluded.

Fox was, of course, constantly there; and with him generally came the Prince of Wales, Sheridan, Burke, and the other satellites who were wont to revolve round the royal presence at Carlton House and the Brighton Pavilion. In short, his Majesty's Opposition in both Houses of Parliament found the mansion in Piccadilly far more attractive than the club-houses in St. James' Street, during the Pitt and Addington administrations; and in the short interval during which Fox held the post of Secretary of State for Foreign Affairs, and was the real director of "All the Talents," the Devonshire re-unions were more thronged than ever. The beautiful duchess, however, died in the year in which "the Man of the People," of whose cause her Grace had been so zealous an advocate, returned to office; and the event cast a gloom upon the triumphant party, which was only exceeded by the demise of its leader a few months later.

The lady who excited the most observation was the

long celebrated Mrs. Fitzherbert. She resided at this time principally at Brighton, in a small house near the Pavilion. Among the large and distinguished circle of her friends, it was believed that she had been married privately to the Prince of Wales. Notwithstanding this, his Royal Highness had since become both a husband and a father. The first appeared to be regarded in the light of those convenient arrangements familiar at most of the German courts, as a marriage with the left hand. Although a book has been written by a relative of the lady to prove that a more legitimate union was contracted, it states only that a paper exists among the collection of MS. treasures preserved at Coutts' Banking-house, which, though no one appears to have examined it, is sealed up and endorsed, " Marriage Certificate."

It has been said that a Roman Catholic performed the ceremony, the lady being a member of that faith, but this is not affirmed in the book, for had it been the case, there could be no difficulty in naming the priest. It was, as frequently stated, that a particular clergyman of the Church of England so officiated: but his name having transpired, Sir John Shelley wrote a letter to the *Times*, on the authority of his wife's father, the said clergyman, denying that he had anything to do with the transaction. Nevertheless, Lord Stanhope, in his life of Pitt, vol. i., p. 322, asserts that, "on the 21st of December, 1785, the ceremony was performed by a clergyman of the Church of England, and in the form prescribed by the book of Common Prayer; and the certificate, bearing the same date, was attested by two witnesses." No authority is given for the statement.

There is very little reason to doubt that the eager bridegroom was his own clergyman, as well as his own registrar; and the assurance the lady gave a friend of Lord Holland, that she had sacrificed herself to evince her devotion to her royal lover, should be balanced with the assurance she many years later gave her kinsman, Lord Stormont, that she had been married in her drawing-room, in the presence of two of her relatives. Even had such a ceremony been properly performed, she must have been well aware that the Royal Marriage Act had made it null and void, and that it was nothing better than a sham.

Not only respect, but a sort of homage was paid the Prince and Mrs. Fitzherbert, whenever they appeared together in public. At Brighton they were the lions of the place, and the common theme of conversation in public circles. Their privacy, however, was held sacred by even the most privileged of their circle of intimates; nevertheless, it did once or twice happen that one of those daring spirits who hang loose upon society, chose to invade it. A story went the round of the clubs of an incident of this nature, that we have not seen in print :—

One evening the Prince of Wales was enjoying his *otium cum dignitate* with his temporary *cara sposa*, when his ears were suddenly startled by the sounds of a guitar under the window.

"Who the deuce can that be?" he inquired, sharply.

"Only some poor *emigré*," replied the lady.

The music continued, and presently a male voice commenced a French *chanson* of an amorous nature, pretty well known on both sides the channel.

"Confound his impudence!" cried his Royal Highness.

The lady laughed, with her habitual good-nature. Twang! twang! continued the instrument, and the refrain was repeated over and over again,

"*Chere amie! chere amie!*"

The Prince looked annoyed, though his fair companion did not, and said all she could to make him regard the thing as a joke. He was curious to know the audacious serenader, but did not like to present himself at the window.

Twang! twang! continued the guitar.

"*Chere amie! chere amie!*" repeated the voice, with increased fervour.

The singer was a young man apparently, but his

features were concealed by a large wide-brimmed hat, and his figure by the folds of an ample roquelaire. As he kept his eyes directed towards the window above him, there could be no mistake as to the object of his gallantry.

"Twang! twang!" went the accompaniment for the twentieth time. "*Chere amie! chere amie!*" added the voice.

The window above cautiously opened, and a head enveloped in an unquestionably feminine cap, with the upper part of the body to which it belonged wrapped in a white dressing-gown, appeared holding a letter in the left hand. The back being to the light, the figure could be but imperfectly seen from the dark street; but the *billet-doux* was clearly discernible, and immediately it was shown, the serenader sprung eagerly forward, and placed himself close under the window to receive it.

"*Chere amie!*" murmured a soft voice from above.

"Here, adorable creature!" replied the serenader, passionately, stretching out his arms to receive the billet.

"Share that!" added more masculine tones, and on the head of the serenader descended the contents of a large water-jug. The sudden movement disarranged the head-dress, and a formidable pair of whiskers became visible. A burst of loud laughter, as the window descended, added to the discomfiture of the too daring gallant. But worse than all were the congratulations of certain of his intimate friends, who, from a distance, had been watching the experiment.

Next day the story was known all over Brighton; the cavalier, who had met with so cool a reception, proved to be Lord Barrymore, who, for once in his life at least, received a fitting reward for his indiscretion.

The Prince did not content himself with his left-handed bride. In wedlock, if he can be said to have been ambi-dextrous, he was certainly more than ambi-sinistrous. In short, the sinister handlings of his Royal Highness are not easily to be computed. The song of the rural swain, in a well-known opera, might have been sung by the royal gallant,

"I've kissed and I've prattled with fifty fair maids,
And changed them as oft—do ye see."

There was, however, an important difference; his preference was in favour of wives or widows. The royal roses, indeed, were all full blown. His Royal Highness heeded not the advice of the cavalier poet,

"Gather ye rose-buds while ye may."

It was a great mistake on the part of those who had arranged his legal marriage, in selecting the bride. Lord Malmesbury, who was sent to Brunswick to conduct the Princess to England, saw at almost the first interview that she was totally unfit for the position she had been called upon to fill. Her coarseness and her levity shocked him, but he did not dare to take upon himself the responsibility of stating his impressions to his Government. The Princess outraged his ideas of refinement by having a decayed tooth extracted and sending it to him as a present, and it was only by the most urgent remonstrances that he avoided her entreaties to become her companion in the travelling carriage.

On her first interview with the Prince of Wales after her arrival in England, the royal bridegroom's impression was declared, after an affectionate embrace, in the appeal, " Harris ! give me a glass of brandy." It was no secret that the slovenly and untidy habits in which she had been brought up occasioned this exclamation. Unfortunately the Princess continued careless regarding her toilette, and the distaste which the first meeting had excited continued till after the birth of a daughter, when the Prince publicly notified his intention of separating himself from her. No affection could ever have existed between them, and the bitterest hostility now marked their feelings towards each other.

While the Prince attracted round him at Carlton

House and the Brighton Pavilion the celebrities of fashion, male and female, the Princess held a similar court of her own at Blackheath or Connaught House, which, if not so well attended by dandies and married ladies of title of doubtful reputation, could always boast of a large literary element, as well as a tolerable show of rising politicians belonging to the Opposition. There was sure to be seen a little dark man, who had got into Parliament, but was more widely known by his novels than by his speeches. This was Mr. Matthew Lewis, whose imagination displayed in such works as "The Monk," shocked the virtuous and delighted the vicious part of the community. Lord Byron was also to be met there, but it was not till his subsequent publication of "Don Juan" that his lordship established his claim to such association.

Thomas Moore, who had published a collection of amorous poetry under the *nom de plume* of "Thomas Little," was a frequent visitor. The arts were represented by Sir William Gell, Sir Henry Englefield, and sometimes Sir Thomas Lawrence. The wits were Luttrell, Ward, and a few other men about town who retailed the gossip of the clubs. Among the ladies were Lady Oxford, Lady Glenbernie, Lady Caroline Lamb, Lady Charlotte Campbell, and Lady Ann Hamilton, many of whom possessed talents of a high order; consequently, the conversational displays, in which the mistress of the mansion, in broken English or equally dilapidated French, took part, were sure to be sufficiently lively if not particularly edifying.

The following lines by Monk Lewis characterize the court ladies of this period:—

> "To form a fair one all complete,
> Regard the following receipt:—
> Take noble Devon's lovely face;
> Take Marlborough's dignity and grace;
> A grain of Lady Bridget's wit;[*]
> The shape and elegance of Pitt;[†]
> From Smyth take every polished art
> That youth and genius can impart;
> From Cath'rine[‡] take th' historic page;
> From Pool what love will most assuage;
> From Townshend's eye take Cupid's dart,
> Make Lothian fix it in the heart;
> What well will every care beguile
> Must be collected from Carlisle;
> From Pembroke's conduct lessons take
> To mould and mend a noble rake;
> Dawkins Hymen's torch shall lend;
> From Langhorne learn to be a friend;
> Minerva's talents take from Guise;
> Take brilliancy from Clayton's eyes;
> A little dash of Fitzroy's[§] spirit,
> Craven's wish and Milford's merit;
> Take Cranbourne's[‖] lively wit and sense,
> With fair Louisa's[¶] innocence;
> Let Acheson the mind improve,
> And Joddrel fan the flame of love;

[*] Lady Bridget Tollemache.   [†] Lady Rivers.
[‡] Mrs. Macaulay.   [§] Lady Southampton.
[‖] Lady Salisbury.   [¶] Lady Shelburne.

Let Bulkley lend the wedding chain;
Ask Milner how a heart to gain;
From Baily learn a heart to keep,
And honey take from Beauchamp's lip;
Take softness from Carmarthen's* dame,
And Philps to crown the lover's fame;
Let Crespigny by magic powers,
Fill up and smooth domestic hours;
Granby shall loves and graces spare,
And Hobart banish every care;
Let Vaughan conduct the marriage reins,
And Meynell ease a lover's pains.
Taste you will find in Derby's school;
Let Bampfield teach you how to rule;
And Thanet all that gladdens life,
In friend, in mistress, or in wife."

There were other persons who were permitted to become intimate with the Princess of Wales, whose recommendations to her notice even, were very slight; yet the familiar footing on which they continued to establish themselves was a fruitful source of scandal. It appeared, however, to her attendants that their Royal mistress took a perverse pleasure in outraging the proprieties of her position and her sex; but whether this was by way of giving annoyance to her fastidious *caro sposo*, or from a morbid inclination for vulgar gratifications, her Royal Highness's offences in this way were too notorious to escape remark. Of course, gossiping tongues made the most of such scandal; and the Prince heard exaggerated accounts of them, as the Princess heard

* Lady Conyers.

similar exaggerations respecting his equally objectionable proceedings. The relations of the separated pair were in this way embittered from day to day.

But this was not all the evil. The gossip from both sources circulated to almost every family in the kingdom—exciting the partizans of the husband and the wife to increased hostility; it gained access to the servants' hall as well as to the drawing-room, generally creating more ridicule than indignation. As a matter of course, it penetrated to Richmond House, and found its way to Goodwood; and before the last piece of scandal had been thoroughly discussed downstairs by the seniors of the family, it was pretty certain of being put forward in a juvenile edition for the entertainment of the children. I could not help hearing the thousand and one Carlton and Blackheath tales. They rivalled in popularity those of the Arabian Nights.

To these illustrations of the social characteristics of the time must be added a brief notice of the costume. Towards the latter end of the preceding century, the ladies had been undergoing many external changes, each of which at the present day would be as much the wonder as the ridicule of fashionable *modistes*. Towering head-dresses at last came down, and all the abominations consequent on the neglect of cleanliness and the superabundant use of pomade and powder were got rid of. The hair was frizzled all over with falling curls on the shoulders and back. A plume of white ostrich feathers, or a single one of a bright colour, drooped over the back in evening or Court dress, or stood upright straight above the forehead; a bag-shaped bonnet, liberally trimmed with ribbons and lace, came half down the face. Recently these had been made of straw, but frequently it was more a cap than a bonnet, with a gauze veil suspended at the back, and bearing an enormous freight of feathers, bows, ribbons, and tassels. On the body was a sort of jacket, so very short-waisted, that an Arcadian poetess, in one of the contemporary publications, is made to say:

> "Shepherds, I have lost my waist,
> Have you seen my body?"

a parody on the "Banks of Banna," a popular pastoral. The sleeves were loose, and generally very short; a long black scarf was flung over the shoulders, or a shawl of a gay colour. The dress, fitting close to the hips, fell in a straight line to the heels. The Court dress, however, was usually expanded by means of an enormous hoop, rivalling the most fully-blown crinoline of our own time; and the swelling fabric was made more outrageous by prodigious wreaths, tassels, cords, and other trimmings.

A better taste began to prevail with the infant

years of the new century; the waists lengthened, excessive ornament was discarded, and a simplicity of toilette studied, though extravagance was not uncommon among those ladies who desired to attract attention, whose "monstrosities" were well caricatured.

Men contrived to gain a name in society, with claims as equivocal as those of Monk Lewis. Beau Brummell, like Beau Nash, seems to have reached his elevation without special advantages of family or fortune—wealth alone, however, was becoming a powerful auxiliary to greatness; and this was proved in the person of a young West Indian, who, towards the conclusion of the first decade of my career, had contrived to become the town talk. If I remember right, he was first heard of at Bath, and, at the theatre there, appeared in the character of *Romeo*, in Shakspeare's well-known play. It was for some charitable purpose, but the amateur performer had filled the Bath gossips with his fame as a millionaire, and by his eccentricity in the lavish display of his wealth. Public curiosity in that long-established field of display for fashionables, and would-be fashionables, was much excited: but when the aspirant for histrionic fame presented himself in the most charming of sentimental dramas, with the complexion of a Creole, set off by a woolly head of hair, in a suit of spangled white satin, that made him appear doubly dingy, the surprise was more evident than the gratification. The studied attitudinising, and the singular ranting of the ardent lover, became more and more ridiculous as the play proceeded. His voice had a strange metallic twang, and his figure, though not bad, was constantly falling into the time-honoured positions of boarding-school declamation, which had a very ludicrous effect. So prodigious, however, was the effect produced by the performance, that it deserved a new Bath Guide entirely to itself, for it was as much the laugh as the talk of the entire community.

He soon afterwards made himself conspicuous in London by driving through the principal thoroughfares a very handsome equipage—a curricle, shaped like a shell, drawn by a pair of fine horses, richly caparisoned, the silver-mounted harness profusely decorated with a cock, by way of crest, having the legend— .

"While I live, I'll crow!"

His Bath performance was repeated at the Haymarket Theatre with increased effect—with such effect, indeed, that his dying scene—an outrageous burlesque—was encored; and in compliance with the enthusiastic call, as he considered it, the delighted actor died over again. His expenditure was extravagant as his acting; he indulged himself in a diamond-hilted sword, and other costly ornaments for the decoration of his person. The object he aimed at—notoriety—was so far achieved, that his portrait, as "The Amateur of Fashion," was engraved and published in one of the magazines; and his fortune, his equipage, his dress, and his jewels, were common topics of conversation.

He aimed at something higher. He was not satisfied with sporting his well-befrogged surtout, tight pantaloons, and tasseled Hessians, to middle-class coteries in second-rate streets; the West Indian, now pretty well known about town as "Romeo Coates," from his theatrical performances, aspired to move in more elevated society; in short, in the exalted society of the Court. It seemed, however, that the noblemen and gentlemen of social influence voted him a plebeian, ridiculed his pretensions to gentility, and black-balled him when he tried to get admission into their clubs.

The darling object of his ambition was to be presented to the Prince of Wales, which, for a long time, he in vain made known to his confidential associates. At last it seemed as if his Royal Highness had heard of his wishes, and kindly sent Mr. Coates a card of invitation to Carlton House. Great was the preparation made by the "Amateur of Fashion," as he delighted in being styled, to distinguish himself on this glorious occasion; but, on presenting himself at the Prince's mansion, he had the mortification of learning that he had been hoaxed. The clubs made much of the joke next day; it was attributed to Sheridan.

Romeo Coates, notwithstanding this mortification, continued to dash along Bond Street in his gay curricle, to flash his diamonds in Baker Street assemblies; and play the lover of *Juliet* wherever a company of poorly-patronised Thespians were to be found, to whom the chance of a full house was too rare an occurrence to be neglected.

During the same period the costume of gentlemen had varied considerably. The expensive suits of velvet, and other costly fabrics that had formerly enriched the tailors, and impoverished many of their customers, were superseded by coats of broad-cloth; buck-skin breeches buttoned to the middle of the calf, where they were met by top-boots, in a few years began to give way to pantaloons, and Hessian boots much crinkled at the top; waist-coats were of satin, or embroidered cloth. The cocked hat was disappearing before the round; the hair was worn in a club behind, tied with a ribbon—pig-tails being abandoned to the gentlemen of the old school. Ruffles were still worn, but they were small; but the pride of the wearer was a high-collared shirt, and a cambric cravat of voluminous folds, tied with a prodigious bow in front. To get this made stiff enough was the object of daily solicitude, paper stiffeners being employed to make it sit properly round the neck. It was said of one of the dandies, who was the envy of his contemporaries for his unrivalled display of cravat, that on being urged, at his death-bed, to divulge the secret of his success, he whispered in solemn tones to his eager listener—" Starch is the Man."

The shape of the coat, which had varied from a sort of Newmarket cut-away to a short-waisted thing with tails descending to the ankles, *à la Robespierre*, now received a great deal of attention. A young man of no family pretensions, had contrived to get into the highest society, where he became quite an oracle of fashion. The dandies of the day, not satisfied with taking him as their model, regarded him as their king; even the Prince of Wales, who aspired to the character of being the best-dressed man in his royal father's dominions, was content to take the pattern of his garments from this influential personage. This was Mr. George Brummell.

The most popular entertainment of the time was the Theatre. The great talents of various members of the Kemble family had increased the amount of public favour which Garrick had attracted towards it. They were well supported by several of their contemporaries—male and female—both in tragedy and comedy; indeed, it would be difficult to make any play-goer of this decade believe that the master-pieces of Shakspeare could be better cast than they were in the great days of John Philip Kemble and Mrs. Siddons. But it was not only the works of the master-mind

"Which so did take Eliza and our James,"

that enjoyed the favour of the public at this period.

The genteel comedy of the eighteenth century was represented with equal force and truth by Sheridan. This accomplished wit and brilliant orator had added largely to his popularity by producing for the stage "The Rivals" and "The School for Scandal." Surprising as were his oratorical displays in the Warren Hastings prosecution, their beneficial effect was insignificant, compared with the results of his dramatic production. As an associate of the Prince of Wales, his name had the advantage of fashionable repute; but the merit of his writings required no such assistance to place them in the exalted position they have since held. With them, modern English Comedy began and ended.

"She Stoops to Conquer" of his predecessor Goldsmith, and "The Road to Ruin" of his contemporary Holcroft, are among the very few dramatic illustrations of English character of the same age that maintained their popularity for the next half century. Less legitimate productions, such as "The Castle Spectre," and "Timour the Tartar," both by Monk Lewis, for a time carried on a successful rivalry with them; but they lived the spasmodic life of sensation dramas. The former, however, has recently been restored at one of our minor theatres.

Increasing favour was shown towards stage representations, in which music was the chief attraction. This was owing in some degree to the admirable English singers, who sustained the principal parts. For instance, of men there were Incledon, Braham, Bannister, Johnstone, Edwin, Vernon, and Harrison; of women, Mrs. Billington, Madame Mara, Signora Storace, Mrs. Bland, Miss de Camp, Miss Poole, and Mrs. Cronch.

Braham was as successful when he came before the public as a musician as he had been as a vocalist; for the music of the operatic piece brought out in 1804, "The English Fleet," he received the unprecedented sum of one thousand guineas. Henry Bishop, who was possessed of far higher ability, made one of his earliest efforts towards gaining the fame he sought from his countrymen, in the year 1809. The opera was called "Kais; or, Love in the Desert." Less than a fortnight afterwards, he produced the music of "The Circassian Bride." The prima donna, Miss Lyon, became the composer's first wife. The opera was eminently successful; but on the night after the first representation, the theatre, Covent Garden, was destroyed by a conflagration, that consumed the music as well as the properties.

Dibdin was another popular composer, but rather as a song writer than as a musician. He and Hook (the father of the novelist), who wrote ballads for Vauxhall, rivalled each other in the variety of their productions; but the musical songs of the one took a hold upon the popular mind, which the less patriotic compositions of the other never acquired. Shield, Michael Kelly, Mazzinghi, Reeve, Attwood, and Davy, were also favourite contributors of what was then considered to be operatic music.

Such satisfied the general public, but the fashionable circle, including the *cognoscenti*, preferred deriving their musical gratification from the Italian Opera, as performed at the King's Theatre in the Haymarket. Here the strife of Tweedle-dum and Tweedle-dee had raged since the days of Handel and Bononcini, but the source of contention was usually the rival pretensions of the principal *cantatrici*. Mara, towards the close of the last century, had to make way for Banti, Storace, and Billington; the last, on her return from Italy, in 1804, was so improved that she appeared to distance all competition, till Grassini, and subsequently Catalani, were heard, and superseded her.

Concerts and operas increased in fashion, and the aspirants for *ton* were not always satisfied with patronizing the artist—some of them sought proficiency in the art. The Royal Family were conspicuous for this amateurship. The Duke of Cumberland gave his leisure to the violin; whilst the Prince of Wales, and the Duke of Gloucester practised quite as zealously on the violoncello. The Prince, too, possessed an excellent voice, which had been cultivated by Latour, the Court music-master, and his Royal Highness organized a private orchestra in Carlton House, to which he lent his assistance. The Duke of Queensberry, the Marquis of Buckingham, Lord Boyle, Lord Hampden, and many other leading personages in society, were in the habit of entertaining their company with concerts, for which the greatest attraction in the musical world, vocal and instrumental, was sure to be engaged. The compositions most in favour were those of Handel and Mozart, Cimarosa and Glück, Paesiello, Sacchini, Sarti, Winter, and Haydn.

Several ladies of rank not only played well on the pianoforte, an improvement on the harpsichord, but wrote many pleasing melodies—the beautiful Georgiana, Duchess of Devonshire, for instance, set to music Sheridan's melancholy lyric, "I have a silent sorrow here." A sentimental effusion equally in favour with the fair of May Fair was, "The Banks of Allan Water," written by Monk Lewis. The Prince of Wales obtained the reputation of having been the author of "The Lass of Richmond Hill," which was said to have been inspired by Mrs. Fitzherbert, then a resident in that picturesque neighbourhood; but, independently of the absurdity of calling a woman of thirty a lass, must be added this singular combination of negatives. The scene of the ballad was not Richmond Hill, Surrey, but Richmond Hill, Yorkshire. The heroine of the ballad was not a fashionable widow, but a damsel in her teens—a Miss I'Anson; and the author was not an heir-apparent who had crowns to resign, but a briefless Irish Barrister, whose half-crowns only, and those perhaps not without some reluctance, could have been parted with to gain the desired object. He was Bernard McNally, known in Ireland as the advocate of the Irish rebels—known in England as the author of the libretto of a comic opera called "Robin Hood," and of various fugitive pieces of poetry.

CHAPTER III.

MY EARLY EDUCATION — WESTMINSTER SCHOOL — ITS DISTINGUISHED SCHOLARS — VERY OLD WESTMINSTERS — TRAVELLING TO IRELAND — HOLIDAYS AT THE PHŒNIX PARK, DUBLIN — MY PANTOMIME — REVELRIES AT THE CASTLE — MY INTRODUCTION TO SIR ARTHUR WELLESLEY BET OF THE LORD LIEUTENANT WITH SIR EDWARD CROFTON — RETURN TO GOODWOOD — THE MANSION AND ESTATE — THE KENNEL — TOM GRANT — HUNTING AT STOKE — RACING AT GOODWOOD — RICHMOND HOUSE — WHITEHALL — RIVAL BEAUTIES — FEMALE ADMIRERS OF MR. PITT AND MR. FOX — POETICAL DESCRIPTION OF THE FAIR FOXITES — THEIR LOSS TO SOCIETY.

CHAPTER III.

I HAVE a decided impression that my early education was neither systematic nor strict. The rudimentary process was not so carefully attended to in the nursery as it ought to have been, and at our transplantation to Goodwood, I am afraid that the favourite preceptor of myself and brothers was to be found in the stable rather than in the schoolroom. We certainly in our tenderest years acquired some information of a scholastic kind, but invariably got on better on a pony than with our ordinary lessons. Our proficiency, however, in riding across country did not quite satisfy our natural guardian, and we were sent to attain more essential accomplishments at one of the most famous of English public schools.

This establishment had proved itself worthy of the affectionate care of its founder—the peerless Queen Elizabeth—by producing a list of intellectual celebrities, such as other institutions would find it difficult to match: Camden, John Dryden, Abraham Cowley, John Locke, Mathew Prior, Sir Christopher Wren, Nicholas Rowe, the two Colmans, Churchill, Cowper, Gibbon, Horne Tooke, and Southey; of statesmen —Burghley, Lord Chancellor Finch, William Murray, Lord Mansfield; Harley, earl of Oxford, Sir Francis Burdett, Lord Broughton, the Marquis of Lansdowne, and Earl Russell; in the army—the Marquis of Anglesey, and Lord Raglan; and in the Church— Dr. South, Harcourt Vernon, Archbishop of York, Bishop Cary—besides a host of others of less distinction.

The masters in Westminster school in my time, if they did not rival Udall, Camden, and Busby, were classed among the ablest teachers of their age. With such assistance and such stimulants, I acknowledge that I ought to have profited largely, but there were some obstacles in the way of my success I found it impossible to surmount.

During the Christmas holidays, I was in the habit of travelling to Ireland with one of my brothers, to pass them with my family at Dublin. The mode of transit was very different to what it is at present, and the journey generally took us a week to accomplish the distance between Dean's Yard, Westminster, and the Phœnix Park, Dublin. As it was considered rather *infra dig* for two such personages to travel by mail-coach or stage, which we should have very much preferred, "their lordships" were handed over to the care of a Monsieur Victor, a French refugee, who acted as a sort of private tutor. Through the kindness of the head-master, we were always allowed an extra week for going and one for returning; and so anxious were we (schoolboy-like) to get home, that we put up with every sort of inconvenience to arrive at our destination in the least possible interval of time. I need scarcely add, that we were rather more dilatory when Black Monday arrived.

Our conveyance was a post-chaise and pair, which we had to change at least two or three times throughout the day, and the best part of an hour was usually lost in unstrapping and restrapping a portmanteau and two wooden boxes.

The present generation of home travellers can form no conception of the state of the roads in some parts of our route. The system in general use of keeping the highways in repair, was very imperfectly known in my juvenile days; and the consequence was, that in many places the passage was difficult for any wheeled vehicle, and in some parts dangerous. Having got bumped over ruts, or dragged through quagmires, with many miraculous escapes to axle-tree, springs, wheels, and harness, we had hardly congratulated ourselves on still possessing whole bones, when a greater peril had to be surmounted in the shape of highwaymen, who infested every well-travelled thoroughfare in England, and levied contributions, pistol in hand.

Henley was invariably the place selected to sleep at, on the first night, and if comfort and attention on the part of the host and hostess, Mr. and Mrs. Dixon, could have made up for what we looked upon as a great waste of time, in not starting earlier, and proceeding further, we should have met with ample consolation. No sooner had we arrived at the "Red Lion," than we urged our preceptor to proceed early the following morning; but Monsieur Victor Signé, as he called himself, liked a light supper, and a good night's rest, so we could never succeed in getting down to breakfast much before seven o'clock.

Between that hour and eight we started, but owing to the state of the roads, three insides, and our luggage, we made, as the sailors say, " very little way." Then an hour was devoted to dinner, as the Frenchman dreaded an attack of indigestion; and about nine at night his inner man yearned for a roast fowl and some pork sausages.

Without tiring my readers with all the delays and inconveniences we had to put up with, or describing the piercing cold of this rattling shaking dice-box on wheels, I will bring them to the time when, after having undergone the horrors of an open boat in crossing the Menai Straits, we reached Holyhead.

"At what time does the packet start?" we eagerly inquired.

"Captain Skinner has been expecting you, my lords," was the reply, "and she will get under-way the moment your lordships are on board."

"Hurrah!" we shouted.

Monsieur Victor looked the picture of despair; for a sea passage to him, at all times, was most hateful, and he disliked it tenfold more when it was undertaken, as it must be in this instance, on an empty stomach.

From fifteen to four-and-twenty hours was the usual time occupied in crossing, and assuredly the cabin was as disagreeable as that of the Margate hoy, immortalized in song by the father of Charles Mathews. I pass over the horrors of it, and bring myself and my companions to the moment when, upon reaching the shores of ould Ireland, we found the Lord-Lieutenant's carriage waiting for us. We quite forgot our cold, miserable journey, and our sickness, and, with light hearts, stepped into the handsome equipage, which rattled us through the streets of Dublin to the Phœnix Park, after a journey of five days and a half on the road, and fourteen hours on the sea.

The delights of these holidays cannot easily be described. I and my brother accompanied my father in his shooting expeditions; and daily enjoyed the luxuries of a good dessert and a glass of wine. We were taken to all the sights in the metropolis, and in its neighbourhood: to the plains of the Curragh; the waters of the Avoca; the falls of Powerscourt; and last, not least, in our estimation, we attended the theatre on the night of the Viceroyal "Bespeak," and were allowed to go there upon numerous other occasions. Miss Walstein, and that clever actress, Miss O'Neil, were the stars of that day—while Farren, Conway, and T. P. Cooke, added much to the gratification of the Dublin audiences in their respective personifications. "The Lady of the Lake," and "Harlequin and Mother Goose," were our favourite plays.

It was my first year at Westminster. There are few passions that grow upon youth with such strength as a love of theatricals, and from this time my passion for the drama was intense. During the few months I had been at this great metropolitan school, I had not only attended the then celebrated dramatic booths of Scowton, Saunders, Richardson, and Gyngel, at Tothill Fields Fair, but was constantly present at Covent Garden, Sadler's Wells, and Astley's theatres.

My uncle, the Duke of Bedford, having a box at Covent Garden, I was allowed to go there every Saturday—I "going home," as the phrase went, to

Richmond House, from Saturday, after school hours, until Monday morning.

My late brother Frederick and myself had got up certain scenes from Shakspeare, as well as from certain blood-stained melo-dramas popular at Astley's, and from some of Richardson's best comic pantomimes. In the latter we felt ourselves extremely strong; we were not so effective in the former, if we were to judge of the laughter we created—in short, like the performance of a late celebrated amateur and M.P., who undertook the parts of *Richard III.* and *Caleb Quotem*, the risible muscles of the audience were excited to such an alarming extent in the tragedy, that there was not so much as a smile left for the farce.

Pantomime, then, was unquestionably our *forte*. One night—for after a Lord-Lieutenant's dinner in 1808, dining as they did at six or half-past, it was generally about eleven when the gentlemen joined the ladies—a dramatic performance was announced. It consisted of a melodramatic romance, entitled "Manfredi and Rosalva, or The Spectre Monk," which we had concocted from three or four we had seen at Tothill Fields Fair; and a new comic Christmas Pantomime called "The Lake of Diamonds, or Harlequin and the Fairy Fish."

In the first there was a grand combat with shield

and battle-axe, borrowed, of course, from Astley's; and between the play and pantomime a sailor's hornpipe was danced by the writer of these pages. Volunteer boys and girls were engaged for that occasion only. The entertainment was exceedingly successful, and the curtain fell amidst shouts of laughter and applause. For unfortunately the long white sheet that was to hide the body of the Spectre Monk became unpinned, and, falling down, disclosed the spangled dress of a juvenile harlequin, who, as double to the real one, was to support me in the pantomime.

A few glasses of negus and potheen and water having been handed round, and the national air of "St. Patrick's day in the morning" having been played, the curtain was drawn aside for the harlequinade.

I need not sketch the opening scene, but proceed to the grand transformation one, when, doffing our magnificent Eastern dresses, my brother, myself, and a dummy or double, appeared as pantaloon, clown, and harlequin—a young lady, who, at so great a distance of time, it would be ungallant to mention, taking the part of columbine.

I must here explain that, in my own estimation, I was as good a harlequin as clown, and, by a well-arranged plan, was what the actors call to "double" the parts; as a matter of course, it was necessary occasionally that the pilferer of sausages and *Spangles* should appear together, when, under these circumstances, the dummy was called into action, and, being about my size, he was not taken for the counterfeit.

My dress was a loose white clown's attire, which by aid of strings could be doffed in a second; so, with the assistance of the pantaloon, who occupied the time of change with what is termed in theatrical language, "business," I never stopped the performance.

The great feat of the evening was a leap through a huge painted transparent clock; and for months and months, I had practised it at Dean's Yard, by taking "headers" through hoops into my bed. When the scene came on, I, as *Spangles* evading pantaloon, took the leap amidst the shouts of the audience. The watchmaker came out to see what was going on; pantaloon, to give me time, made sundry essays to follow, and failed—when I, dressed as clown—the second harlequin sitting at a window, daring me to take the jump, for with his wand the clock had ascended—took what would now be termed the "sensation" leap, and surprised many of the audience.

Among them was Sir Arthur Wellesley, who, from his earliest years, was a supporter of athletic games and feats of agility. He burst forth into a loud exclamation of "Bravo! bravo!" Elated with my success, I was transforming myself into harlequin, when another mishap occurred. Our temporary scene-shifter, in removing the clock scene, which had been made out of an old screen, quite forgot that I was partly undressing behind it; and, instead of the next and last grand tableau of the Lake of Diamonds, the audience perceived, in one corner "dummy" harlequin kneeling to the fairy gold-fish—and I, half clown, half harlequin, enjoying a glass of Dublin porter out of the pewter, while my attendants were arranging my dress. The quick eye of Wellesley at once discovered the "artful device,"—"dodge" it would now be called—and loudly applauded it.

"Clown and harlequin in one!" he said, in his quick manner; "capital! capital!"

The clock and myself moved off, and in I rushed, throwing a somersault, and uttering one of the clown's time-honoured jokes, while, with open mouth, knees and toes stuck in, I made extraordinary contortions, after the most popular models; and down went the curtain.

Owing to the length of the performance, and the mistakes that had occurred, some of the company had hinted that "a grilled bone" would not be objected to; and as my father was ever ready to promote hilarity and conviviality, supper was ordered. By the time the *dramatis personæ* had got rid of the chalk, paint, and dirt, attached to their hands and faces, and decked themselves in their neat frocks and smart jackets, supper was announced; and one of the earliest toasts—for the days, or rather nights, were those of toasting and hard drinking—was "the dramatic company," with an especial allusion to the grace of columbine, the extraordinary cleverness of clown, as well as an equally complimentary notice of pantaloon, who, really, from having to fill up the pauses, had a most onerous duty.

Sir Arthur, who was next my mother, called us both up, complimented us on our success, and playfully said to the Duchess:

"You had better send them to Covent Garden or Sadler's Wells—especially William."

"I hope better things for him," responded my mother; "he desires a commission in the army—don't you?"

Of course I said I did.

"Well, we'll see what can be done. How old is he?"

"Just eight."

"Plenty of time before him," responded Sir Arthur.

No further notice appeared to be taken of this matter. It was not, however, forgotten by the

Secretary, though it did not have any result till my distinguished friend had long left behind him the pleasant scenes of his Irish official duties, and had completed his grand career in the Peninsula.

During this winter a bet was made by my father and Sir Edward Crofton for £500, that the latter should not produce a horse who could leap, in fair Irish sporting style (which allows just touching with the hind feet), a wall seven feet high. Sir Edward produced a half-bred animal, called "Turnip," by Turnip, a thorough-bred son of the celebrated Pot. 8. O's, that was brought to Dublin by Colonel Hyde, his dam a common Irish mare.

On the day appointed, a gate was removed from its place in a very high park wall, near the Phœnix Park, and men and stones being ready, was built up to the required height, in the presence of my father. Whilst this was being rapidly done by men used to build such walls, Turnip was walking about, rode by a common groom, in jacket and cap.

When all was ready, and the signal given, over he went, but had so little run, that my father, thinking the rider was going to turn him round and give him a race at it, moved his head at the moment, and did not see the leap. To re-assure him, however, the horse was rode over it again. He was a slow horse, and died afterwards from the effects of a severe run with the Kildare hounds in an open country—where, though the fences would in England be reckoned severe, they were nothing to the walls of Roscommon and Galway.

Attractive as was our residence at the Phœnix Park, and the pleasures of the Irish capital, they did not lessen our affection for our English home. Dublin made a delightful change, but on our revisiting Goodwood we seemed to become only the more sensible of its innumerable gratifications. The greater portion of these were of recent origin, having been produced only a few years before by my father's predecessor in the title. After my great-uncle had retired from public life, he had devoted himself to the enlargement and improvement of his estates, and to the building and furnishing a mansion which should correspond with their extent. Halnaker and Westhampnett—the last an addition of upwards of 1800 acres—were added to his patrimony.

The house was originally designed by Sir William Chambers, but owes its more important additions to the genius of Mr. James Wyatt. It is rich in every kind of decoration, among which must be named a collection of more than two hundred and thirty paintings: a large portion of these are of the English school, masterpieces of Reynolds, Gainsborough, Barry, Romney, Lawrence, Hogarth, Ward, Jackson, and Beechey, with numerous interesting productions by Stubbs, Lambert, Wootton, Allan Ramsay, Hudson, John and George Smith, Scott, and Pond. There are also amongst them several fine pictures by the old masters, both of the Italian and Dutch schools.

A library has been accumulating since the period of the last of the Stuart sovereigns; but while my uncle cultivated a taste for literature, his love of field sports was pursued with remarkable ardour. He kept one of the finest packs of fox-hounds in the kingdom, and the arrangements made for their accommodation were on a scale that astonished every visitor. The kennel is erected on a rising ground, about a mile from the house. It is in length about one hundred and forty-eight feet, the height of the centre is twenty-eight feet, and of the wings eighteen feet, measured from the crown of the arches upon which it is built. The distribution of the building is in four kennels; two of them thirty-six feet by fifteen, and two others thirty feet by fifteen; there are two feeding rooms, twenty-eight feet by fifteen, in each of which is a ventilator placed at the top, and there are stoves to warm them in winter, or air them in damp weather.

The huntsman, old Tom Grant, and his good wife, had very snug quarters in the kennel; Tom's parlour was sporting all over, the walls being covered with hunting pictures and prints. There might be seen the "turn-out" of the days of yore, when the huntsmen and whippers-in were decked in gorgeous liveries and huge cocked hats, down to the fashion of the day, "a bit of pink," and a black velvet cap. But let me describe the place as I found it.

Conspicuous on the side-board are two large silver goblets, made in the shape of foxes' heads, and a tankard of the same metal, on which is inscribed— "From the members of the Goodwood Hunt to Thomas Grant, as a slight memorial of their respect."

Foxes' brushes are to be seen in every direction— the bell-ropes even are made of them, and with them two easy chairs on each side of the fire-place are beautifully trimmed and ornamented. A large deer-skin covers the hearth-stone, the gift of a brother huntsman in the North; upon it lie extended two as "varmint" looking terriers as ever were seen in the purlieus of Tothill Street, Westminster. To complete the picture, Mrs. Grant is knitting a red worsted comforter for her old man, and Tom himself is busily employed copying the hunting appointments to send to the county press—for in those days the "meets" were not to be found in the London newspapers. The inkstand, be it mentioned, was made out of the hoof of "Honest Robin," a favourite hunter, that had carried Grant for many a season without a fall; this he prizes as much as the temporary holder of the Eclipse trophy, or the owner of Marengo's foot (Napoleon's Waterloo horse) do their possessions.

Tom at this time was no chicken, and began his career betimes, for early in life his talents shewed forth as whipper-in to a pack of harriers.

Never shall I forget the day, when, passing the Christmas holidays at Stoke, I was fortunate enough to get a mount with the Goodwood fox hounds, and never will the impression of that event be effaced from my memory. Since that period I have visited Holland, Belgium, France, Germany, Canada, and the United States; have been present as a non-combatant on the ensanguined field of Waterloo, have marched into Paris with the victorious allied army under Wellington, have hunted the deer in the royal forests of France, and been in at the death of a fox on the banks of the Danube, have massacred innumerable quantities of hares at the tame *battues* near Vienna, have fished for cod on the banks of Newfoundland, have speared salmon in Lake Ontario, have caught beavers in the country of the Hudson's Bay Company, have wandered for hours at sunrise and by moonlight beneath the foam of the mighty Niagara, have drank sherry cobbler on the banks of the Huron, have smoked the calumet of peace with many a North American Indian, and yet, vivid as is the recollection of all the above "sensation" scenes of my life, my first day with the fox hounds is even more strongly impressed upon my mind, and is as fresh upon it in 1863 as it was fifty years ago, when I astonished my brother boarders at Mrs. Packharness's, Great Dean's Yard, Westminster, with the account of the run.

The hounds met at the Valdoe, a tolerably sized wood near Goodwood House, and in less than ten minutes the tones of poor old Tom Grant, the huntsman, were heard, shouting "Gone away!"

"Hold hard, gentlemen!" cried that first-rate sportswoman, Miss Le Clerk, afterwards the wife of General Dorrien, as she herself was preparing for a start.

"Give 'em time," he added, approaching me; for, rather abashed upon this my first appearance, I had shrunk behind the red coats, whom I then looked up to with the greatest awe and respect.

"Come along, youngster, I'll show you the way; there, down that ride, turn short to the right, the fox is sure to sink the wind; set your pony's head straight, he'll refuse nothing, and you'll get the brush."

Encouraged by this friendly hint, I lost no time, and, upon emerging from the wood, found myself close to the hounds.

"Capital, youngster!" shouted Tom, as I took the first fence—a flight of stiffish rails—into one of the paddocks.

I looked back and found only the huntsman, first

whipper-in, the lady I have already alluded to, and some five or six men in pink, with the hounds. Having once got the lead, and being admirably mounted, I determined to try and keep it; and as the pony I was mounted upon, was one of the best fencers in the country, I had little difficulty, with my light weight, in accomplishing this my most anxious desire. We approached Halnaker Park. Part of the high deer palings had been broken down by a tree falling upon them. I spied the gap, and went at it, as Tom Grant afterwards said, "like a Briton." The fact is, that, though reduced as was the fence, it was an awful leap. The huntsman followed me; while the others, not seeing the place we had taken, turned away, and skirted the park.

"Bravo, young 'un!" shouted Tom, "you're one of the right sort; we've set the field—the gate's open —steady, there's a nasty gap on the other side of that quick-set hedge."

The greatest conqueror of ancient or modern times was not prouder than I was of this my first victory.

I will not tire my readers with details of this memorable run; suffice it to say, that the fox ran straight down wind ten miles, over a beautiful flat country, the hounds running into him upon Houghton Bridge, as he was about to cross the Arundel river. No one except the huntsman, the first whipper-in, and myself were up, the field having been thrown out at Halnaker Park. The brush was presented to me with warm congratulations, and to this day I retain it as a proud and well-earned trophy.

Racing was cultivated quite as zealously as hunting —the Goodwood Races having been established in the year 1802, probably to gratify the members of the Goodwood Hunt, and the officers of the Sussex Militia, all of whom looked up to the Duke of Richmond as their chief. Of "the Hunt" so long and justly celebrated throughout the county, and by every lover of British field-sports, crayon portraits are preserved in the house. The ladies who were the ornaments of it, were the Ladies Louisa and Mary Lennox, the Dowager Lady King, Mrs. General Dorrien, whose full length by Romney hangs on the staircase, and Mesdames Tredcroft and Leeves; the noblemen and gentlemen were the Earl of Egremont, Lords King and Pelham, Sir H. Featherstonhaugh, Honourable T. Steele, Colonel Teesdale, Reverend Messrs. Toghill and Alcock, and Messrs. Steele, Peckham, Tredcroft, and Leeves.

Stubbs was called upon to place upon canvas the best of the Duke's stud. The result may be seen in his picture of "Race Horses training," including portraits of the Duchess, and Lady Louisa, wife of my grandfather, Lord George H. Lennox; her Grace's portrait has also been painted by Angelica Kauffman. There are four other equine portraits by Wootton, of about the same period.

On the first year of the races, which continued for three days, April 28 to 30, the money run for amounted to £1001; the Duke's horses "Cedar" and "You know me" were winners; but the Prince of Wales's "Rebel" by "Trumpeter" beat the former, and Mr. Byndloss's "Sir Simon" beat another of the Duke's horses—"Goodwood." "Cedar" was again beaten next year. Two of his Grace's stud, "You know me" and "Rollo," were winners in 1805, and one colt won in 1807. Lord Egremont and other proprietors of racing stock, attended these meetings—and ran matches, and the gentry and farmers of the county flocked to them as the great sporting event of the year.

The stables, from the design of Sir William Chambers, contain stalls for fifty-four horses.

My recollection of Old Richmond House is not very distinct, as it was burnt down when I was young. But it is well known to have been the headquarters of successive generations of fashionable visitors. Some slight idea may be gathered of its position from Canaletti's pictures, "A view of London from the Terrace at Richmond House," and " A view in London, including the Gardens at Richmond House,

White Hall, and the Old Treasury Gate"—preserved at Goodwood. They belong to those fine illustrations of the Thames architecture which the artist was employed to paint during his residence in England. Though not to be compared with his Venetian pictures, of which there are a pair of his best, representing the Rialto and the Custom-House in the same collection—they are interesting works.

From the days of the "Merry Monarch," the site has been the scene of court gaieties almost innumerable—nor did they fall off very much in the more sober Georgian era; if the gossip of Walpole, Mrs. Delaney, and other careful recorders of the small events of fashionable life is to be accepted. Whatever attractions it may have boasted in the reigns of Queens Anne and Caroline, in that of Queen Charlotte it seems to have rivalled Devonshire House in the brilliant assemblages it attracted. In my early time, however, they were of very opposite character—the Whigs making their rendezvous in Piccadilly, and the Tories their's in Whitehall; the friends of my cousin Fox filling the one—the friends of my godfather Pitt crowding the other. Rival beauties, too, were as attractive an element as rival politicians; and there are reasons for believing that it was not exclusively the influence of Government or of Opposition that reigned at these fashionable re-unions.

Among them at Richmond House must not be forgotten the fairest ornaments of the Court, irreverently described in the "Rolliad" as—

> "Ye gentle Maids of Honour in stiff hoops,
> Buried alive up to your necks,
> Who, chaste as phœnixes in coops,
> Know not the danger that awaits your sex."

The indifference of my godfather to female blandishments was proverbial, and brought on him a perpetual shower of indecent epigrams. The fame of my kinsman was as opposite to it as the poles, and the Whig versifiers made the most of his popularity with the fair. The best effusion of this kind thus records the names of the ladies who were the most zealous Foxites:—

> "Avaunt! ye profane—the fair pageantry moves,
> An entry of Venus, led on by the loves!
> Behold how the urchins round Devonshire press,
> For orders submissive, her eyes they address;
> She assumes her command with a diffident smile,
> And leads, thus attended, the pride of the isle.
> Oh, now for the pencil of Guido to trace
> Of Keppel the features, of Waldegrave the grace;
> Of Fitzroy the bloom, the May morning to vie,
> Of Sefton the air, of Duncannon the eye;
> Of Loftus the smiles (though with preference proud
> She gives ten to her husband for one to the crowd);
> Of Portland the manner that steals on the breast,
> But is too much her own to be caught or expressed.
> The charms that with sentiment Bouverie blends,
> The fairest of forms and the truest of friends;

The look that in Warburton, humble and chaste,
Speaks candour and truth, and discretion and taste;
Or with equal expression in Horton combined
Vivacity's dimples with reason defined.

Reynolds, haste to my aid for a figure divine,
Where the pencil of Guido has yielded to thine;
Bear witness the canvas where Sheridan lives,
And with angels the lovely competitor strives—
While earth claims her beauty, and heaven her strain,
Be it mine to adore every link of the chain.

But new claimants appear ere the lyre is unstrung—
Can Payne be passed by? shall not Milner be sung?
See Delmé and Howard, a favourite pair,
For grace of both classes, the zealous and fair;
A verse for Morant, like her wit may it please,
Another for Braddyll, of elegant ease,
For Bamfylde a simile worthy her frame—
Quick! quick! I have yet half a hundred to name.
Not Parnassus in concert could answer the call,
Nor multiplied muses do justice to all.

Then follow the throng, where with festal delight,
More pleasing than Hebe, Crewe opens the night;
Not the goblet nectareous of welcome and joy,
That Dido prepared for the hero of Troy;
Not fiction describing the banquets above,
Where goddesses mix at the table of Jove,
Could afford to the soul more ambroseal cheer
Than attends on the fairer associates here.
But Crewe with a mortal's distinction content,
Bounds her claims to the rites of this happy event;
For the hero to twine civic garlands of fame
With the laurel and rose interweaving his name;
And while Io Pæans his merits avow,
As the Queen of the feast place the wreath on his brow."*

* Political Miscellanies, "The Westminster Guide," Part II.

A pretty description of a very attractive assemblage. Alas, that there should be so little left of either the poet or the sources of his inspiration! The artist whom the poet summoned to his aid has left us a few of this *belle assemblée,* whose lovely features he transferred to canvas, at an average expense of about thirty pounds sterling to each beautiful sitter; and when such portraits come under the observation of Messrs. Christie and Manson, they are pretty sure of realising for the fortunate possessor something nearer an average of a thousand guineas; and the equally faithful pencil of Gainsborough has preserved for us a few more; but the bright galaxy are but feebly represented by these resemblances. Charming pictures though they are, admirable works of art, exquisite examples of a style of portrait painting which has rarely been excelled—what do they give us of the fascination, the wit, the grace, or the merit of their originals?

We may look in vain for the brilliant leader of that bright social circle—for the devoted wife, for the affectionate daughter, for the earnest friend! Their reflections are on the canvas, and Time has dealt with many of these beauties ungallantly—their names are in the Peerage, and Lodge has been but niggardly in his estimate of their nobility. Yet with such memorials, and a little gossip to be picked up occasionally here and there, a later generation must be content. We may visit their tombs, we may gather what consolation we can in knowing that they are dust, and in reading their epitaphs, but we had better be satisfied with the gossip and the portraits. To the old who can remember such precious sources of gratification, there is nothing to reconcile him for their loss.

CHAPTER IV.

THOUGHTS OF A PROFESSION—BUILDING CASTLES—LIFE OF A WESTMINSTER BOY—FAGGING—MY SCHOOL CONTEMPORARIES—THE MARGRAVINE OF ANSPACH—DUBLIN SOCIETY—LADY MORGAN'S STATEMENTS—MISS OWENSON, THE WILD IRISH GIRL—MARCHIONESS OF ABERCORN—DR. MORGAN—HE IS KNIGHTED BY MY FATHER, AND MARRIES MISS OWENSON—DR. CARY, THE HEAD MASTER OF WESTMINSTER SCHOOL—RESULTS OF GOING OUT OF BOUNDS—I AM BETRAYED—MY TUTOR—FELLOW PUPILS—THEATRE AT NEWBURY—"HAMLET" INTERRUPTED.

CHAPTER IV.

I HAD not been quite so idle as many of my readers may perhaps imagine. I enjoyed myself as far as my opportunities permitted, but, numerous as they were, they left me a little time for serious reflection; and much though I may have enjoyed my present, I was not without thoughts for my future. I speculated on my career. My ideas did not turn with particular zest towards the business of the State. The fact is, the illustrious statesman whose name I had the honour of bearing, had passed away from the scene of his anxious labours and his glorious triumphs, where his distinguished rival, my kinsman, Fox, had followed him. Political patronage from either, therefore, was out of the question; even had the latter survived, the political opinions of my family were so opposed to his that I could not have expected his support.

I had long placed my affections on a military life

—from which several of my family had derived very high honours, but, in consequence of my father's quarrel with the Duke of York, my prospects at the Horse Guards were thought to be exceedingly unpromising. The exposure of the traffic in commissions with which Mrs. Mary Anne Clarke had astonished a Committee of Enquiry in the House of Commons, in this year 1809, did not afford me much encouragement, but I knew I must wait some years before my chance would come, if it came at all. So I continued at Westminster, building castles in the air that would have done credit to Vauban.

The life of a Westminster boy, by the way, is not all *couleur de rose*; indeed, while he remains a fag, it presents a totally different complexion—at least it did in my time. The young gentleman was then obliged to rise at six in summer, and seven in winter. He commenced the labours of the day by fetching water from the pump in Dean's Yard, and then applied himself to light his master's fire—usually with an insufficient allowance of wood. He next boiled his water, and prepared his breakfast. Later in the day he had to fag for him at cricket or fives, or run messages, and do his little marketings for sausages, rolls, muffins, tarts, and fruits, with the risk, if caught out of bounds, of having a flogging, to encourage the others, as a Frenchman said of the execution of Admiral

Byng. He had also to prepare tea and supper, to brush boots and clothes, and clean cord breeches, and top-boots, gridiron, frying-pan and all other cooking utensils, the property of his master. As a recompense for these multifarious duties the fag sometimes obtained ten shillings or a guinea at Christmas—more frequently the reversion of an old tea-pot. Such suit and service I performed for the Honourable Mr. Erskine, afterwards Earl of Mar. The nature and extent of my reversionary interests I cannot remember, but I doubt whether they were more munificent than those which fell to the other juvenile victims of the system—a system, however, which was carried out in my time far more harshly than I believe it is now.

One day when I was to fight a boy "after four," Erskine sent for me.

"If you don't lick him," said he, "I'll lick you!"

I fought till I was blind, and was vanquished. When on the sick-list in the housekeeper's room, Erskine came in.

"You fought well," said he, "I shan't fag you for a week; here's half-a-guinea for you."

Tyrant as I had considered him, and not without cause, his kindness won me, and I slaved on for him so long as I remained in the lower school, without a murmur.

I was also fag to the Honourable William Coventry, who is still, I am happy to say, flourishing, and for whom I entertain the highest regard. It was only last Christmas I reminded him, at dinner before his wife and family, that his punishment, when I failed to give a bright polish to his boots, was to take down every boot and shoe and trample on them, to provide me with so much extra labour.

The Marquis of Westminster, then Lord Belgrave, I remember as a kind-hearted, good-natured boy; qualities he retains as a man. The Marquis of Anglesey, then Lord Paget, was an excellent runner, cricketer, and good sparrer. In one contest the Paget blood came out, and he fought as his gallant father did at Benevente and Sahagun. He still exists—no one more popular than the owner of Beaudesert.

Lord Lucan, then Lord Bingham, was a warm-hearted youth. He has proved himself a distinguished cavalry officer. Lord Mayo, then "Big Burke," is as fine a specimen of an Irishman as can be seen anywhere.

I well remember the Margravine of Anspach. I was taken to visit her at Brandenburg House, afterwards immortalized by Theodore Hook, in his *John Bull* song upon Queen Caroline's visitors:

"And frothy Grey Bennet,
That very day se'night,
Drove down in his dennet, to Brandenburg House."

And this reminds me that one day Hook sang me the above song; and upon my delicately asking who was the author of that and other writings in *John Bull* about Queen Caroline, replied, " Occasionally hints were given and sent me, but this finger and thumb wrote every line."

The Margravine showed us her Bijou Theatre, and then suggested a visit to another of greater celebrity. One curious feature there was at this popular place of public entertainment: the names of the respective plays were painted in gold characters, and exhibited from beneath the royal arms in the middle of the proscenium.

The Margravine assembled a large juvenile party, consisting of myself, brothers, and sisters, to go to Sadler's Wells, and great was our delight to see two grand carriages arrive at Richmond House, the servants wearing royal liveries.

I jumped on the box of one, much to the surprise of the burly coachman who occupied it. And so unaccustomed was I to sit on a driving-box, that I was almost jolted off it during the long drive from Privy Gardens to the New River Head. The manager of the theatre was in readiness to receive us in royal state; and with old Joe Grimaldi in the comic pantomime, and an aquatic melodrama, in which a naval engagement took place, and amphibious actors were immersed in the real water, then rescued from it, we were enchanted.

The Margravine was a kind-hearted, good-natured old lady, with a decided touch of eccentricity. Her vanity, too, was evident enough, particularly in the private theatrical performances which rendered Brandenburg House famous in the annals of fashion; for, by the particular desire of herself, she performed plays of her own composition—melodramatic attempts founded on the then popular productions of Schiller and Kotzebue. She subsequently went abroad and died in Italy, under circumstances recorded in the Private Diary of the Duke of Buckingham, published a year or two back.

My godfather sometimes called on me at Richmond House, on his way to the House of Commons. I perfectly recollect his tall, thin figure, powdered head, and flushed face, eloquent of his favourite beverage— port. His manner to me whilst he lived was invariably kind, and at his death he left me a sword— probably the one he wore as Colonel of the Cinque Port Volunteers—and a brooch with his head set in gold. He did not "tip" at his visits—an unpardonable fault in the eyes of Westminster Boys. In contrast to him in this respect was the late Sir Robert Peel, who, upon two different occasions, when my brother and myself had to call upon him, on our way from school, made our pockets heavier by a guinea each.

I did not want friends during my school career, therefore was kept pretty liberally supplied with the circulating medium, which enabled me to enjoy a tolerably extensive acquaintance with juvenile pleasures. But it was at the period of the Winter and Midsummer vacations that we youngsters enjoyed life thoroughly. How we enjoyed it, can scarcely be appreciated without a tolerable knowledge of the state of things in the Irish metropolis while my father filled the office of Viceroy.

There was certainly a good deal of vivacity in the best Dublin Society at this period. To do at Rome as the Romans did, seemed an axiom that might be transferred to the Irish capital, therefore the family of the Lord Lieutenant, as far as was expedient, attempted to do at Dublin what was done there by its principal people. Lady Morgan has ventured to state that a Mr. Bathurst, a member of the Duke's suite, used to astonish the Irish ladies by entering the drawing-room performing a succession of somersaults; but of this I have no recollection; nor do I believe another assertion of her ladyship's, that "there were in the Castle circle a *posse* of titled women of bold reputation, who had the uncontrolled sway in everything." She adds, "These ladies introduced a kind of savage dance, or rather romp, called "Cutchakutchoo." This was performed by the parties squatting themselves on the floor, both their arms underneath their legs, and changing places with their partners as well as they could in such a posture. In short, the Dublin Court of that period was like the manners described in Grammont's Memoirs."*

I have no hesitation in stating my opinion that this is a gross exaggeration. What the Irish ladies were with whom Glorvina most frequently associated, I cannot say. It is clear, from her own admissions, that much romping and flirting went on wherever she was present; but such "Irish ladies" were not the associates of my mother and sisters; and where they presided, though any harmless frolic was sanctioned, there was never the slightest approach to the vicious manners of Charles the Second's Court, as described by the dissolute Count Grammont.

While my family were stationed at Dublin, its members became more or less acquainted with all the noble and intellectual, gentle and simple of the Irish metropolis and neighbourhood, who desired to be presented to the Viceroy. Among these were Lady Moira, Catherine Countess of Charleville, with the Marquis and Marchioness of Abercorn—the former

---

* Lady Morgan's "Memoirs. Autobiography, Diaries, and Correspondence." Vol. ii., p. 244.

a superlatively fine gentleman of the olden time, who, in his exceedingly studied get up, looked so superior an article of humanity, as was only fit to be seen under a glass shade. His lady was quite as elegant and refined in her costume—indeed, aspired to set the fashion at the Irish Court in manners as well as dress.

In their suite they had secured a young woman who had obtained no small degree of celebrity as a writer of fiction. She was one of the two daughters of a person named Owenson, who had been a farmer, a wine merchant, and an actor—but was much more widely known on the boards of one of the Dublin theatres, than as a trader or agriculturist. Like scores of similar adventurers of the same class and country, he had always been better acquainted with Fortune's eldest daughter than herself—nevertheless, being an amusing fellow, he was frequently found in good society. Though he could not afford to give his children a regular education, they contrived to acquire as much of it as fitted them to play a respectable part on the great stage of life. Indeed, one got on so far in reading and writing, that when she ought to have been at school, she took a situation as governess; and when she should have been qualifying for so onerous a post, she was writing a novel.

Imaginative literature was at a very low ebb in the

sister island—" The sorrows of Werter," and the "Poems of Ossian," were the chief sources of sentiment and taste; and Sydney Owenson, having fallen in love with a clerk, wrote the result of her experience and her reading, in a tale called " St. Clair, or First Love," which was published in Dublin in 1802. The moderate success which attended this production emboldened her to try another venture, and she produced "The Novice of St. Dominic," which had the distinction of being brought out by a London publisher, Sir Richard Phillip's, to whom it was taken by the authoress in person, in 1805. This had a much more extended success. It has been affirmed that Mr. Pitt was delighted with it, and re-perused its pages when suffering from the illness that proved fatal. Dr. Johnson, we know, was equally enraptured with Miss Burney's early attempt at fiction. The literary merit of both works, notwithstanding, has long ceased to be appreciated.

It was Miss Owenson's third venture, " The Wild Irish Girl," that established her fame as an Irish novelist. The extent of her imaginative power may be understood from the fact, that in the story she represents the rollicking Dublin actor and bankrupt tradesman, her father, as the " Prince of Innismore," herself as Glorvina the Princess; a man of the name of Everard, and his scape grace son, with whom she had been carrying on an amorous correspondence, as an English nobleman, Lord M., and his heir.

Never before or since had such homely materials been so transformed. They took the shape of a melo-dramatic romance written, in a series of letters—a favourite mode of romance writing in the last century, the best example of which exists in Smollett's "Humphrey Clinker." The work had a success equal to the best of Maturin's equally flighty productions, and the reputation it brought, gave Miss Owenson easy access to the best Irish society. Ladies of rank were glad to patronize the popular authoress—as she became a *lionne* in their circle, and was so completely identified with her own heroine, that everyone called her Glorvina. Whether her father was similarly elevated, is not affirmed.

Lord and Lady Abercorn took Miss Owenson into their establishment " to amuse them ;" and it is but justice to say, that she entertained them and their friends, amazingly. She was always ready to make herself generally entertaining, if not generally useful, to the throngs of gay Irishmen and Irishwomen who filled the fashionable drawing-rooms of her patrons. She played tunes on the harp, sang Irish songs, and danced Irish jigs, with equal vivacity. Her small figure, dark complexion, round head of curly hair, and languishing eyes, being displayed to the best advantge, but with a theatrical manner that could only have been tolerated in "A Wild Irish Girl" and a "genius."

The ladies were more amused than edified by her exhibitions—in truth, some of them thought her a quiz, and ridiculed her displays. The gentlemen professed immense admiration, particularly those with whom she flirted, which was said to include every one who required, or was thought to require, a wife. It so happened that the more desirable of her numerous admirers looked at the enticing bait, but did not seem to care to be hooked. Stories were in circulation respecting a poor subaltern who had drowned himself, and a small poet who had pined away for the peerless Glorvina, which may probably account for the reticence of her fashionable adorers.

I remember well the fun my brothers and I found as spectators of the young lady's performances. To us schoolboys they afforded a rich treat. Nothing we had seen of Irish life we found half so amusing.

Lady Abercorn at last became afraid that her lovely *protegée* might get herself into a scrape, if she did not make some effort to have her respectably off her hands. So, after long consultations with her husband, and subsequent conferences with my father, it was determined to marry her to Lord Abercorn's family doctor, who, forming a part of his lordship's establishment, was at hand for the much-desired purpose.

The young lady's friends, however, were well aware that she was ambitious—that in her heart she had cultivated the hope of realizing the aristocratic pretensions of her " Wild Irish Girl." The Marquis and Marchioness therefore made earnest suit to the Lord Lieutenant, that he would assist them to elevate the amusing Glorvina. This petition he could not very well deny, as he just before, in his Vice-regal capacity, had done the same service for her sister, by knighting a certain Dr. Clarke, whom that young lady had married. It was therefore resolved that Dr. Morgan should straightway be made Sir Charles, and that he should be the husband of Sydney Owenson. This programme was fulfilled, and in the month of January, of the year 1812, she became Lady Morgan; after having been seriously abjured by her considerate friends to give up flirting, and mind her ps and qs—for her reluctance to abandon her ambitious aspirations was evident to them all.

My profession having been decided on, I somewhat prematurely gave myself airs of manhood. I had received a commission, and therefore considered myself independent of scholastic rules.

A few days previous to the " breaking up " for the midsummer holidays in 1813, Dr. Cary, the head-master of Westminster school, sent for me, and addressed me nearly in the following words:

"Since you have been gazetted to the Blues, your conduct has not been so steady as I expected it would be. I do not wish to lead you into a trap, but I have every reason to believe that you and Mallory went to the theatre last Tuesday; and that you, somehow or other, managed to get out of your boarding-house after answering to your names. I have made it a rule never to act as a spy, or employ others so to do, nor did I court the information that reached me. I own that the channel through which it was conveyed was an improper one, still the statement that you both were seen at Covent Garden Theatre, that you afterwards supped and slept at an hotel in Bridge Street, was so circumstantial, that there can be in my mind no doubt as to the correctness of it. I have not followed the affair up as I might have done, for I hope and believe that you would not condescend to tell a lie. I ask for no disclosure—your silence will be sufficient."

"It is true—all true," I responded, "but none of the servants at Mrs. Packharness's were to blame; we answered to our names, got through Dr. Dodd's room, and escaped out of the window and across the area."

"I suspected as much," replied the gentlemanlike head-master. "Under the circumstances, I think it will be advisable for you not to return here after the holidays—you will require some military instruction before you enter your new career—I hope it may be attended with credit to yourself. I have written to the Duke, pointing out the advantages that may be gained by a course of study under some experienced private tutor, and have not hinted at the cause of my decision. Mallory will have to write out a hundred verses from Virgil during the holidays. You may leave me now."

Upon joining my comrade in disgrace, we put our heads together, and certainly they seemed to have been made of a like material as those of certain parish authorities. They were advocating Macadamizing a street, which drew from Sydney Smith the remark, "Gentlemen, if you require a hard road, you had better put your heads together." It took us some time to make out who had betrayed our secret. We had confided it to one or two "cronies," but we knew that they were too honourable to peach.

At length we remembered meeting a gentleman, or a person dressed like one, at Ginger's hotel in Bridge Street, who addressed us in the coffee-room, remarking that he had sat near us at the theatre. In the exuberance of our spirits we invited him to have a glass of Bishop, to which he assented. It was during this flow of soul and bowl that he drew from us that we were truant Westminster boys, and added, as the saying goes, insult to injury, by drinking our beverage and then informing against us.

From that day to this we never knew who our treacherous friend was; but that it was the man we suspected, in some measure was confirmed by Dr. Cary, who, having heard that we had suspected a schoolfellow, assured us that he had nothing to do with it. We regretted that the spy did not make his appearance in Dean's Yard, for he would have unquestionably undergone that remedy not then so popular as it has been since—the cold water cure under the pump.

In consequence of the above, I never returned to Westminster, but was sent, early in August, to the Rev. Mr. Knollis's, at Littlewick Green, Maidenhead Thicket. There I found half a dozen youths of about my own age, all of whom were destined for a military life. Among them were James Lord Hay, and Jasper Hall, afterwards in the Guards; all of them I often met afterwards. In January, 1814, Mr. Knollis removed to Donnington, near Newbury, and there I remained, but it was not to be for long.

During the time I was at Donnington, I had frequent opportunities of carrying out my early passion for theatricals and field-sports. Our worthy Dominie expected a certain amount of work to be done every day, and the moment that was concluded, we were permitted to join in the chase with Mr. Charles Craven's fox-hounds, to attend the coursing meetings in the neighbourhood, and to patronize the theatre at Newbury, which was then under the management of Mr. Barnett. In those days Shakspeare had not been driven from the provincial boards, and the audiences much preferred "Macbeth," "The Merchant of Venice," "Hamlet," and "Othello" to the then sensation dramas of "The Murder by the Lone House," "The Wizard of the Wave," "The Duel in the Snow," "Idiot Witness," "Son of the Wilderness," and "Children of the Castle."

One evening, Mrs. Barnett, a clever actress, was acting the *Queen* in "Hamlet," when, just previous to the exit of the player *Queen*, something had tickled our fancy and raised our risibility much. Indeed, the whole scene of a small stage on a small stage had been absurd to the greatest degree, and one and all of us occupying the proscenium-box broke out, to our shame be it spoken, into a loud laugh. Mrs. Barnett looked daggers at us.

"Beautiful!—what stage effect!" I cried.

Upon which, when, in reply to the King's question, "How like you the play, madam?" Mrs. Barnett, instead of replying at once, "The lady doth protest too much, methinks," came sweeping down to the lamps, and, turning to us, said, in a high-flown tone, "Puppies are no judges of stage effect!" and then proceeded with the text. Fortunately for us, the audience were too dense to think the remark applied to us, or, as the Barnetts were especial favourites, we might have been hooted out of the house.

CHAPTER V.

THE DUKE OF WELLINGTON—MY FIRST LETTER FROM HIS GRACE—MY FIRST INTERVIEW—AM APPOINTED TO JOIN THE EMBASSY AT PARIS AS ATTACHÉ—JOURNEY FROM ENGLAND WITH THE DUKE—ON BOARD THE "GRIFFIN"—THE DUKE AT BERGEN-OP-ZOOM—ENTERTAINMENTS AT BRUSSELS—PRESENTATION OF THE ORDER OF THE BATH TO THE PRINCE OF ORANGE—THE DUKE AND THE NEWSPAPERS—INSPECTION OF FORTRESSES—MISTAKEN FOR A GREAT MAN—JOURNEY TO PARIS—STATE RECEPTION OF THE DUKE OF WELLINGTON BY LOUIS XVIII.—FETE OF ST. LOUIS—FRENCH PLAYS—MY FRENCH MASTER, M. GALLOIS.

CHAPTER V.

FROM the year 1808, all I had heard of the admirer of my pantomimic efforts at the Phœnix Park Christmas entertainments, was through the public journals, which in due course of time announced the reception of the hero at Dover, on the 23rd of June, 1814. One morning, when looking out for the arrival of the post—for I was anxiously expecting a remittance from home—a franked letter, among others, was given me. As in those days it did not at all follow that the communication was from the same pen as the franker—this not being the case in ninety cases out of a hundred—I read my other correspondents' effusions first. They consisted of an application for payment of a small account at Maidenhead, which had escaped my memory, and two or three scrawls from old cronies at Westminster.

At last I turned to the franked letter, and, upon

looking at the seal, saw that it bore a ducal coronet. Upon opening it, great was my surprise to see " Dear William," in a hand unknown to me, and greater still was it when I read as follows:

"The Duke and Duchess have consented to your accompanying me to Paris. You must lose no time in getting ready for the journey. When you arrive in London, call here. Yours affectionately,

"WELLINGTON."

"Hamilton Place."

At first I fancied the whole affair a hoax, but showing the document to Mr. Knollis, he at once pronounced it to be genuine. While receiving the congratulations of my young comrades, a parcel was brought me from the coach-office, which contained a few lines from my uncle, the late Duke of Gordon, then Marquis of Huntley, saying that he was going through Newbury to London, taking Ascot by the way, and promising, if I would be ready by three o'clock, he would meet me at the Pelican Inn, where we could have an early dinner, and then proceed to Wokingham, where we were to sleep, reaching London the following afternoon. He concluded by wishing me joy of my appointment to the duke's embassy.

Taking a hasty leave of my tutor and young companions, I joined my uncle, and in less than eight-and-forty hours found myself at Richmond House, where my father and mother were residing, and they soon assisted me in making preparations for my journey to Paris.

The London season had been one of the greatest gaiety. Napoleon had abdicated the throne of the world—the Bourbons had been restored—Louis XVIII. had quitted England—the warehouse for bonded sovereigns (as it had been called)—"to relieve France," so wrote Berthier, "from the weight of misfortunes under which she had for five-and-twenty years been groaning." Kings, emperors, princes, potentates, had flocked to London, which was thronged with the votaries of fashion and pleasure. Fêtes, operas, balls, masquerades, dinners, concerts, illuminations, naval and military reviews, formed the order of the day and night. Everybody was dining out, supping out, driving out, and hunting the royal and imperial lions.

Upon the 6th of August, I received orders to be with the Duke of Wellington the following day, at two o'clock in the afternoon. Need I say, that punctually at that hour I drove up to the door of his Grace's temporary residence in Hamilton Place, Piccadilly? I was ushered into his presence, and there saw the great conqueror seated at his writing-table, placing some manuscripts in a large despatch box. The room was strewed with covers of letters, printed forms, and papers.

After a most kind reception, his Grace desired me to order the carriage round at three o'clock, and then proceeded to arrange his documents, give his directions, and make preparations for his departure. As the clock was about to strike three, Wellington rose from his chair, and, having previously taken leave of relations and friends there assembled, walked to the door of his carriage.

In less time than I can take to record it, my brother *attaché*, Lord Downes, then Sir Ulysses de Burgh, and myself, had followed, and were seated opposite him. The servants had mounted the rumble; and the carriage, a perfectly plain one, drove off, with four good posters, on the road to Coombe Wood, where we were to dine and sleep.

During our journey the Duke conversed affably upon a variety of subjects; he told us that at half-past ten in the morning he had been honoured by an audience with the Prince Regent, and that he had remained nearly an hour with his Royal Highness. He mentioned that, upon the previous day, after reviewing the Blues, and dining with the officers, he had a narrow escape from a serious accident. In driving through Brentford, upon his return from Windsor, about nine o'clock at night, the linchpin came out of the fore-wheel of his carriage, by which it was nearly upset. In consequence of this, he was detained at Brentford until the damage was repaired; and it was with some difficulty that he could prevail on the populace to relinquish their desire of drawing him to the metropolis.

At our destination, the Earl of Liverpool was in waiting to receive his Grace, and a small party were assembled for dinner. Nothing could exceed the good-humour and affability of the great man, who told anecdotes of the late war, laughed, jested, and kept the whole company in a state of delight. At an early hour next morning we left for Dover.

The Duke was received everywhere on the road with the highest enthusiasm; the gathering multitude pressing, clinging, struggling around the carriage at every change of horses. In the language of Southey —"The people would not be debarred from gazing, till the last moment, upon the hero—the darling hero of England!"

At three o'clock a salute from the batteries announced the arrival of Wellington at Dover. He alighted at Wright's Hotel, and partook of some refreshment, but finding that the wind was blowing very fresh from the west-south-west, and the weather too boisterous to embark at that port, his Grace proceeded on to Deal, about five o'clock. Vice-Admiral Foley preceded the Duke about an hour, in order to give the necessary directions for his reception on board the *Griffon*, sloop of war, Captain Hewson.

Upon reaching Deal, where his Grace was received by all ranks with every demonstration of joy and respect, we found the Vice-Admiral in waiting; and, accompanied by that gallant officer, and a great concourse of the inhabitants, we proceeded to the boat prepared to take us off to the ship. Here, again, the Duke was heartily cheered.

No sooner were we on board the *Griffon*, than she got under weigh, and, with a strong wind, steered for Ostend.

There was nothing peculiarly attractive about the *Griffon*, and, as the captain had not sufficient time to prepare for so distinguished a guest, the Duke had to rough it, upon the ordinary sea provisions. There was a circumstance, however, connected with this vessel, which did not escape the acuteness of Wellington, and to which he referred in the handsomest manner, upon taking leave of Captain Hewson and his officers. It appeared that, in 1813, a malicious report had found its way into the newspapers, stating that there had been a mutiny of the crew, and that the vessel had been carried by them into the port of Boulogne. This led to a letter being addressed by the crew to their commander:

"H.M.S. *Griffon*,
"Dungeness, January 6, 1813.

"Sir,—A report of a most disagreeable nature having

been circulated, greatly to our disadvantage, in representing us as having 'taken H.M.S. *Griffon* from our officers, and carried her into Boulogne'—we, the petty officers, seamen, and marines, of the said sloop, most humbly beg to represent that, far from having any cause of discontent either with our captain or officers, we feel obliged to them for their lenity during the present short-handed state of the vessel; and hope it will please the Commander-in-Chief, or the Lords of the Admiralty, to prosecute the author of so scandalous and malicious a report, tending so greatly to our prejudice, and that of the service.

"We remain, honoured Sir,
"Your most obedient humble servants,
[Signed by the whole ship's company].
" To George Trollope, Esq.,
"Captain of H.M.S. *Griffon*."

In recording this portion of my early career with Wellington, the following extract from the log of the ship in which we embarked will tend to illustrate what occurred on our crossing the Channel:

"H.M.S. ship *Griffon*,
"Monday, August 8, 1814.

"A.M.—Strong winds and squally weather; at 9, weighed, and made sail under the courses and close reef topsails; at noon, strong gales and clear weather.

"P.M.—Strong gales and cloudy; at 2.30, bore up; at 3.30, sent the gig on shore to Dover; at 5, wind W.S.W., gig returned, filled and made sail for the Downs; at 5.30, shortened sail, and came to (small bower) Walmer Mill, on the west end of the Hospital; at 6, answered telegraph made by 'Monmouth;' at 6.20, embarked the Duke of Wellington and suite for Ostend, fired a salute of fifteen guns; at 7.30, weighed and made sail; at 9, North Foreland Light, N.W.; North Sandhead Light, S. by W.; at 12, fresh gales and cleared.

"August 9, 1814.

"A.M.—Fresh breezes and cloudy; at 1.30, hove to; at 1.50, filled; at 3.30, bore up for the Boom Pot; at 4, watch up top gallant yards, sounded every half hour, lost by accident one head and hand line, strong gales and cloudy; at 7.30, made the land; at 8.30, West Kapelle, S.S.E., distance eight or nine miles, strong gales and cloudy weather, attended with heavy squalls; at 10, made signal for pilot with several guns; at noon, strong gales and cloudy.

"P.M.—Strong gales and cloudy weather; at 1, hove to, close by Zierckzee Pier Head, sent the boat on shore for a pilot, made sail; at 5, shortened sail and came to, moored ship at Bergen-op-Zoom; at 6, disembarked the Duke of Wellington and suite, cheered, and fired a salute of fifteen guns."

On landing at Bergen-op-Zoom, the Duke beheld the scene of that untoward and fatal enterprise, under Sir Thomas Graham (afterwards Lord Lynedoch), wherein Skerret, the intrepid defender of Tarifa, led the attack and fell; as did Gore, Mercer, Carleton, and McDonald. He saw the spot where three hundred were killed, and eighteen hundred wounded; and mourned over the siege, which, although it promised at the onset complete success, failed in the end, from the loss of the principal officers of the right column, which caused it to fall into disorder, and from the left column being weakened by the loss of a detachment of the guards, cut off by the enemy.

It was with the deepest interest that Wellington inspected the town and fortress; he minutely examined the different points at which the gallant Graham had attempted to carry the place by storm; he gazed upon the spot between the Antwerp and Water Port gates, where Cooke, despite the difficulty of passing the ditch, on account of the ice, succeeded in establishing his column on the ramparts; and stopped opposite the Stenbergen gate, where the faint attack was to be made by the third column.

He paused for some time to the right of the New gate, where the second column, under Colonel Morrice, was compelled, from the heavy fire of the enemy, to retire; but the point that seemed to attract his all-absorbing attention was at the entrance of the harbour, fordable alone at low water. Here the right column, under Skerret and Gore, had forced their way into the body of the place, but the death of the latter, and the severe wounds of the former, had (as I have stated) caused the troops under their command to fall into disorder, and to suffer a great loss in killed, wounded, and prisoners.

The whole road from Bergen-op-Zoom to Antwerp was a scene of the greatest gaiety; "the bees had expelled the bear that broke open their hive;" "Orange Boven!" was shouted everywhere; the bluff burghers were puffing freedom out of their short tobacco pipes, and drinking success to it in draughts of schiedam.

On the 10th, we reached Antwerp; as my chief was in plain clothes, he was not immediately recognized, but the moment he was discovered he was very much cheered, especially by the English. His Grace shook hands most cordially with many of his fair countrywomen.

On the following day, I accompanied the Duke in his visit to the dockyard and arsenal; and, about one o'clock, having previously seen the cathedral, we set out for Brussels. Here it was a most gratifying scene to see the young and gallant Prince of Orange, afterwards King of Holland, who had served in the Peninsula as aid-de-camp to the great Duke, welcome his former chief to the country to which he had been so lately restored.

On the night of our arrival in Brussels, I had the honour of attending the Duke to the theatre, where we occupied the box of the Sovereign Prince. Notwithstanding Wellington's unassuming exterior, he was soon recognized, and the orchestra struck up, "See the conquering hero comes!" and other English and Dutch national airs.

On the 12th we attended the *fête* given by Lord Clancarty, in honour of the Regent's birthday, when at least four hundred persons were present. In the morning, there had been a parade of the English guards and artillery, and the Hanoverian and Belgian regiments. The Duke, and the hereditary Prince of Orange, with a brilliant staff, passed the troops in review.

A short time after our arrival, a most interesting ceremony took place, when the hereditary Prince of Orange was invested with the order of the Bath. Lord Castlereagh, in presenting the insignia to his royal highness, addressed him in a very appropriate speech, in which he dwelt with admiration upon his conduct during the Peninsular campaign; adding a confident assurance that the same zeal would be displayed by him, in his newly-restored country, should its safety or the repose of Europe be endangered.

Within ten months, the battle of Waterloo afforded the Prince an opportunity of evincing his zeal, where this gallant soldier covered himself with glory, and proved that the lessons he had learned, when upon the staff of Wellington, had not been obliterated from his mind. To add to the gaiety of Brussels, the late kind-hearted, affable Duke of Cambridge was present, regulating the arrival of a large Hanoverian army, which was to be stationed in the Netherlands.

The talented authoress of " Evelina" gives the following graphic description of Wellington, who, despite the presence of English and foreign royalty, was still the magnet of attraction:

" Our last entertainment here was a concert, in the

public and fine room appropriated for music or dancing. The celebrated Madame Catalani had a benefit, at which the Queen of the Netherlands was present—not, however, in state, though not *incognito;* and the King of Warriors, Marshal Lord Wellington, surrounded by his staff, and all the officers and first persons here, whether Belgians, Prussians, Hanoverians, or English. I looked at Lord Wellington watchfully, and was charmed with every turn of his countenance, with his noble, and singular physiognomy, and his eagle eye. He was gay, even to sportiveness, all the evening; conversing with the officers around him. He never was seated, not even for a moment, though I saw seats vacated to offer to him, frequently. He seemed enthusiastically charmed with Catalani, ardently applauding whatever she sang, except the 'Rule Britannia'; and then, with sagacious reserve, he listened in utter silence. Who ordered it, I know not, but he felt it was injudicious, in every country but our own, to give out a chorus of ' Rule, Britannia ! Britannia rules the waves !'

" And when an *encore* began to be vociferated from his officers, he instantly crushed it by a commanding air of disapprobation; and thus afforded me an opportunity of seeing how magnificently he could quit his convivial familiarity for imperious domain, when occasion might call for the transformation."

One morning, when I was occupied in answering some invitations for my chief—for at that period I had no more important correspondence entrusted to me—I saw that the Duke was enjoying some paragraphs that appeared in the English papers, and which caused him to burst out into a loud fit of laughter.

"William," said he, "you will soon be at home again, for I find the following notice in the paper of last week:

"'It seems as if the Duke of Wellington's embassy to Paris was not to be of long duration. His Grace has taken Goodwood, the Duke of Richmond's seat in Sussex, for three years, during which time the latter intends to remain in France.'

"And I find, too," he continued, smiling, "that the Duchess will be in Paris before us, for the *Courier* announces 'that the Duchess of Wellington left London on Wednesday the 10th of August, in a travelling carriage and six, attended by some of the Royal Horse Guards (Blues) for Dover, on her way to Paris.'"

A monosyllable, which sounded in my ears very expressive when preceding the word "nonsense," proved the value the Duke placed upon two such absurd statements.

After a moment's pause, his Grace said—

"The first shall be contradicted officially—the latter

is not worth a moment's thought;" then turning to me, remarked—"I think the first stage to Dartford would blow your old bangtails, especially if they had to keep up with the six posters."

Shortly after this conversation, the Government organs of the press contradicted one report by authority, and the Duchess falsified the other by not landing at Calais until the 7th of October.

On the 17th of August, I was, as they say in the army, "told off" to attend the Duke, who, accompanied by the hereditary Prince of Orange, was to visit Namur; the object being to examine the situation of that city, and the remains of the works, as well as the fort upon the hill, at the conflux of the Sambre and Meuse.

The Prince and the "hero of a hundred fights" were received with inconceivable joy. The Dutch garrison, with the commandant, General Stedman, at their head, were under arms. The people took the horses from the carriage, and drew it, amidst the loudest acclamations—amid the ringing of bells, and firing of cannon—to the hotel.

The hereditary Prince and the Duke employed two days examining this place, attended by some officers of the English engineers; and we were generally, with the exception of time allowed for a slight midday refreshment, in our saddles from dawn to dusk.

Troop horses from a regiment in garrison were allotted to us, and greater brutes I never had the misfortune to ride. Upon one occasion Wellington mounted an officer's charger, but as he was worse than any of those in the ranks, he was abandoned.

From Namur, the Prince of Orange and the Duke proceeded to Charleroi, Mons, Tournay, Courtrai, Menin, Ypres, Furnes, and Nieuport, and the same routine went on day after day. An early and excellent breakfast, a long morning's ride, a "snack," an afternoon's ride, a public dinner, and the theatre in the evening.

His Grace's presence in the Netherlands was viewed with jealousy by France, for it was well known at Paris that the Duke was actively employed in giving advice with respect to the fortifications, and suggesting measures for strengthening that formidable line, which was to form a barrier on the French frontier from Namur to the ocean.

This line, embracing the above-mentioned towns, was parallel with that of the French fortresses, which, extending from Phillippeville, runs through Maubeuge, Valenciennes, Lisle and Capelle, to Dunkirk. Hence these fortresses were to be kept in check, and any sudden attack upon the Netherlands was rendered difficult, if not impracticable.

The theatre in the Park was open, under the

management of Mr. Penley, with a company of English players. "John Bull" was represented on the first night of performance, and, owing to its name, attracted a most crowded and fashionable audience. Throughout the day it had been hinted at the box-office, that the Duke of Wellington had acceded to the request of the manager, and that he would probably honour the evening's entertainment with his presence; and under this hope a private box had been retained. The Duke's avocations, however, prevented his making his appearance upon this occasion, as he had already intimated when asked to patronize the play. This led to a ludicrous mistake: A brother officer and myself had been dining in company with the Duke, and, with that good-nature and consideration for which he was famed, his Grace gave us permission to attend the theatre, telling us we might make use of his carriage after it had set him down at home.

Upon reaching the Park, the carriage was recognized, and a crowd immediately followed it. As we gained the entrance of the theatre, the name of Wellington rent the air. This was communicated to the manager, who thrust his head out from behind the curtain, to give a signal to the leader of the band to play "See the conquering hero comes!" The report that his Grace was about to make his appearance spread like wild-fire. The performances ceased—all eyes were anxiously fixed on the vacant box.

In the meantime, my companion and myself had jumped out of the carriage, had tendered our money, and were surprised at the obsequiousness of the box-keeper, who, thinking we were the precursors of the Duke, begged us at once to walk into the lobby. The manager, or some official personage, had rushed into the private box to prepare the seats, and there, candles in hand, awaited the welcome visitor.

It was now easy to see the mistake that we had unwittingly caused, and, anxious to explain it, we approached the now open box-door. No sooner were our uniforms visible than the band struck up the heart-stirring melody. In vain did we strive to correct the error; the audience had risen *en masse;* shouts re-echoed throughout the house; the curtain was drawn up, and the company came forward to sing the national air of " God save the King!" but no representative of the sovereign to the newly-restored monarch of France appeared.

For some minutes the cheers continued. At length it was announced from the stage that a slight mistake had occurred—that the engagements of the noble Duke prevented his attendance upon that evening, and that due notice would be given should he condescend to give a bespeak.

After the excitement had a little subsided, my young friend and myself sneaked quietly into the box, placing ourselves behind the curtain, and enjoyed all the fun produced in the afterpiece. Fearful of calling the attention of the public to two mere urchins, who had unintentionally very nearly received the honours justly due to their illustrious chief, we refrained from all applause, and subdued as much as possible the laughter that we should otherwise have bestowed upon the immortal Thomas Thumb.

The time now approached for the Duke's departure from Brussels, and on the 23rd of August, after as rapid a journey as could be made in those days of heavy horses, bad roads, and huge jack-booted postilions, we reached Paris, and took possession of the Hôtel Borghese, Rue de Faubourg St. Honoré, formerly the residence of the beautiful princess of that name; and upon the following day his Grace was presented in great state to Louis XVIII. and the royal family.

The Duc de Noailles, peer of France, whom the King had appointed to accompany the Duke of Wellington, Messieurs de Lalin and Dargainaraty, repaired to the ambassador's hotel, with three royal carriages, each drawn by eight horses, to conduct his Excellency to an audience of his Majesty at the palace of the Tuileries. In addition to the royal carriages, the cavalcade was composed of three splendid court carriages belonging to the newly-appointed ambassador, the state coach of the Duc de Noailles, and that of Monsieur de Lalin, each drawn by six horses, and followed by a number of servants in handsome liveries.

In the first carriage were the present Lord Downes and Monsieur Dargainaraty. In the second was the hero, accompanied by the Duc de Noailles and Monsieur de Lalin; the late General Fremantle, and Colonel Percy, attached to the embassy, with the writer of these pages, occupied the third royal carriage. The whole party alighted at the grand vestibule of the Tuileries, and proceeded to the Hall of Ambassadors.

The guards at the palace were under arms, and the King having returned from mass to his apartments, the ambassador and suite were conducted to the audience. The Marquise de Breyé, grand master of the ceremonies of France, with his assistants, received the duke at the foot of the staircase, and accompanied him to the presence chamber. The Duc de Luxembourg, captain of Guards, came to meet his Excellency outside the Hall of Guards. The bodyguard were under arms, and formed a passage for him.

The King was on his throne, having on his right and left the princes of the royal family and the princes of the blood. The great officers of the crown were placed behind his Majesty's throne.

On entering the presence chamber, the ambassador made a profound obeisance to the King, who rose and uncovered. His Excellency, having reached the foot of the throne, was presented to his Majesty by Monsieur de Lalin.

After this presentation, the King sat down, put on his hat, and made a sign to Wellington to do the same. The princes were also covered. The ambassador then addressed a speech to the King, after which his Excellency presented his credentials: his Majesty received and handed them to the Secretary of State for Foreign Affairs.

The audience being closed, the ambassador and his suite retired in the same order as on their entrance, and they were afterwards conducted to the presence of their royal highnesses, Monsieur, Madame la Duchesse d'Angoulême, the Duc d'Angoulême, and the Duc de Berri. "The King," said Monsieur, "and all the royal family, view with the most lively pleasure the selection which the Prince Regent has made of a hero worthy to represent him. It is our wish and our hope to see a durable peace established between two nations, made rather for mutual esteem than hostility."

The Fête St. Louis followed shortly after; for a length of time the celebration of this festival had not been suffered to take place. This august name, which reminded the Frenchmen of a brilliant epoch in their history, had for a number of years been only inwardly breathed by them. The enthusiasm for the patron saint revived; and many a Frenchman's heart beat high at the recollection of St. Louis, who was not doomed to be the last martyr of his race—at the recollection of Louis XII., the father of his people; of Louis XIV., the pride of France; of Louis XV., under whose reign the arts and sciences flourished; or in some degree at the name of Louis XVIII., whose return to the throne of his ancestors was to a majority of the nation a pledge of peace and happiness.

On the 25th of August, the Fête St. Louis was celebrated at Paris, and never did the Court of the Tuileries exhibit a more brilliant spectacle. The great orders of the state, the diplomatic body, the French marshals, the general officers, the various civil and military authorities, the courts of justice, the tribunals, and all the distinguished foreigners that had now flocked to the "city of frivolity," were admitted to offer their felicitations and homage to his Majesty. On returning from mass, the King and the royal family presented themselves at the balcony of the gallery of the chapel, and were enthusiastically received by that populace. Nothing could exceed the expressions of love and devotion which, on that day, the Parisians evinced towards Louis le Désiré and the Bourbons.

The multitude of citizens of all classes presented a picture full of interest to those who could not be aware of the "hollow hearts" that reigned within. Joy, confidence, and happiness were depicted in every countenance.

At the Opera House "Pelage, ou, le Roi et la Paix," was represented, and at the Feydeau "Les Heritiers Michaux" was performed. The allusions presented by these two pieces were eagerly seized and appreciated by the people. *Le Tartuffe* of Molière— was not there a latent satire in the title?—was acted at the Théâtre François, where I had fortunately secured a place; and on the delivery of the line,

"Nous vivons sous un Prince, enemi de la fraude,"

the whole audience rose, and received the sentiment with a burst of applause.

Upon this occasion all the theatres were opened gratuitously to the public, who filled them at an early hour. Those who were not lucky enough to obtain seats, consoled themselves with walking about the town to witness the illuminations, which were general and most brilliant. Among the transparencies were many bearing inscriptions that testified, as far as oiled paper and paint went, the love of the people towards their long wished-for ruler.

I was indebted for my seat, for a subsequent walk through the city, and for an excellent supper, to a gentleman who had been engaged in the morning by the duke to instruct me in French. By the greatest luck imaginable I met Monsieur Galley at the entrance of the theatre; he recognised me, and understanding that the ambassador had retained a private box for the season, and that he was engaged to dinner and an evening party, soon persuaded the Cerberus who watched over the box department to admit "le jeune milord" and himself. There we sat comfortably during the evening, my future dominie enjoying the racy wit of Molière while I indulged in a nap.

CHAPTER VI.

FRANCE IN 1815—COMTE D'ORSAY—THE LATE DUKE OF CAMBRIDGE—DISTRIBUTION AND CONSECRATION OF THE COLOURS OF THE NATIONAL GUARD IN THE CHAMP DE MARS—THE APPROACH OF NAPOLEON—MEET OF THE ROYAL HOUNDS AT GROSBOIS AND RAMBOUILLET—THE DUKE'S TURN OUT AS A HUNTSMAN IN THE STYLE OF THE FRENCH COURT—ST. GERMAIN-EN-LAYE—TAKING FRENCH LEAVE OF MY FRENCH MASTER—THE CHATEAU OF CHANTILLY—A DAY'S HUNTING AT VERSAILLES—I ACCIDENTALLY LAME ONE OF THE DUKE'S HORSES—TALMA IN ORESTE—THE DUKE'S KINDNESS OF MANNER—FRENCH STAG-HUNTING WITH ROYAL SPORTSMEN—THE DUC DE BERRI—THE DUC D'ANGOULEME—THE DUC DE GRAMMONT—VERSAILLES—MADAME GRASSINI.

CHAPTER VI.

FRANCE, at this period, could boast of its royal hunt; the season commenced towards the end of August, and on the 27th the Duc de Berri, accompanied by the Prince of the Moskowa (Ney) hunted in the Bois de Boulogne. Wellington, who had an excellent stud of English hunters, kindly mounted me, as he did during the whole time he took part in the pleasures of the chase. Wellington and Ney met in friendly intercourse by the covert's side. What extraordinary events occurred between the "meet" at the Bois de Boulogne, on the 27th of August, and the "meet" on the plains of Waterloo on the 18th of June! How much happened in that interval! The hunt was attended by all the sporting *élite* of Paris, and there, not the least curious part was to witness the two great generals riding side by side in amicable converse.

One youth attracted great attention that day from his handsome appearance, his gentlemanlike bearing, his faultless dress, and the splendid English hunter he was mounted upon. This was the late Alfred d'Orsay, afterwards so well known in London society. De Grammont, who some few years after married his sister, had sent him from England a first-rate Leicestershire hunter, whose fine shape, simple saddle and bridle, contrasted favourably with the heavy animals, and smart caparisons, then in fashion with the Parisian Nimrods.

The count was presented to Wellington and his staff, and from that moment he became a constant guest at the Hôtel Borghese. The sport, owing to the numerous field, was very indifferent; the deer was headed, the hounds ridden over, nor could the vehement action, vociferous shouts, and unqualified oaths of the royal duke, preserve the slightest order. Under these circumstances, the hounds were taken home, and the antlered monarch of the woods allowed " to live to *run* another day."

The late Duke of Cambridge visited Paris, and often honoured Wellington with his presence at dinner and the opera; but a greater hero to English eyes than had hitherto appeared, arrived in Paris from Rennes on the 4th of September—Soult.

On the following day, Divine service was held, for

the first time, at the British ambassador's hotel. The English residents, amounting to more than a hundred, assembled in the great dining-room, where the service was performed by the duke's chaplain, the Reverend Mr. Briscall, in the presence of his Grace.

On the 7th of September, the ceremony of the distribution and consecration of the colours of the National Guard took place in the Champ de Mars; my chief was present, and I had the good fortune to attend him. The King left the Tuileries at ten o'clock, accompanied by a magnificent retinue, and was loudly cheered as he reached the ground. After the benediction had been given by the Archbishop of Rheims, M. de Talleyrand, his Majesty addressed himself as follows to the chiefs of the Legion and the officers of the National Guard:—" Gentlemen, this is a delightful day to me; it is a new tie which I contract with my brave National Guard. What may not be expected from the French, when one sees such troops whom zeal alone has formed? Let the enemy come when he will—but he will not come, we have none but friends."

At the conclusion of this speech, a thousand voices repeated—" Vive le Roi!" " Vive Monsieur!" " Vive Madame!"

Monsieur, then turning towards the King, said:— " Sire, the National Guard is deeply sensible of the great honour your Majesty has done it by presenting it with the colours yourself. I can assure you, Sire, that it is worthy of it. All are prepared to die for the person of your Majesty; and among so many faithful subjects, there is no one more devoted than their Colonel General."

All hands were now raised—" Yes, we swear it! Vive le Roi!"

Touched by these sentiments of affection, the King held out his arms to Monsieur, who flew into them with transport; his Majesty pressed him to his heart, and tears flowed from many an eye.

Louis XVIII. was but a poor prophet in making the above harangue, for within a few months he was doomed to listen to the spirit, if not the letter, of the following unpalatable remarks, and of which we venture a translation:—

"Sire, he whom you call at Paris the Corsican ogre, who is still styled the usurper at Revers, is already called Bonaparte at Lyons, and the Emperor at Grenoble—he whom you regard as surrounded, pursued, put to flight, careers onwards swift as the eagle, whose emblem he bears. His soldiers, whom you believe to be dying of hunger, exhausted by fatigue, and ready to desert him, augment like the snow-flakes around the revolving ball. Sire, depart: resign France to her legitimate ruler—to him who has conquered. Depart, Sire, not because you are likely to encounter any danger—your adversary is strong enough to protect you; but because it would be humiliating in a grandson of St. Louis to owe his life to the hero of Arcole, Marengo, and Austerlitz."

On the 9th September, the royal hounds met at Grosbois, about four leagues south-east of Paris, a residence which had been occupied by Louis XVIII. when Count of Provence. The Duc de Berri, Wellington, and De Grammont, already referred to, who had served in the 10th Hussars, with a variety of English and French sportsmen, attended this *chasse*. The object of the sons of our island, and one in which I took a deep interest, was to get the deer to break cover, but so surrounded were we with huntsmen and gens-d'armes, that upon this occasion we found it impossible to carry out our wishes.

Nothing occurred during the day's sport to merit any particular comment; perhaps the most amusing part of it was our "lark" home across the country, when myself, Fremantle, and other *attachés* of the English embassy, led some half dozen Frenchmen a rather stiffish line of stone walls and brooks. Among the latter was D'Orsay, who, albeit unaccustomed to go "across country," was always in the "first flight," making up by hard riding whatever he may have lacked in judgment; he afterwards lived to be an excellent sportsman and a good rider to hounds. Since this time "horsemanship," whether in the hunting field, in the steeple-chase, or flat race, has made rapid progress in France, and there are now many men to be found who would hold their own with our countrymen.

Rambouillet was to be our next "meet." There is nothing remarkable in this place, which is a dull town, with the exception of the Château, the residence of the kings of France down to the time of Charles X., who, after the revolution of July, 1830, signed, in conjunction with the Duc d'Angoulême, his abdication of the throne of his ancestors. The monarch was led to this step by the rumour that the mob at Paris were upon the road to Rambouillet, armed, and threatening results not dissimilar to those which befel Louis XVI. at Versailles in 1789. The Château is a gloomy building of red brick, flanked with towers of stone; it contains an apartment still shown, in which Francis I. died in 1547. The extensive forest is well adapted for the chase, and was the favourite sporting ground of the Bourbon princes.

It was here that, early in October, Wellington met the hounds, equipped, out of compliment to the Royal Dukes, for the first time in the French hunting costume—cocked hat, gold-laced coat, *couteau de chasse* and leather jack-boots. Never shall I forget the smile that beamed upon his countenance, when he saw Fremantle decked out in a similar costume.

"What would they say in England?" he asked, as he took a full view of his ex-aid-de-camp.

I had the honour of driving the Duke, as was my custom, to the "meet" in his curricle and pair, and in my own estimation I fancied the "pink" coat, white cords, and top-boots, I sported, in neatness far eclipsed my chief's dress. Although the ambassador did not object to be thus himself accoutred, he spared his gallant steed the fancy costume, and instead of the velvet saddle, the costly housings, the embroidered crupper, the emblazoned pistol holsters, and the richly ornamented bridle, the noble animal appeared with a plain English saddle and bridle.

The following week the Duke hunted at St. Germain-en-Laye, and I had again the honour to be charioteer. The town, interesting from its historical recollections, although large, has a melancholy air of desolation in its grass-grown streets and straggling edifices. The royal Château, once the favourite residence of Marguerite de Valois, Henry II., Henry IV., Francis I., and the birth-place of Charles IX. and Louis XIV., had been converted into a military prison, surrounded for security by a high wall.

The forest occupies a promontory formed by a sweeping bend of the river Seine, and is one of the largest in France, having a circuit of twenty-one miles. In the centre is the Pavillon de la Meute, begun by Francis I., whose refined taste is proverbial throughout his own country, and whose style is now so much appreciated in England.

No one enjoyed a joke more than my illustrious chief, and I will record one that caused him great merriment. Upon arriving at Paris, anxious that my education should not be neglected, the Duke gave his domestic chaplain instructions to read with me three or four times a week, made arrangements with Franconi to give me riding lessons, with a Monsieur Brideaux to teach me to fence, with Monsieur Deschamps to attend to the Terpsichorean department, while to Monsieur Galley, already alluded to, I was to look for instruction in the French language. Monsieur Galley was a great admirer of French tragedy, and was constantly in the habit, after my lessons were over, of spouting from Racine and Corneille.

One morning when we were to hunt at Chantilly, the Duke sent for me, and inquired at what hour I was to take my French lesson. I replied at nine o'clock, but that I had overnight worked very hard to prepare a translation from La Henriade, a copy of which, neatly written out, I presented to his Grace.

"Under those circumstances," said he, "you can go—lose no time in your equipment, for the carriage will be round ten minutes before nine : Don't forget," he added, calling me back, "to write a line to Mr. Galley, excusing yourself."

Off I ran to my room, was soon booted and spurred, and then sat down to indite a few lines, which, being in a poetical, or rather doggrel, vein, I thus accomplished, knowing full well how pleased my dominie had always expressed himself at any attempt at poetry. The lines ran as follows :—

"J'ai rien a vous dire, mon cher Monsieur Galley,
Que je vais a la chasse, et pous pouvez en aller."

Which in English would mean—

"To the chase forth I sally,
So I wish you good morning, my dear Monsieur Galley.
With Phædra, Medea, I can no longer dally,
Here's success to the chase! Tally ho! Monsieur Galley."

Just as I had finished the lines, Fremantle entered the room to tell me I had not a moment to spare.

"What! what are these?" said he, taking up the paper, and reading them aloud. "I must commit them to memory;" so, reciting them to himself until we entered the carriage, he repeated them to the Duke, whose risible faculties were so excited, that he quite forgot the disrespect I had shown my worthy tutor; and if he once called upon me to repeat the verses in the course of the day, and after dinner, he did so twenty times. Monsieur Galley was not at all displeased at having a holiday, and enjoyed greatly the first attempt of his pupil at French versification.

We dined and slept at Chantilly, and early in the morning, thanks to the kindness of one of the *aides-de-camp* of the Duc de Berri, I was conducted over the Château. Here may be seen the hall of the celebrated valorous, generous, Francis, of Angoulême, the bed-chamber of the beautiful devoted la Vallière, and the identical trap-door through which the youthful Louis gained entrance into her dormitory, after his mother had caused the door of the stairs to be bricked up; there, may also be seen the oratory of James II., and the chamber in which he breathed his last, September 16, 1701, the palace having been assigned to the exiled king by Louis XIV.

The old Château of Chantilly, built by the great Condé, and in which, after retiring from military life, he spent his latter years in the society of Racine, Boileau, and other literary characters of his age, was levelled by the mob during the Revolution. The stables alone remain, a splendid pile, capable of containing nearly two hundred horses.

I was reminded—for my French history would not in the present day have received many marks at a Burlington House examination—that here the immortal culinary artist, Le Grand Vatel, committed suicide by running himself through with his sword (the spit would have been a more appropriate weapon), in despair, because the fish did not arrive in time for dinner, upon the occasion of his sovereign's visit in 1671.

In spite of the devastation of the Revolution, Chantilly at this period was a most lovely spot; the present building was full of memorials of Condé; and the gardens, park, and grounds, as beautiful as green turf, fragrant flowers, noble trees, and limpid streams, could make them. The forest extends to 6,700 acres; in the midst of it is a small gothic building, flanked by four towers at the corners, and built, it is said, by Blanche of Castile; its carved ornaments of snakes, frogs, lizards, snails, intermixed with water lilies, and other aquatic plants, produce a most pleasing effect, and tend to show that it was originally built as a fishing lodge.

One morning, late in December, the curricle was at the door, and I was in readiness to drive the duke to the place of meeting—Versailles, when his valet approached, and said his Grace wished to see me. I lost no time in attending to the summons, and found my chief equipped for hunting, but very busy over some papers.

"I shall not be able to go to-day," said he; "but you can have the curricle. Tell the royal Dukes I have some letters to write, as the courier starts at two o'clock, which will prevent my meeting their royal highnesses. 'Elmore' is sent on for me, but as he is short of work, you had better ride him. Don't knock him about, for he has not quite got over his journey."

I briefly expressed my thanks; and started for the *rendezvous*, where I delivered my message, and mounted the far-famed horse, lately purchased in England from Elmore, the horse-dealer, and named after him.

We had an excellent run twenty minutes in the forest and fifteen across the country, which being tolerably well enclosed, gave me an opportunity of testing the animal's merits, and of distinguishing myself. This I may be permitted to say without any appearance of vapouring, as I was splendidly mounted, and rode under ten stone.

Although the fencing and pace had choked off all the royal Nimrods, they arrived in time to be in at the death. The deer that had given us so good a run had taken to the water, and shortly after fell a victim to the unerring aim of the Duc d'Angoulême's *garde chasse,* who, perceiving the Prince's bullet misdirected, quietly, and unknown to many, lodged a bullet in the centre of the noble animal's forehead.

"Monseigneur tire parfaitement," said the keeper, to his royal master, who seemed highly gratified with the success of his shot.

It was quite evident that the majority of the field were anxious to possess Elmore—indeed, it was hinted to me that the Duke could command a very high sum for him.

Delighted with the character the new purchase had established, I started to ride gently home by myself; but when within half a league of Paris, in crossing a small grip on the side of the road, I found that my horse went lame. At once I dismounted to inspect his foot, but could detect nothing wrong. No alternative, then, was left me but to lead the limping animal home to his stables. This I did, amidst the taunts and jeers of the rabble; but their insults were trifling compared to the annoyance I felt at this untoward termination of the day's sport.

Directly I reached the Hôtel Borghese, I sent for the head groom and the Duke's coachman, and explained to them all that had occurred.

"Well, you have gone and done it," said the latter personage, Turnham, who was a great character in his way; "why, his Grace would not have taken two hundred for that horse."

The groom, however, seeing that I was in a state of great mental agony, comforted me a little by saying he trusted it was nothing. He would have the shoe taken off, and hoped all would be right.

Happily for me, the Duke, who had been occupied all day, was out riding, and I did not see him until dinner-time. I had fully made up my mind to mention the accident, but wished to wait till nine o'clock, when I was to have a bulletin of Elmore's state.

As a large party were assembled, little was said about the hunting during the time the ladies remained at table. On their retirement, I was called upon to give a full, true, and particular account of it. I mentioned the brilliant manner in which the horse had gone, and the panegyrics he had received from all.

"A splendid animal," said my chief; "I hope to ride him next Monday at Fontainebleau."

My heart quailed within me.

At this moment the butler, who had heard of the mishap, gave me a message from the groom, that the horse was a little better, from some treatment that had been adopted.

"You look quite knocked up—dead beat!" cried one of my friends, as he observed the dull state I was in; little knowing that the mind, not the body, was suffering.

"I can take you to the theatre," added his Grace, presently, "the cabriolet is at the door."

We drove there. I was, as usual, the charioteer upon such occasions, but so distracted was I, that I nearly grazed the curb-stone at starting, and was within an inch of knocking over one of the *gens-d'armes*, as we approached the theatre.

It was late when we arrived; the last act of "Oreste" was going on, with Talma as the hero; then followed the inimitable Mademoiselle Mars in "La Jeunesse de Henri V.," from which piece the English version of "Charles II." has been adapted. To account for this change of monarchs, and to explain the inconsistency of having the "wicked Earl of Rochester" the companion of "sweet Prince Hal," we may remark that, when the drama was first about to be brought forward in Paris, during the reign of Napoleon I., the licenser objected to the introduction of Charles, he being a restored monarch; so the author had no alternative left him but to re-write the whole, or change his hero. The latter course he adopted, trusting that a Parisian audience would not detect the anachronisms.

The perfect acting of Talma had no charm for me, and when the after-piece began, I was too wretched to laugh at the *bonhommie* of the actor who represented Captain Copp, or the archness of that child of nature, Mademoiselle Mars, in " Betty."

" I am afraid you are quite knocked up," observed the Duke, as, seated by his side, I drove him from the theatre.

My only answer was a deep sigh; then, making a sudden resolution, I screwed my courage to the sticking place, and recounted the whole of the day's adventure, and the accident that had befallen me.

" Can't be helped," said the Duke, in his usual quick voice. " Hope it is not as bad as you think—accidents will happen."

The tone and manner in which the above phrases were delivered, and my inward satisfaction of feeling my conscience unburthened, in a great degree restored me to some sense of comfort. This was not a little increased by the kind way in which my patron wished me good night.

The fatigue and excitement of the hunt soon caused me to fall asleep, and I was awoke out of a heavy slumber, during which the transactions of the day had all flitted across me, by the entrance of the trusty porter, who waited upon me, announcing that it had just struck six. I had ordered myself to be called at that early hour, being anxious to attend the stables and hear the report of the groom as to Elmore's state.

To my great dismay, I found my worst fears realized—the horse was dead lame. From seven till ten o'clock, I wandered about the house, like a perturbed spirit, when I received a message to attend his Grace in his morning room. I entered the Duke's presence like a condemned criminal.

"Turnham tells me Elmore must be blistered and turned out!"

I quaked in my shoes; independently of the annoyance of having been the cause of so much mischief, I thought to myself that my hunting days were over.

"I've heard all particulars; you're not to blame—you did your best." The Duke had been informed of my early visit. "But"—the thought of Othello's remark, "Never more be officer of mine," came across my mind—"but," continued the chief, "I can't afford to run the chance of losing all my best horses; so in future,"—the climax is coming, thought I, I shall have no more hunting—"so, in future, you shall have the brown horse and the chestnut mare, and if you knock them up, you must afterwards mount yourself."

I was so overcome with this noble and liberal conduct, that I could scarcely stammer out my thanks.

"There, take this to the office, and give it to

Fremantle. We shall hunt, dine, and sleep, on Monday, at Fontainebleau."

I left the kind-hearted Duke with but one sentiment—that of overpowering gratitude, and felt that he was as good in all the generous offices of social intercourse as he was great in the most onerous duties of the battle-field.

Not only upon this, but upon a variety of other occasions, I found Wellington of a most considerate and forgiving temper.

Monday arrived, and at an early hour the Duke and myself left the hotel in a travelling carriage and four for Fontainebleau. After passing Chailly, where there was one rather extraordinary feature at the posting-house, namely, that the master of it kept nothing but grey horses, of which he had more than fifty, we entered the forest about thirteen leagues from Paris.

This extends over an area of 23,700 hectares (about 55,000 acres) and contains oaks and beech of majestic size. A large space is covered with broom, heath, and underwood, with extensive plantations of black fir. Here may be found red deer in great abundance, as wild as hawks, for they instantly fly at the approach of man. No part of France can boast of more picturesque and romantic scenery than this neighbourhood.

At this period the forest was the favourite "meet" of the then royal family of France. I may here state that, since the Revolution of 1830, the deer have been exterminated, and this attractive hunting ground, once the resort of the Kings of France, hears the "ring of a hunter's peal" no more.

In a sporting point of view, the French system of stag hunting is far preferable to our own; for instead of turning a poor, scared, home-fed "calf" out of a covered cart, in which he has been jolted for some half-dozen or dozen miles, the deer in France is singled, and driven early in the morning into a particular district, near the *rendezvous*, where the hounds are laid on, and find their own game.

The *rendezvous* on the present occasion was at La Croix du Grand Veneur, an obelisk placed where four roads meet, and which, according to an ancient legend, receives its name from a spectral black huntsman, who was supposed to haunt the vicinity—the same that appeared to Henry IV. shortly before his assassination.

No sooner had we all descended from the carriage, and were about to mount our hunters—(I had the chestnut mare, and called her "Forgiveness," in compliment to my chief)—than up galloped an advance guard of cuirassiers, sword in hand, the officer desiring us to draw up in a line, as the King and Royal

Family were approaching. We had scarcely time to comply with this order, before a body-guard of Lancers clattered past us, at a tremendous pace; immediately after them followed a magnificent carriage, the whole body covered with gold, and the arms of France emblazoned upon the panels—having four tall footmen, in state liveries, perched up behind.

This monster coach was drawn by eight short-tailed brown English horses, six in hand (a feat worthy of Cooke's circus), and a postilion on the leaders, wearing a huge cocked hat, with powdered head, a blue jacket covered with silver lace, and a Brobdignag pair of jack-boots. In the carriage were his Majesty, the Duc and Duchesse D'Angoulême, and the Comte D'Artois—the equerries in waiting riding by the side. Then came another carriage and eight, containing the Duc de Berri and his aide-de-camp. Two empty landaus followed, in case of accidents; a very necessary precaution, considering the badness of the roads, and the weight of what the London coachman call "live lumber" that occupied them. A strong body of heavy dragoons brought up the rear.

The French princes, having warmly recognized the Duke, now mounted their English thorough-bred hunters, and prepared themselves for the chase. The King and Duchesse D'Angoulême, after calling Wellington to the carriage, exchanged their costly

Lord Mayor's coach for a light open barouche, and, attended by the ranger and deputy-ranger of the forest in uniform, and by an escort of gendarmerie, drew up by the cover's side.

The hounds, though the piqueur declared they were genuine natives, had evidently a cross of our fox-hound. The huntsman was magnificently " got up," in a long blue coat, covered with lace, jack-boots, chain spurs, and sported a powdered peruke, and a gold-laced cocked hat, worthy of a London sweep on a May-day morning. A large French horn was hung over his shoulder, and a *couteau de chasse* hung by his side. His horse, looking as if he had been fatted for a Smithfield cattle-show, was as fine as red velvet housings, leather holsters, gold-embossed bridle and crupper, could make him.

The *valets des chiens* wore cocked hats, scarlet jackets, white unmentionables, silk stockings and pumps. A few heavy *gens-d'armes*, on long-tailed, black-job looking horses, were in attendance, to protect royalty from the pressure of mobility.

The hounds were now laid on, and all remained breathlessly straining their ears to catch the "*à droits*" and "*à gauches*" which were hallooed out to intimate which way the deer was running. At length the Duc de Berri gave a shout, worthy of being taken for the war-cry of the Ojibbeway Indians, and clapping spurs to his horse, started off at the rate of twenty miles an hour, followed by the *gens-d'armes*, who in vain tried to keep up with the royal sportsman.

"Hold hard, give them time!" he shouted, interspersing his injunctions with certain expressive English execrations, which proved his royal highness to be perfectly conversant with our vulgar tongue.

In a second, away went the whole field, deer, hounds, huntsmen, sportsmen—royal, noble, and simple—equestrians, pedestrians, amidst the shout of the gathered multitude.

For awhile, the deer kept to the forest; but finding himself hotly pressed, took to the open country, followed by all our own countrymen, with De Grammout, D'Orsay, and a few others who were mounted on English hunters.

"Hold hard!" bellowed the Duc de Berri.

"*Arretez*, Messieurs!" cried the piqueur.

"Turn him back to de wood!" ejaculated the huntsman.

Despite, however, of all these injunctions, and the volleys of foreign maledictions, we succeeded in keeping the pack in full cry over a fair hunting country, taking regular French leave of the royal sportsmen. The plain was passed, a small thickly-grown wood skirted, a brook with steep and deep banks crossed, some swampy meadows traversed, when a lake appeared in view.

"He's dead beat!" shouted the self-elected huntsman, Jack Fremantle, as he was familiarly called.

So it was, for the words were scarcely uttered when the deer was seen, evidently distressed, the hounds almost within sight of him.

From scent to view was beautiful.

"Hark, forward!" was echoed around.

Wellington was in the first flight—Fremantle and myself acting as huntsman and whipper-in.

The stag now gained the lake, and plunged in.

Anxious to save the noble animal, the Duke and Fremantle whipped off the hounds, while De Grammont, D'Orsay, and myself dashed up to our middles in water, attempting, with a lasso formed of stirrup leathers, to secure the "poor sequestered stag."

At that moment the Duc de Berri, accompanied by his royal brother, and an *aide-de-camp*, galloped up. We all shrank back, expecting a severe rebuke, when, to our great surprise, a saccharine smile beamed upon the royal countenances.

"Well, Duke, this is an English run!" exclaimed the good-humoured Duc de Berri.

Our Duke made a suitable reply.

"How splendidly your horse took the last fence!"

said the *aide-de-camp*. We looked around; it was scarcely four feet high.

"And the brook, your Royal Highness!" exclaimed one of the most impudent of the lot—need I name him. "It was a regular Wissendine."

The *piqueurs, gens-d'armes,* and the rest of the field came tailing up, all describing their prowess over *les grand fosses,* and declaring that the *chasse* was *magnifique.*

To account for the arrival of these worthies, I must mention that a road ran nearly parallel with the line we had taken. Upon nearing us, they gave up their "high-way system," and some of the hard riders had selected a narrow part of a small stream, and a couple of fences, to show off their riding.

During the time of these boastings, the Duc d'Angoulême had with a rifle given (as the courtiers said) the *coup-de-grace* to the hunted animal, whose "heart's best blood was on the waters." Quicker eyes and less flattering tongues more truly attributed the murderous deed to the keeper, who fired at the same moment.

We then wended our way to the Château; and, after leaving our steeds at the stables, strolled into the gardens, in expectation of seeing the Fountaine belle Eau, which gave the name to the palace; but the spot had long since ceased to exist. We then reached the house, where, after indulging in that luxury of luxuries, a warm bath, we were allowed to occupy our time until dinner in exploring the ancient building.

I was fortunate enough to get hold of an attendant who had been an exile in England, and who showed me over this venerable seat of the French kings. I shall merely say that Louis VII., in 1162, first built a castle here; and that it is indebted to Francis I. for its chief extension and improvement. Further additions were made to it by Henri IV., Louis XIV., and Louis XV. The Chapelle de St. Saturnin is said to be of the time of Louis VII., but the improvements of Francis I. have quite obliterated its original structure.

In the Chapelle de la Trinité the marriage of Louis XV. with Maria Lechzinska, took place in 1725, as did that of the ill-fated Duc d'Orleans in 1837. In the apartments des Reines Mères, Pope Pius VII. was lodged, rejecting all the magnificence prepared for him by his imperial jailor. The Boudoir de la Reine was occupied by the unfortunate Marie Antoinette; and the metal window bolts were said to have been wrought by the hand of Louis XVI. The Galerie de Henri II. is the most splendid room in the palace; everywhere appears the crescent of Diana de Poitiers and her initials linked with that of her royal lover.

We reserved the two most interesting apartments to the last—namely, the Galerie des Cerfs, and the Cabinet de Travail. The former was the scene of the atrocious murder of Monaldeschi, at the command of Christina of Sweden, at that time residing at the Château as the guest of Louis XIII.

The Cabinet de Travail contained the little mahogany round table at which Napoleon, a few months before, had signed his abdication. The Emperor's bed-room remained nearly in the same state as he had left it.

I need scarcely add, that the dinner was excellent, and as foreign cooking was little known in England at that time, it is not to be wondered at, that the Duke's party thoroughly appreciated the culinary talent of the King's Cordon Bleu.

I knew almost everybody in Paris, who might be considered worth knowing; celebrities of almost every variety. Talma I saw as often as I could; but there was another theatrical star of whom I saw a good deal more.

Madame Grassini has since paid the debt of nature at Milan. She was about seventy-eight years old, but looked scarcely fifty, so wonderfully well had she preserved her attractions as a beautiful and accomplished vocalist.

This admirable lady possessed in the highest degree

the art of touching the feelings. Talma used to say of her that he had never seen any other actress—not even Mars, Duval, or Duchesnois—endowed with a physiognomy so expressive and so mutable.

Her *profile*, with its Grecian outline, her fine marble brow, and dark hair, which formed a frame of ebony about it—her incomparable eye-brows, her black gipsy eyes, now flashing with the fiery passions of tragedy, then languishing with the tender emotions of love—and that astonishing *ensemble* of perfection which nature had collected in her, as if to review all her gifts in one woman, exercised on the spectator a charm he found it impossible to resist.

One evening in 1810, Grassini and Crescentini were singing Romeo and Juliet, at the Tuileries. After the admirable scene in the third act, Napoleon, transported, and forgetting the rules of etiquette, clapped and shouted like a school-boy.

Talma was weeping, seated on a bench near the orchestra. The great tragedian confessed that he had never felt anything so deeply in his life before as what he now felt after listening to the syren.

As soon as the performance was over, the Emperor sent Crescentini the order of the Iron Crown. Not being able to decorate Grassini in the same way, he enclosed to her a slip of paper, on which he had written with his own hand:

"Bon pour vingt mille livres.—NAPOLEON."

Crescentini, who was frantic with joy at the unexpected favour conferred upon himself, could not help peeping at the lady's note.

"Twenty thousand francs!" cried he; "that's a large sum."

"It is the marriage portion of one of my nieces," replied Grassini.

Indeed no artist could be more generous or more indulgent than she was to her own family.

Long after the Empire had been swept away, as the great actress chanced to be at Bologna, they presented another niece to her, who was also to be provided for. The girl was extremely pretty, but she lacked spirit and tone of voice, they said, to take to the stage. "She is a spoiled contralto," they added.

"Let me hear her," said Grassini.

No sooner had the girl emitted her first note, than she threw her arms about her neck, and said:

"Dear child, you require none of my assistance to get you on in your vocation. Your voice is not a contralto; it is the finest soprano in the world, and far stronger than mine. Labour well, my little darling, there is a rich bank in your throat."

The young girl to whom Madame Grassini predicted so brilliant a destiny was Giulia Grisi.

CHAPTER VII.

PARISIAN ENJOYMENTS—PROPOSED CONGRESS—THE DUKE OF WELLINGTON TAKES LEAVE OF LOUIS XVIII.—JOURNEY TO VIENNA—SOCIETY IN THE AUSTRIAN CAPITAL—DISTINGUISHED PERSONAGES—GRAND TOURNAMENT—THE IMPERIAL PALACE—ROYAL FAMILIES OF AUSTRIA, PRUSSIA AND RUSSIA—COURT BALL—DEATH OF PRINCE D'ARENBERG—INTRODUCTION TO THE KING OF ROME—LORD STEWART'S FOX-HOUNDS—PRINCE EUGENE BEAUHARNOIS—FREDERICK VON GENTZ—VISCOUNT CASTLEREAGH—PRINCE TALLEYRAND—INTERRUPTION OF THE CONGRESS—ISABEY'S PICTURE OF THE CONGRESS OF VIENNA—ENGLISH QUIZZING.

CHAPTER VII.

My sojourn in the French capital had been one of unalloyed gratification. Paris then was possibly more thoroughly the head-quarters of pleasure than it had ever been before; for the continent, having hitherto been closed against the English, those who possessed the means seemed determined to make up for their long deprivation of its far-famed gratifications. English "my lords" abounded; and the prodigality of many as much astonished the Parisians as their ignorance of social refinement. The French got as much money as they could from their visitors, and testified their gratitude in jokes, verbal and pictorial. John Bull, however, did not care about the caricature, and did not understand a *jeu d'esprit*. He hurried from one attraction to another; testifying his "insular prejudices" and partialities without the slightest reserve.

I enjoyed the novelty as much as any of my compatriots, and had advantages over the majority which I fully appreciated. But those delights could not be expected to last for ever.

The Congress of Paris settled several things, but left many unsettled, and it was arranged that a Congress should be held at Vienna where all undecided questions should be disposed of. The great European monarchies appointed one or more representatives to look after their interests at this conference; and among those selected by the English Government for this duty, was the Duke of Wellington.

On the 23d of January, 1815, the Duke of Wellington took leave of the king in a secret audience, which lasted a considerable time. The late Lord Raglan, then Lord Fitzroy Somerset, secretary of legation, was to act for the ambassador in his absence. Upon his Grace's return to his hotel, I was apprised that, upon the following morning, Colonel Fremantle and myself were te have the honour of accompanying Wellington to Vienna.

Our journey was a most delightful one, and often do I look back with feelings of unmingled gratitude and pleasure to the good fortune that enabled me to participate in so covetable a privilege as being the companion of the great hero.

The Duke travelled in an English carriage, with his

valet Tesson on a seat upon the roof, and a courier in advance. Anxious to lose no time on the road, we breakfasted and dined in the carriage; our meals consisting of game pies, cold fowls and tongue, *terrine de foie gras*, with the choicest pure claret and hock from the Duke's own cellars.

With the exception of four hours during the night, we never stopped upon the road, except to change horses, between Paris and Vienna; and here the Duke's power of falling at once to sleep came into effect, for no sooner did we reach the inn, than, the courier having made preparations, his Grace retired to bed; and at the hour named for starting, he appeared perfectly refreshed, having slept, dressed, and breakfasted during that brief period; while we, the two *attachés*, looked what is called, with more truth than elegance, "awfully seedy," having passed our time in eating supper, and then lying down in our clothes before the hot German stove, until it was time to make our toilet, previously to departure.

I pass over the first three days of our journey, as they produced little of interest; on the 27th of January we reached Strasburg, and crossed the Rhine without stopping, sleeping at Saverne in Alsace; on the 28th we were at Stutgart; on the 29th we passed Augsburg, and reached Munich—there, after remaining a short time, with Sir George Rose, we continued our journey. On the 30th we slept at Braunau, reaching Vienna on the 2nd of February.

Vienna at this time, was the concentrating point where Greeks, Turks, Jews, and Italians met, for the arrangement of their mercantile affairs throughout the continent of Europe. There you were constantly struck with the number and variety of characters that you daily met. The Greek and Albanian, with their short cloaks, edged with sable and ermine, delicately trimmed mustachio, and exposed throat; long robes, trimmed with tarnished gold or silver, with thickly-folded girdles and turbans, and beards of unrestrained growth, pointed out the majestic Turk. The olive-tinted visage, the full, keen, dark eye, and a costume half Greek and half Turkish, distinguished the citizen of Venice or Verona.

I soon found myself a welcome guest in the imperial circle, and in the brilliant coteries of the Esterhazys and Schwartzenbergs. The days were passed in morning drives and rides to the Prater and Aungarten, in the promenade of the Rempart and Belvedère Gardens; in evening assemblies, select dinners, splendid balls, *petits soupers*, theatrical and operatic representations.

The gay and busy appearance of Vienna, peopled with sovereigns, ambassadors, ministers, and generals; its bustling activity; the streets crowded with people, groups of military parading the city; the balconies filled with fair spectators; beating of drums, firing of cannons, ringing of bells;—all added to the joyous life of the scene.

Although at that period of my life I could scarcely be called a lover of the fine arts, I accompanied a young Englishman, now, alas! no more, to the gallery of the Duke Albert of Saxe Teschen, to see the imperial collection of paintings at the Belvedère, and the private cabinets of Prince Esterhazy, Liechtenstein, Schönborn, and Count Lamberg.

I visited the two arsenals, the city and the imperial one, and with an enthusiastic guide by my side, forgot the present in the past. In the former I was shown the head of Kara Mustapha, who conducted the siege of 1683, and was strangled the following year at Belgrade by the order of the Sultan; and in the latter, memorials of many distinguished men, including the armour of the celebrated crusader, Godfrey de Bouillon, the servant of the Holy Temple, of Frederick Barbarossa, and the Emperor Charles V.; the leathern jacket and the hat worn by the great Gustavus Adolphus at the battle of Lützen, where he was killed; the helmet of Prince Eugene of Savoy, the companion-in-arms of Marlborough; and the balloon used by the French at the battle of Fleurus, in 1793.

Worked up to enthusiasm by my cicisbeo, impressionable and imaginative as I then was, I could dwell upon the pious, though mistaken zeal, of the crowd of warriors who devoted their lives and their fortunes to the recovery of the sacred city from the hands of the Paynim. I fancied I beheld the venerable hermit, Walter the Moneyless, the Counts Toulouse, Fermandoise, and Blois, and the careless and gallant Robert of Normandy. In my "mind's eye" I had glimpses of the siege of Nice; the re-capture and re-taking of Jerusalem; the crusade of the Emperor Conrad and Louis VII. I shuddered when I thought of the assassination of the brave Marquis of Montserrat; despised the weak Austria and the envious Philip, and my heart swelled at the noble daring and gallant exploits of Richard Cœur de Lion, and the Soldan Saladin.

A tolerable sprinkling of young Englishmen had congregated in the imperial capital, some being attached to the embassy, others had wended their way there for pleasure. Independent of the great men, Wellington, Castlereagh, Sir Charles Stewart, we had Lord Paget, one of the smartest hussars in the service, Earls Bathurst and Clanwilliam, Lords Mount Edgecumbe and Rancliffe, Fremantle, Francis Forbes, and others. As all the sights were open to us, we lost no opportunity of visiting the most attractive.

It was with no small degree of interest that I attended the *fête* given in honour of the victory of Leipsic, which took place on the second morning after my arrival. On this occasion twenty thousand men were assembled in the Prater; at eleven o'clock in the forenoon, the Emperors, Kings, and allied Sovereigns, the Empresses, and Queens, came upon the ground with a very numerous and brilliant *suite*. The troops having formed an immense square, the *Te Deum* was chaunted by innumerable voices, after which the troops defiled in presence of their Majesties—the Arch-Duke Constantine being at the head of his regiment of Cuirassiers.

Wellington was present, and attracted universal attention.

Dinner was then served to the Sovereigns, the officers, and the men. The royalties dined in the villa at one end of the Prater, and the troops on the field.

Nothing could exceed the gaiety of the city; multitudes collected to see the Sovereigns, and were coming and going every moment; the drums were beating; the men under arms; the people were in masses on foot, on horseback, and in carriages, jostling each other in every direction; four royal guards were mounted on the Grand Square—" *Wache heraus!*"—" Guard turn out!"—was uttered almost every five minutes, as Kings, Royal Dukes, and military heroes passed through the city during this International Exhibition.

Amongst other entertainments which had been provided for the amusement of Royalty and their guests, nothing could surpass the splendour of a tournament, which took place in the Imperial riding-school, to which I was fortunate enough to get a ticket of admission, to the seats reserved for the Ambassadors, Plenipotentiaries, and their *suites*. Upon reaching the building, I found that the sides were filled with a dense mass of well-dressed spectators. At each end, galleries had been erected, decorated with party-coloured festoons and draperies of silk; the pillars that supported them were covered with floating pennons, bearing gallant mottoes, and the flags of all nations. These galleries were filled with the distinguished representatives of all the most noble families; one being reserved for the reception of the Court.

The arrival of the Empress, who was to appropriate the rewards, escorted by the noble Hungarian guard, in their uniforms of green and silver, with their leopard-skin accoutrements, and mounted on grey chargers, was announced by a clamorous blast of warlike music, playing the national anthem—several thousands of male voices joining in the choral chaunt.

The train that attended the imperial *cortège* on this occasion consisted of the bravest and the fairest, the wisest counsellors, and the highest born nobles in the land.

A flourish of trumpets announced the approach of those who were to take part in the tournament. The massive gates were then thrown open, and the knights, preceded by heralds and pursuivants-at-arms, entered in long procession, forming up in line of double file in front of the Imperial tent, the leader of each party being in the centre of the foremost rank. All had their swords drawn, and their lances upright, their bright points glancing in the sun.

> "Their armour, as it caught the rays,
> Flash'd back again the general blaze,
> In lines of dazzling light."

There they remained until the Sovereigns had inspected the ranks.

The joustings then began. Every knight who wished to enter the lists approached the barrier, throwing down his gauntlet of defiance. The herald's attendant then came forward and registered his name or armorial bearings. Many were the "gages" showered into the lists. Those who were to contend, were then admitted at separate barriers; after paying their respects to the Sovereigns and ladies, they took their respective stations, then, as the trumpets sounded, couching their lances, and spurring their horses, "the faint image of war" commenced.

For some moments the dust raised by the clattering steeds darkened the air; when the tourney became visible, many knights had been shaken from their saddles, armour was shattered, and lances splintered. A truce was now sounded, the successful champions filing by and saluting the imperial party.

The lists being removed, other war-like feats commenced. The air was rent with the clamorous shout of exultation. Ladies waved their embroidered scarfs, military music was sounded, and banners and pennons floated in the wind. The knights then dismounted, removing their helmets, and, kneeling at the foot of the throne, the prizes were awarded.

The imperial palace was crowded with crowned heads. It contained two emperors, two empresses, four kings and a queen; two hereditary princes, the one imperial, the other royal; two grand duchesses, and two princes. The building, I may here observe, forms a rectangled parallelogram; on one of the great sides is the palace properly so called, and on the other, opposite to it, are the buildings for the council of state. The Amelia and Swiss palaces form the wings. The Emperor and Empress of Russia inhabited the second story of the Amelia palace. The

King of Wurtemburg occupied the first. The King and Queen of Bavaria, with the princes their sons, and the grand Duchess of Weimar, tenanted the council buildings. The King of Denmark had that part of the Swiss palace which looks towards the bastions; and the King of Prussia that which faces the city. The hereditary Prince of Prussia resided with the latter. The Emperor and Empress of Austria, the grand Duchess of Oldenburgh, and the hereditary Prince of Austria, occupied what is properly called the palace. The young Archdukes and Archduchesses were at Schönbrun.

The witty, and not less true, saying of Talleyrand, " Le Congrès danse, mais il ne marche pas," was strikingly illustrated. At a party given by Prince Metternich, the gay and courtly throng imparted life and animation to the scene; but all the nobles, by the express wish of the Emperor, appeared in the costumes of their respective peasants.

The ball given by Prince Razamousky, the Russian ambassador, was followed by a magnificent banquet, at which eight hundred guests were comfortably seated at the tables; how unlike a London ball supper, where scrambling is the order of the night!

The most splendid entertainment was the Court ball. It was indeed one of unequalled brilliancy. There were foreigners present of every European nation—the magnificent Russian, the proud Austrian, natives of Prussia and Poland, Englishmen, Frenchmen, Danes, Swedes, Portuguese, Italians, Greeks, and Spaniards. The entire suite of long and handsome apartments were thrown open. The antechambers and corridors were lined with the noble Hungarian Guard, in their richest uniforms. The saloon in which the Empress and her ladies were seated, was a dazzling scene of pomp; there were feathers waving, diamonds glittering, lustres gleaming, music swelling, and last, not least admired, fair lips prattling.

The roof, supported by pillars, in imitation of finely polished white Parian marble, reflected the lustres by which it was decorated; the ladies were richly adorned with diamonds; kings, nobles, and ambassadors with orders, and were dressed in military uniforms, embroidered with gold, clasped with pearls; plumes, stars, and orders were in extraordinary profusion. There might be seen the grave courtier and the stern patriot, with the scions of the noblesse just launched upon the ensnaring blandishments and gaieties of the world; the youthful belle, the faded beauty, the aged chaperone; while emperors and empresses, kings and queens, warriors, and statesmen, mingled with the galaxy of beauty.

Mazurkas, polonaises, and waltzing, were danced to perfection, and the music was admirable.

There, amidst *la crême de la crême,* might be seen the shrunken figure and sallow features of the Emperor of Austria; the manly presence of the great autocrat of Russia; the solemn gait of the King of Prussia, whose height made a striking contrast to Denmark's diminutive sovereign; the English-looking face of the King of Bavaria; the fine persons of the Duke of Saxe-Coburg, and his brother the Prince Leopold, the present King of the Belgians; the handsome features and military figure of the Viceroy of Italy, Eugène Beauharnois; and the simple, manly, unassuming yet dignified bearing of Wellington.

But it would be an endless task to enumerate the lions of the night. It was a vast regal menagerie; and perhaps any one of them, had he but made his appearance during a London season, would have been run after with that avidity with which John Bull always welcomes novelty, whether in the shape of a Don Cossack, a Hottentot Venus, an *anatomie vivant,* a Swiss giantess, a Polish dwarf, a Blondin, a Leotard, a gorilla, or a band of French Guides.

The frost had now set in; the ground was covered with snow; all the wheeled carriages, even to the hackney coaches, had disappeared, and the streets were crowded with sledges. The Emperor had appointed a day for a party at one of his palaces, some distance from the city. At two o'clock, on a bright cloudless day, the procession, consisting of forty sledges, left the palace; preceded and followed by a band of music, and an escort of cavalry. Nothing could be more animated than the appearance of the *traineaux*—their brilliant colours, their ornaments of gold and silver, lined throughout with the richest velvets, and most expensive furs. The horses were caparisoned in embroidered cloth of gold, with plumes upon their heads and necks; their manes and tails plaited with ribands, and bearing a mass of silver or gilded bells across their shoulders. The picturesque costumes of the servants in their cloaks of sable, and of the chasseurs and equerries in the uniforms and liveries of their respective masters, were strikingly effective. The return of the procession by torchlight had also a most imposing effect.

A cloud was about this time spread over Vienna by the death of the Prince d'Aremberg. A very spirited horse which he was riding in St. Joseph Platz knocked down a woman. The Prince alighted to inquire into her condition; fortunately she had received no serious injury. The young Prince again mounted his horse, which shortly reared and fell back on its rider. He was conveyed in a lifeless state to the Palace of Prince Schwartzenberg.

A fatality seems to have attended the Prince's family. His father received, when shooting, a gunshot in his eye, by which he was deprived of his sight; his mother died on the guillotine; his brother was banished in consequence of a duel, in which he had the misfortune to kill his adversary; and finally, his sister perished in the fire which broke out in the house of Prince Schwartzenberg, at Paris. Apparently this was a doomed house!

The object of my greatest solicitude, and one for which I felt the deepest commiseration, was that inestimable mourner, the dethroned Empress of the world—the imperial daughter, the imperial bride, the imperial victim, sacrificed to pride; whose lot it was, midst the festivities, the rejoicings, with which her father's court re-echoed, to maintain the dignity of misfortune. "Proud Austria's mournful flower," the Empress Marie Louise, with her guiltless son, to whom, but a few months before, the eyes of the world had been directed—now lived in seclusion at Schönbrun, a phantom of departed glory and greatness.

Tempted by the interest of the object, an *attaché* to the British Ambassador, and myself, so far transgressed the limit of etiquette, as to request an introduction to the juvenile King of Rome, then styled the Prince of Parma.

"The boy,
The young Astyanax of modern Troy."

With some diplomacy, and after a great deal of

difficulty, our request was acceded to. We were conducted to the garden, where, dressed in the uniform of a hussar, with a profusion of light curly hair falling upon his neck, and with an engaging though bashful appearance, the son of *l'homme du Siècle* was occupied in the childish occupation of playing some newly-invented game. A dozen Frenchmen, still wearing the liveries of the fallen Emperor, and a few faithful friends, were all that remained of the court of the Empress.

After a brief interview, during which the Prince was most natural and affable, we took our leave; and for hours I could not help reflecting on the rapid and eventful changes that a few short years had worked in the destiny of Marie Louise. Nine years had only elapsed since the French army had entered Vienna in triumph, headed by him who had overrun Europe from the Tagus to the Kremlin—nay, within five the city had again been taken possession of by Napoleon's all-conquering arms. It was here, too, that the prediction was realised, that his life would be exposed to the chances to which despots are ever liable, by the dagger of some political or religious enthusiast. In the very palace of Schönbrun, where I had so lately been, he had established his head-quarters, and dictated the terms of peace to the imperial house of Austria.

I reflected on the bitter pang the daughter of that

house must feel at the *fêtes* given in honour of the downfall of the father of her son; of him from whom her own unexampled greatness had sprung; I reflected on the abject misery, the hopelessness, which the now deserted mother,

"The theme of pity, and the wreck of power,"

must have experienced, when in a gallery in the same palace, where, five years previously, on a sick bed, she had obtained the sympathy of Napoleon, in diverting the bombardment from the quarter in which she resided, and where, four years ago, she had witnessed the august ceremony of her espousals, she had concealed herself to behold the allied Sovereigns, who had deposed her husband, and driven him from the great Empire his genius had created.

The circumstances that attended the escape of Napoleon from Elba are too well known to require much notice; suffice it to say, that news reached Vienna that, on the 14th of February, he had sailed from Porto Ferrajo, in one of his own brigs, the "Inconstant," followed by six smaller vessels. A few Frenchmen, several Corsicans, Elbese, and Poles, to the number of one thousand, accompanied him. It was stated that, after encountering two great risks—first, in meeting a royal French frigate, which hailed the Inconstant; and secondly, in the pursuit of the

British sloop of war, the "Partridge," which had followed with the determination to capture or sink the flotilla—he had landed at Cannes, in the Gulf of St. Juan, in Provence, between Frejus and Antibes, and on the next day had continued his route, escorted only by a few Polish lancers.

He had passed the town of Grasse without entering it, and in the two following days had proceeded by Sisteron and Gap, across the mountains to Grenoble, where the 7th Regiment, with their colonel, Labedoyère, joined his ranks, and on the 8th of March the whole garrison had opened the gates to him. He then advanced with his eagles to Lyons, which he entered at the head of six hundred horse, when he was joined by the troops in garrison; thence to Mâcon and Chalons. At Laons de Saulnier, "the bravest of the brave," Ney, who had declared that he would bring Bonaparte to Paris, like a wild beast in a cage, recognized his superiority, and again became his satellite. In a few days his advanced guard was at Auxerre, forty leagues from Paris; and before the end of the month he had reached Fontainebleau, near which, at Melun, one hundred thousand men were posted.

Young as I was, I naturally thought more of pleasure than the political state of Europe, and looked forward with far greater delight to the prospect of a fox-hunt, than to running down "the Corsican Ogre," with a combined pack of one hundred and fifty thousand men, which Great Britain, Austria, Russia, and Prussia, were to furnish. I, therefore, paid little attention to the treaty, which placed the first Napoleon, without the pale of civil and social relations, as an enemy and destroyer of the tranquillity of the world.

I ought here to inform my readers, that Lord Stewart, the late Marquis of Londonderry, who was ambassador at Vienna, kept a pack of fox-hounds for the purpose of hunting deer, and during Wellington's stay in the Austrian capital, he went out constantly with them. As wild foxes were not very plentiful, in the event of the deer being taken early in the day, we always secured bag ones; the distinguished honour of conveying the "wily animal" to the meet, devolved upon me.

It was on the morning of the 9th of March, that, at an early hour, a britchka was at the door of the Duke of Wellington's residence, to transport me and my vulpine companions to a small *cabaret* near Eisenstadt, the magnificent residence of Prince Esterhazy. Just before I got into the carriage, my brother *attaché*, Fremantle, gave me a hint that the "Beau"—the name the Peninsular campaigners gave to their chief— might probably be unable to attend the hunt, and that I was to inform the Prince that despatches of some importance had arrived, which called for his immediate attention.

Off I started, and reached my destination soon after ten o'clock. A goodly assemblage of sportsmen kept anxiously looking out—not, reader, for me, but for my freight—and as the brace of foxes I had escorted from Vienna looked strong and healthy, much sport was expected. I was upon most intimate terms with Eugene Beauharnois, and, upon mounting my hunter, which had been kindly lent me by Lord Bathurst, then Lord Apsley, the Viceroy joined me.

"Is the Duke coming to-day?" he anxiously inquired.

"It is very doubtful," I replied; "some important despatches were brought to him this morning."

"That confirms all I have heard," responded Eugene; then, turning to me, he abruptly asked, "Have you heard any rumour of Napoleon's escape from Elba?"

"No," I rejoined; "yet stay," I continued, "Fremantle told Valletort that war was inevitable."

"Ah!" exclaimed Beauharnois, aloud, while he gave vent to his thoughts in Italian, a language I did not understand. "Do not allude to the subject," the Viceroy presently added, "there's Lord Stewart, and Prince Esterhazy."

At eleven o'clock a noble stag was turned out, and went away in gallant style. When viewed at the distance of about two miles, the hounds were laid on, and after a little time, challenged in good form. The crash was awful—

> "A cry more tuneable
> Never was hallooed to, or cheered with horn."

"Forward, forward!" resounded through the plain. Away they went at an English pace, over a fine galloping country, through the extensive wilds of Margarethen, toward the lake of Sultz; there the stag took the water, the hounds followed, their noble master, Prince Esterhazy, and a few daring riders dashing in with them.

The scene was now most animating—a stag swimming a lake more than a mile from one shore to the other, a gallant pack following, encouraged by the fearless riders. Happily they all landed safely, and, after a few moments' pause, the hounds challenged, and ran in a direct line for nearly two miles; there, the deer was headed, and bent his course back towards the lake, which he made a desperate effort to gain—but in vain, for before he could reach the water's edge, his pursuers had pulled down their game. Here our long-lost companions joined the chosen few, among which I happened fortunately to be one.

I will not describe the dismay of my noble relative, who entertained some little fear that his favourite hunter, and perhaps his beloved cousin, might meet with a watery bier; excellent sportsman as was Lord Apsley, he was not amphibious enough to prefer swimming a lake to a gallop on *terra firma*.

I now proposed turning out one of the "bagmen," but soon found that events of a more important nature occupied the minds of all present: they had heard of the escape of him who for years had "kept the world at bay." His country's Cæsar, Europe's Hannibal—

"Whose game was empires, and whose stakes were thrones,
Whose table earth—whose dice were human bones."

The report was true: a courier had reached the Duke of Wellington, bearing despatches from Lord Burghersh, that gave an official account of Bonaparte's escape from his exile.

Most of the members of the Congress were personally known to me, but I was at the time a youth, much more ready to enjoy whatever diversion seemed most easily accessible than to take advantage of my opportunities of recommending myself to such great men as Esterhazy, Nesselrode, Schwartzenberg, Metternich, and Talleyrand. I cannot, therefore, say much about either. Indeed, I was much more in the society of Englishmen, of whom there were many at Vienna. I became acquainted, however, with some of the talented foreigners, with whom in the suite of my chief it was imperative that I should fraternise.

One of the most remarkable men in that remarkable group was Frederick von Gentz. Though he held but the subordinate post of secretary at the conferences of the Congress, he had played an influential, yet certainly not a prominent part in the proceedings that had made such conferences necessary. He was a literary adventurer. As the lance of Hawkwood had been at the service of the best paymaster, equally so appears to have been the pen of Von Gentz; but the indifference to the cause he served, in the German, went a step beyond the English Condittiore, for he accepted retainers from clients whose interests were opposed.

Like the "Intelligencer," of the sixteenth and seventeenth centuries, he occasionally united the profession of news-writer with that of spy. He received large sums from the English Government for information respecting the policy of the German courts, and he seems to have been as liberally paid by the Government at Vienna for describing the policy he betrayed. His patriotism, however, was so far Teutonic, that he was as faithful to German interests as he was to his own—indeed, to such an extent was his devotion to the fatherland carried, that he drew upon himself the personal hostility of its great enemy, Napoleon, by his exposure and denunciations of the Emperor's schemes of aggrandizement.

Gentz, however, was not an Austrian, he having been born in Breslau, and his family had originally settled at Berlin; but the pleasure-loving Viennese suited him better than his more grave compatriots, and amongst these he set up his rest as a journalist, historian, and political writer in general. For twenty years he furnished successive English Administrations with literary materials of various kinds, receiving in return sums of £1,000 or of £500, according, it is supposed, to the extent or value of his labours in their behalf.

Such assistance was well known to his official employers in the Austrian capital, who continued to have recourse to his able pen for the drawing up of state documents of more than usual importance. He moved freely in the highest society, and had easy access to important European secrets, out of which he made so large a capital that he lived in the style of a functionary of the first rank.

His *bonnés fortunes* were as conspicuous in other directions. When past the age of sixty, he fell in love with a beautiful Danseuse—subsequently well known at the Opera house in London, as Fanny Elsler—

whose parents believing him to be wealthy from a knowledge of the appearance he made, and the society in which he moved, permitted her to enter into an arrangement with him, common enough in Vienna as well as elsewhere, between pretty ballet dancers and their rich admirers. Though half the young men of fashion were madly enamoured of her—the Duc de Reichstadt at their head—she is said to have remained faithful to her venerable lover till his death, and showed her respect to his memory by raising a monument, to mark her affection and the place of his interment. It has often been asserted that the son of the first Napoleon, just alluded to, was so much the slave of her charms, that the intensity of his passion for her aggravated the disease of which he died. This, however, is untrue; no communication had ever passed between them. The Duc was never alone with her.

Lord Castlereagh had a difficult part to play in these deliberations. He had not merely to watch over the interests of his own country, he had to maintain the part of Moderator in an assembly in which conflicting interests were aggravated by opposing nationalities, whose antagonism had recently been excited by the most savage ferocities of war. The prominent part which Great Britain had played in the mighty struggle that had just terminated, the enormous extent of the material advantages she had brought into it, should have entititled her to the lion's share in the division of the spoil—but, in the first place, the feeling of his countrymen was against any continental appropriation, or severe measures against a prostrate enemy; in the next, there were other pretenders for the lion's share, who were totally devoid of leonine generosity.

In the arts of diplomacy the English Foreign Secretary might be no match for some of the great masters of the craft to whom he now found himself opposed. In the Russian service those who professionally "lie abroad for the good of their country" are obliged to attain a proficiency which the representative of John Bull, from certain national prejudices, may toil after in vain. Count Nesselrode, in the game, ought to have been a match for a dozen Castlereaghs; but he was assisted by Prince Rasumowsky and Count Stackleberg—a diplomatic trio that ought to have beaten all Europe.

Scarcely less accomplished were the official servants of Austria, of whom Prince Metternich at a conference was as strong as Napoleon at a battle—his colleague, Baron de Wissenberg, should have been unnecessary.

Prussia, as hungry a lion as either of their roaring allies, was, in the persons of Prince Hardenberg and Baron Von Humboldt, equally eager to realise the profits of her share in the adventure.

They were grave statesmen, laying claim apparently to none of the refinement in the exercise of the arts of diplomacy, possessed in so eminent a degree by their Russian and Austrian *confrères*, but they were equally anxious that Prussia should pocket her share of the joint winnings.

France was the prey that had been hunted down. She was now prostrate and helpless; but as she had grown formidable at the expense of her neighbours, those who had suffered most by her vicinity were resolved to reduce her power of evil by depriving her of the territorial additions she had gained by force of arms. She must be reduced to her dimensions as they existed before the Revolutionary War.

Louis XVIII., however, was the friend of the Allies; for his restoration they professed to have been directing hostilities against Bonapartic France, and it would not be benefiting the Bourbon dynasty, for whom they had done so much, if they recalled them to a kingdom deprived of its sources of prosperity. This argument lost nothing in the hands of so able a negociator as Talleyrand, who was worthy to be the opponent of Nesselrode and Metternich. Nevertheless, it would have had but little effect, had not the more generous policy of England prevailed. Lord Castlereagh made it evident that though his Government had employed such extraordinary exertions to carry on the late European struggle, it was only with the object of preventing the rise to a dangerous pre-eminence of an unscrupulous neighbour. Belgium and Holland were therefore detached from the overgrown empire, and such other arrangements insisted on as were thought to afford security for the continuance of peace.

Still, there were rival interests in Germany, that could not be so easily disposed of. In vain did England set the example of restoring the valuable conquests she had made—in vain did she abandon claims for the prodigious monetary assistance she had afforded; the Germanic powers did not appear to appreciate such policy. What they had once grasped they desired to retain—indeed, what they once coveted they determined to possess. It was very difficult to satisfy them that the balance of power demanded that the scales should be trimmed for them as fairly as they had been adjusted for the French empire.

Whilst they were disputing, the Congress was summarily closed by an incident that no one of them had anticipated—the escape of Napoleon from Elba. This made other arrangements imperative.

Before I close this account of my stay in the Austrian capital during this memorable period, I must add a few lines on a subject which is too closely connected with it to be omitted. Isabey, a celebrated French miniature-painter, executed a drawing in which he introduced full-length portraits of all the members of the Congress. From this an engraving was produced in Paris, after the original picture had been exhibited in London, where it attracted much attention, not only as a work of art, but as an interesting historical memorial. A key was published with the print, but as both have become very scarce, and the former is rarely accessible, I shall here name the Plenipotentiaries as the artist has grouped them.

On the extreme left stands my chief, as one of the representatives of Great Britain; and near him are the ambassadors from Portugal, the Counts de Lobo and Saldanha, as well as the Count de Loewenholm from Sweden. The latter came to look after the interests of the Crown Prince, Berdadotte, whose hesitation, arose from certain *arrieres pensées*, which, as a Frenchman, he could not avoid cultivating. The next group consists of Count de Noailles, Prince Metternich, and Counts Du Pin and Nesselrode—the first and third appearing for the restored monarchy of France, the second for Austria, and the last for Russia. A little lower down Count Palmella appears, as a third representative for Portugal. More to the right, Prince Rasumowsky stands for the Czar; with Lord Stewart, the late Marquis of Londonderry, who had been attached to the head-quarters of the

Allies during the campaign that drove Napoleon from the north of Europe to his own capital. At the extreme right, Baron Humboldt and Lord Cathcart represented Prussian and English interests; below them Count Stackelberg made a fourth plenipotentiary for the autocrat of all the Russias; and Talleyrand gave a large increase to the diplomatic talent engaged in behalf of Louis XVIII. To the left, the strongly-marked Celtic features of Lord Clancarty who was our ambassador at the Hague, was represented by the side of M. de Labrador, the solitary Spanish envoy. More towards the centre, the Duc de Dalberg makes a fourth advocate for France, and Baron de Wissenberg the second for Austria. Below them, to the left, is the figure of the English Foreign Secretary, Viscount Castlereagh; and in the foreground, still further to the left, the astute Prussian minister, Chancellor Hardenberg.

These personages form the Congress, but the artist has introduced, at top, near the right-hand corner of the print, the figures of the secretaries, Wacken and Von Gentz, apparently whispering. But there is very little in the picture to show that any business is going on at the conference. There is certainly a table in the apartment used on this memorable occasion, and the open doors of another chamber are seen, and on the table materials for writing may be observed, but, whatever may be said, the group, sitting or standing by, are evidently not disposed, like Captain Cottle, to "make a note of it." Whatever diplomacy may be in progress, must have been thought scarcely worthy of record. In short, everybody is either standing or sitting for his portrait, rather than attempting to establish the balance of power, or harmonize conflicting interests.

Probably M. Isabey was more anxious to make an attractive picture than an exact representation of the proceedings of this distinguished assemblage; and as he has done full justice to the four representatives of England, we ought not to complain. As an illustration of an event of the highest historical importance, the print must be classed with the most valuable that have ever been published, and for the fidelity of the portraits, I can vouch.

Independent of Talleyrand's oft-quoted witticism, the foreign and English newspapers were indulging their satire at the wise heads assembled at Vienna. Among the best was the following, which appeared in the *Morning Chronicle* :—

"We learn from high sources a project is made
How Vienna's grand Congress the Christmas will spend;
Since public affairs have so long been delayed,
They may very well wait till the holidays end.

Kings and Queens to be drawn on a *Saxony Cake*,
    To be gained in one slice—'twill be very much followed,
While a good *Twelfth-night monarch* the ex-king will make,
    In title a king, though his kingdom is swallowed.

The Dane has long played the *Game Royal* of Goose,
    His neighbour, the Swede, as sly *Renard* will labour,
And Prussia's great king, though much out of use,
    Is still reckoned skilful at '*Beggar my neighbour.*'

At *Polish Drafts* Russia his power will try—
    People think he will win the game easy enough;
For England to meet him appears very shy,
    And with the Pope Austria plays *Blindman's Buff*.

France with Naples and Sicily *Forfeits* will play;
    And while thus engaged no person can blame us,
If our ministers here against Christmas-day
    Have rehearsed a long time to perform '*Ignoramus.*'"

CHAPTER VIII.

NAPOLEON'S PROGRESS IN FRANCE—THE EMPRESS MARIE LOUISE AND HER SON AT SCHÖNBRUN—ARRANGEMENTS OF THE ALLIES—THE DUKE OF WELLINGTON LEAVES VIENNA—ARRIVAL AT BRUSSELS—I JOIN GENERAL MAITLAND'S STAFF—RIDING A COSSACK HORSE—MY ACCIDENT—LETTERS FROM THE DUKE OF WELLINGTON AND LORD SALTOUN—PREPARATIONS OF WELLINGTON—NAPOLEON'S ADVANCE—FRENCH ROMANTIC ACCOUNTS OF WATERLOO—M. THIERS—THE DUCHESS OF RICHMOND'S BALL AT BRUSSELS—APPEARANCE OF THE DUKE THERE—A TRAP LAID FOR THE FRENCH EMPEROR—VICTOR HUGO'S ROMANCE OF WATERLOO—VISIT TO THE BATTLE-FIELD DURING THE FRENCH ATTACK—GENERAL ALARM—LORD HAY—SCENE AT BRUSSELS—THE DUKE AFTER THE BATTLE.

CHAPTER VIII.

FROM the 7th of March, the day upon which the courier reached the Duke of Wellington with despatches from Lord Burghersh, the late Earl of Westmoreland, every hour teemed with some new event; and in due course we were informed of Napoleon's progress.

During the time we remained in Vienna, politics alone were discussed, and never was there a scene more replete with interest than was this city during that brief period. In a few days the Powers, who had signed the treaty of Paris, made the celebrated declaration:

"Napoleon Bonaparte, by again appearing in France with projects of confusion and disorder, has deprived himself of the protection of the law, and in consequence has placed himself without the pale of civil and social relations; and, as an enemy and disturber of the tranquillity of the world, has rendered himself liable to public vengeance."

It is impossible to convey an idea of the bustle which prevailed in and about the palace. Multitudes were hourly collecting to see the crowned heads and other great dignitaries. Every five minutes the guards were turned out to pay the proper compliments to the assembled sovereigns; and as the representatives of the Allied Powers made their appearance, they were greeted with the acclamations and cheers of the populace.

Especial attention from all classes was shown to Wellington, Metternich, Nesselrode, Hardenberg, Talleyrand, and Castlereagh, who formed a concentration of political talent that could not be equalled.

Shortly after the declaration was made public, the Powers that signed it bound themselves, on behalf of their respective sovereigns, to maintain inviolably the Treaty of Paris; to keep each one hundred and fifty thousand men in the field, and not to lay down their arms until the peace of Europe was restored by the annihilation of Napoleon Bonaparte.

During this period the Duke remained in constant readiness, expecting every day to leave Vienna; but it was not until the morning of the 29th that, accompanied by Colonel Fremantle, and myself, he finally took his departure. Proceeding without delay, we reached Frankfort on the 2nd, and arrived at Brussels on the 5th of April.

To prove the rapidity of our journey, we passed at Cologne, on the 4th, the courier who had left Vienna on the 28th of March. At the last-mentioned town we ascertained that Napoleon had reached Fontainebleau, near which, at Meulun, one hundred thousand men were posted.

In the meantime, proclamations had been issued by the French Government, declaring Bonaparte a traitor; while counter proclamations to the French people, signed "Napoleon," were dispersed throughout the towns favourable to the late Emperor.

Upon reaching Brussels, Wellington devoted the whole of his time and energies to military preparations. A few days after our arrival, the Duke told me, in the most kind and considerate manner, that as he was anxious to replace on his staff those officers who had served with him in the Peninsula, he could no longer retain me.

At first this sounded like a death-blow to my hopes; my disappointment, however, was considerably lessened by his Grace assuring me " that I should be reappointed to the first vacancy on his staff; " and most strictly was his promise kept. Fortunately for me, General Maitland, who subsequently married my sister Sarah, was in want of an extra aide-de-camp, and kindly gave me the appointment.

After passing a few days in Brussels, I joined General Maitland at Enghien, my old Littlewick acquaintance, Lord Hay, being also aide-de-camp, and Major Gunthorpe (they were both of the Guards) acting as Brigade Major. Never were there a finer body of officers and men assembled together than those who formed the division of Guards, as their prowess afterwards fully proved.

The village of Enghien had nothing particular to recommend itself; but the park, where my general and his personal staff had their quarters, was a most picturesque spot. A portion of it was marked off as a cricket-ground, and a green sward that encircled a large sheet of water, backed by a forest of finely-grown trees, made an excellent gallop for those who wanted to test the merits of their horses.

One morning, when playing a match of cricket, St. John, then an ensign in the Guards, asked me, as the lightest weight, to ride a match round the lake. Unfortunately for me, I consented, little knowing the nature of the animal, a Cossack horse, I was to mount.

As my "side" were in, I tied a silk handkerchief round my head, and was soon in my saddle; at the word off being given, away started the Don " upon the pinions of the wind," and for some time I managed to keep him in the course. The clattering hoofs of my opponent at his heels presently caused him to bolt into the wood, and dash between two trees. The result, as I afterwards discovered—for I was insensible for more than seventy-two hours—was, that my head and arm came in violent contact with the trunk and branch, and I was brought to the ground.

Two medical men, belonging to the brigade, were soon by my side, and I was removed to a summer-house in the park, where they had recourse to the process of trepanning. So hopeless was my case deemed, that my arm, broken in two places, was scarcely attended to.

A soldier was left to nurse and watch over me. About the third morning, greatly to his surprise, I started up in bed, and asked where I was. The man, taking my inquiry literally, rose and saluted me, and answered, " At the head-quarters of His Majesty's brigade of Guards."

He then ran off, and soon returned with one of the surgeons of that regiment, who lost no time in administering to my comforts. The news of my recovery spread through the camp, and many a comrade would have come to shake me by the hand, had not peremptory orders been issued to keep me perfectly quiet.

Although my senses were restored, I was in a precarious state; but, after four and twenty hours of repose, I was pronounced well enough to proceed to my father and mother's home in Brussels. Maitland, who had been very kind, would have accompanied me, had not my father brought his carriage, with a trusty surgeon in it, to attend me on the road, should his services be required.

It was not until I reached home that I was made aware of the mischief the accident had caused. The sight of my right eye was completely gone, and my right arm so contracted and stiff, that for months I could make no use of it. Thanks to the best medical advice, and a good constitution, I recovered partially, but it was nearly two months before I was out of the sick-list, and as many more before I regained my usual strength.

My position excited the anxiety of my friends, and particulars were asked from every one likely to be able to give any information on the subject.

I append a couple of the replies:—

Duke of Wellington to Lady Sarah Lennox (afterwards Lady Sarah Maitland).

"Brussels, April 14th, 1815.

"MY DEAR LADY SARAH,—It is true that William has had a fall from his horse, which appeared yesterday rather a serious one. I am waiting for March to go down to the Duchess to let her know it, and you had better say nothing about it till I shall arrive.

"Ever yours, most sincerely,

"WELLINGTON."

Lord Saltoun had more time at his disposal, and probably had to satisfy a more exacting correspondent, but my position in his communication is much less important than in the preceding.

Lord Saltoun to Lady Saltoun.

"Hove, near Enghien, 15th of April, 1815.

"MY DEAREST WIFE,—We got here to-day, after a very long and tiresome march. I did not mean to write to you before to-morrow, but I am just come back from dining with Maitland, who is about two miles from this, and having there heard that the post goes out to-morrow at nine in the morning, I cannot resist returning to my old practice of night writing, for fear I should not wake early enough in the morning; not that I have any merit in so doing, for think of you I must, at least I can't help it, and writing brings me rather nearer to you, inasmuch as you afterwards get my then thoughts; but this is only the old story, for I used to think so in Spain, and see no reason why I should not continue so to do to the end of the chapter.

"I meant, my dear Kate, to have written you from Ghent, but the day we got there, and joined the Battalion, it received the order for marching, and as I had many things to put in order, I was obliged (as I dare say I shall often have to do hereafter) to give up my own wishes to public duty; but a man must live by his trade, and follow it to get on. As to our present situation, I shall give it you as far as I know. The Guards form the first division of the British army, under General Cooke; our brigade is commanded by my old friend Maitland; our division and another not yet named is to form the right corps of the army, under the Prince of Orange. As yet everything remains quiet, we waiting for the Allies, and old Boney straining every nerve to be able to meet the brush, and I think it will be at least a fortnight before we shall be in a condition to act; the reports to-day, however, state that Murat has declared for Boney, and taken the field in the name of the King of Rome; and they go so far as to state that he has advanced upon Reggio, defeated the Austrians in that part, and is advancing upon Milan. I do not believe this to the extent mentioned in the *Moniteur*, but after what took place at the Congress, no person can doubt which side Murat will take, and Austria is not under existing circumstances likely to act with effect further a field than the Adige. If Italy declares for Napoleon, which is more than likely, we shall have a toughish card to play, but giving him all this advantage, I expect to introduce you to my tenantry at Philorth before the end of September, as it is now certain that the South of France is very favourable to the Bourbons—not that they deserve it, for Louis is but a wooden king; but that is no business of ours, for Bonaparte is our natural and inveterate enemy, and we should never rest till we have not only seen him out of his empire, but well under ground into the bargain.

"I have no news to give you, except that Lord William Lennox, in riding a race on a horse he could not manage, got thrown off against a tree, broke his arm in two places, and so hurt his head, that he now lies in Maitland's quarters in a very dangerous state, as he has a good deal of fever, and the doctor will not be able to tell before to-morrow, whether his skull is fractured or not. From what I hear I am rather afraid of him; however, he is very young, and that goes a great way in these cases.

"Our post days are at present Sundays and Thursdays,— that is, they send letters from this to England, and I shall write to you often, as often as I can; for now, next to hearing from you, writing is my greatest pleasure for

reasons above stated, though now, my dear girl, I must leave off, having been up this morning at half-past three, six hours sooner than our usual breakfast hour, and as it is now two of the night, I must take a sleep to be ready for any thing to-morrow. Let me hear from you, my dear,
And believe me, ever your affectionate husband,
"SALTOUN.

"P.S.—The language of these Belgians is to me quite unintelligible, and their beds have such d—d hard pillows half-way down the bed, that they are perfectly detestable. Good night. God bless you!"

Nothing could exceed the zeal and promptitude displayed by the Duke of Wellington in making preparations for the campaign.

Siborne, in his "History of the War" says :—

"At the moment of the landing of Napoleon on the French shore, the only force in the Netherlands consisted, in addition to the native troops, of a weak Anglo-Hanoverian corps, under the command of his Royal Highness, the Prince of Orange; but the zeal, energy, and activity displayed by the Government of Great Britain, in engrafting upon this nucleus a powerful army, amounting, at the commencement of hostilities, to about 100,000 combatants, notwithstanding the impediments and delays occasioned by the absence of a considerable portion of its troops in America, were truly surprising."

No individual could have been selected with

higher qualifications to take the command of the army in Belgium, than the great Duke. The confidence placed in him by his soldiers—his caution, prudence, sagacity, and unfailing presence of mind—pointed him out as the only man calculated to enter the lists with the next greatest captain of that or any other day.

In the commanders of the Prussian army, Wellington found an able coadjutor in the veteran, Blücher von Wahlstadt, or, as he was called in his own country, from his dashing bravery, "Marschall Vorwarts."

The recent publication of the last volume of M. Thiers' romantic "History of the Consulate and of the Empire," has increased the absorbing interest which Englishmen have felt, and will long continue to feel, in that grandest of grand catastrophies—the Battle of Waterloo. As I may claim the advantage of having, though only for a few hours, been a spectator of the imposing spectacle which closed the magnificent Napoleonic drama, I consider myself in a position to comment, with some authority, on the innumerable fabulous statements respecting it, which the French historian has ventured to publish as facts.

When undertaking this work, M. Thiers seems to have assumed in the eyes of all France the post of Counsel for the Defence. For the French Consulate and Empire had been charged with grave crimes and humiliating offences, for which it had been arraigned at the bar of public opinion, and would have to abide the judgment of posterity. That excellent special pleader, Patriotism, appears to have suggested to him the well-known advice, offered in a similar unsatisfactory cause. " You have no case—abuse the Plaintiff's attorney." But he was far too clever an advocate to confine himself to so narrow a margin for his labours. His own interests, as well as those of his client, demanded that he should represent the defendant as faultless, as the plaintiff, and indeed all who aided and abetted him, were the reverse.

Our old acquaintance, "Perfide Albion," must be recognised as the Plaintiff, and Wellington as the attorney. With this dominant idea all through the Peninsular War, and the operations in the South of France, the Counsel for the Defence does his duty in a manner that ought to realise for him the endorsement of his brief—" Popularity." If he has not rendered France thoroughly contented with his labours in her cause, French vanity must be impossible to satisfy. Whatever gratification the historian's compatriots may have experienced in having their reverses in Portugal, in Spain, and on French territory explained to them—not as those afflictions which are to be accepted as mercies in disguise—but as triumphs that were lost by mistake. The final struggle in Belgium was more important than all the campaigns that preceded it in which England had taken any share. It was directed by the great Napoleon in person, at the head of an army of the finest soldiers in the world. Amply furnished with the best military materiel procurable, that illustrious commander had, moreover, the power of selecting his own time and place for striking a blow that should totally annihilate the most formidable of his antagonists. The modern Cæsar came, saw—and was overthrown.

Nearly half a century has passed since this prodigious conflict took place, and no Frenchman of the type M. Thiers prefers, can hear the name "Waterloo," without a thrill like that with which a sickly stomach rebels against the nastiest of black doses. The historian, therefore, if he hoped to gain the honorarium marked on the back of his brief, must have exerted himself in a truly wonderful manner. He did so, and the result is, that he has drawn on his imagination to an extent that would have afforded provision for a dozen novels. Captain Siborne had the merit of having collected all the facts that could be made to illustrate the event, but M. Thiers has proved that he can be perfectly independent of such common-place assistance.

Even in the numbers of the opposing force, he is as incorrect as he is in the statements he has given of their character. The French army at Waterloo were of one nationality—veteran soldiers, who could be relied upon in any emergency; they formed a gross total of 71,947, of which 15,765 were cavalry, and they had 246 guns. The Duke of Wellington's army numbered 67,661, having 12,408 cavalry, and 156 guns—of these 35,000 English—of which the bulk had never seen a shot fired in anger—with 6,000 King's German Legion, and 32,000 Hanoverians and Brunswickers, could be relied upon. The remainder, some 30,000 Dutch and Belgians, were untried troops.

The allegation that the Emperor surprised the Duke is equally untrue. The Prussian outposts had been driven in at Thuin. The English commander made his preparations to meet the attack, and had arranged with Blücher a regular plan of operations. Orders had been issued by the Duke to provide for the French advance on Charleroi, as early as three o'clock in the afternoon. At ten in the evening he issued further instructions for a concentration at Quatre Bras. Having completed his arrangements, he left his quarters and proceeded to my father's house, to which he had been invited—the Duchess having announced a ball and supper for that evening. He entered the ball-room, paid his respects to my mother with his customary high-bred courtesy, and continued to chat playfully to my sisters, not forgetting a kind pressure of the hand to myself.

While he was enjoying the good things produced for the supper, about midnight, the Prince of Orange, who had left the house two hours before, entered the room, walked up to him, and whispered a few sentences, announcing the capture of Charleroi by the enemy, and his advance towards Fleurus and Gosselies.

"I have no further orders," answered his Grace, aloud; then added kindly, "I think the best thing you can do, is to go to bed."

The Prince attempted no other communication; he at once retired. The information his Royal Highness had brought, though not known to the Commander-in-Chief, had been anticipated. The Duke had done all that was necessary to meet the exigency, and was determined to enjoy the little leisure at his disposal. His Grace, therefore, resumed his conversation with my mother which the Prince of Orange had interrupted, and surrendered himself to the pleasures prepared for him, with perfect confidence and case of manner, for full twenty minutes.

He now rose from his seat, and leaving his place at the supper-table, advanced to his host, to say "Good night." This having been done in his usual manner, he suddenly sunk his voice so as not to be overheard, and asked,

"Have you a good map of the country between here and the French frontier?"

His host quitted the supper-table as the Duke paid his *adieux* to my mother and such members of the family as happened to be near her, and accompanied his guest out of the room; but instead of proceeding to the street-door, my father led him into his private sitting-room.

"Bonaparte has gained a day's march on me," said Wellington, when the door closed behind them.

My father anxiously desired to know what his friend intended to do, to meet the Emperor's attack.

The map was found and spread out before them. The Duke scrutinised it closely.

"I have made arrangements to meet him at Quatre Bras," he observed, " and if I find myself not strong enough to stop him there, I shall fall back towards Blücher, and fight him *here*." The Duke pointed to the open country, where he made a mark with his thumb-nail.

The friends then separated, and my father returned to the supper-room with the map in his hand, and showed the locality of the coming battle, as indicated by his illustrious guest. The field has since enjoyed a world-wide fame. Its name, as is well known, was taken from a village of insignificant houses existing there.

My mother's guests, at least such of them as had become cognizant of the fact, could scarcely be otherwise than uneasy at the near approach of Napoleon to Brussels. The wives and daughters of the English officers who were able to draw a comparison between the combination of inexperienced English troops and unreliable foreign levies, unpossessed of any principle of cohesion, and the flower of the French army fighting under the eyes of their adored chief, might well tremble for the result, particularly when, at the first onset of the latter, some of the Belgians and the valiant Dutch rushed as fast as they could back to Brussels, proclaiming the total defeat of the Allies. But we all had such firm reliance on Wellington's prudence, and military knowledge, gained in so many hard-won triumphs, that we continued to hope, even after others had began to despair. Indeed, a few of the most adventurous, mounted and rode out, and, though non-combatants, met the danger more than half-way. Among these were my father and myself.

The Duke of Wellington was not taken by surprise by his imperial opponent; but Napoleon was surprised by the stand the Duke made at Quatre Bras. The Emperor had planned to separate the armies of Blücher and Wellington, to defeat them both utterly, and enter Brussels in triumph on the 17th June. On the 16th he fancied himself successful. He had attacked the Prussian commander at Ligny before he could be supported, and driven him back; and the English commander, afterwards, at Quatre Bras, with equal fierceness, though with less effect, and the latter also fell back.

Nor was the Duke of Wellington outgeneralled. The Emperor's genius in the art of war had devised a brilliant gambit in this military game of chess, but the Duke had devised a more brilliant defence. In short, the ardour of Napoleon succumbed to the cool sagacity of his opponent. The Duke retreated to a stronger position, having a perfect understanding with his Prussian colleague, and there, permitted his imperial opponent to waste his strength in reckless attacks. When the latter had exhausted his reserves, Wellington gathered together his unbroken battalions and charged the remains of the wearied French army, as his allies came tardily to his support. The fact is, that Napoleon fell into a trap that had been laid for him, and instead of succeeding in driving his two opponents—the one on the Rhine, the other on the Scheldt—he was himself so totally overthrown, that his military career was at an end.

It is scarcely possible to do justice to the imagination of M. Thiers, as he disposes of entire English regiments cut to pieces by his victorious countrymen—their squares broken by cavalry attacks, and their colours taken in extraordinary profusion—

the cuirassiers absolutely penetrating to Wellington's third line, and seizing six standards and sixty guns. We are assured that the Duke had lost 39,000 men, more than half his force, before six o'clock, and had scarcely a troop of cavalry left. Nevertheless, the triumph is finally wrested from the hands of the victors by the apparition of a body of English horse, he estimates as 3000 strong—they really mustered about 6000 sabres—who fell first upon the remnant, only four hundred, of the French cavalry of the Guard, and cut them to pieces; and then, assisted by the Prussians, swept the field of the heroes who had been performing such wonders.

Here it becomes necessary to introduce a word or two respecting another French romancist, who has taken a part of the same defence. More trustworthy chroniclers have stated that, when the Imperial Guard were summoned to acknowledge themselves prisoners, their general answered for them—" The Guard dies, but does not surrender." M. Victor Hugo, in a recent heir of his invention, called " *Les Misérables,*" devotes a hundred pages to a fanciful account of the great battle, wherein he makes General Gambronne, on being so summoned, reply, with a filthy word that no gentleman would either write or speak. Both stories are equally untrue. Those of the soldiers of the Guard who could not escape from the field gladly accepted the mercy of the conquerors, General Gambronne setting the example by surrendering to an English drummer.

This bit of sentiment has only been equalled by the statement respecting the ship "Le Vengeur," going down in the great naval battle of the 1st of June, with all the crew shouting "Vive la République!" That vessel certainly sunk from the effects of the fire of her antagonists, but not till every man on board of her who could swim, had made the most strenuous exertions to get taken into the nearest English ship.

The fact is, this kind of exaggeration is a powerful element in the ordinary French character. It is as much a matter of course as *gloire* rhyming with *victoire*. I remember, in the print-shops in Paris, one of the favourite illustrations of the war was the picture of a French soldier, who appears to have suffered as much as Goldsmith's dwarf, who had a giant for his companion-in-arms. But the mutilated Frenchman had a source of consolation which had been denied the poor mannikin. A legend engraved on the plate makes him state, he had taken so many colours from the enemy, that he could never want bandages for his wounds.

Such appeals to the national vanity were natural enough in shop windows, in the martial times to which

I refer, but I cannot reconcile myself to recourse being had to them, nearly half a century later, by public writers assuming to treat history as romance, or romance as history. No attempts are made in this country to lessen the imperial hero's long list of triumphs. There certainly was a time when "the Corsican ogre" was far from being popular in these islands; even then, however, he had partizans and apologists. Of late years we have done him ample justice. I cannot help, then, protesting against this deplorable littleness of mind in our friendly neighbours and faithful allies. MM. Thiers and Victor Hugo may rest assured, that the battle of Waterloo is an accomplished fact, and, as long as truth will endure, such efforts as theirs will be fruitless to render it an accomplished fiction.

Austerlitz is said to have hastened the dissolution of my god-father. I cannot consider it a less glorious victory on that account. I am induced to think that the spirit of that patriotic statesman must have been fully satisfied when the results of his policy were made manifest on the plains of Waterloo.

Prevented though I had been from doing service in the great battle, I was not to be kept from getting into it. Hearing that my brother aide-de-camp, Lord Hay, had been killed at Quatre Bras, on the 16th, and feeling a restless anxiety to join my general, made me suggest to my father the propriety of at once proceeding to the scene of action. I was told that, so long as I was under the hands of the surgeons, I must attend implicitly to their injunctions—and those injunctions were, that for the present I should remain quiet.

"If, however," continued my father, "you like to ride with me to-morrow morning to the field, where the army will bivouac to-night, there can be no objection to your doing so, and we shall then be better able to judge of your strength and powers on horseback."

To this I cheerfully assented, and at an early hour my first charger—a fine specimen of an English hunter—which the present Lord Bathurst had purchased for me in England, was at the door. There was one peculiarity about this horse; his ears were cropped—a cruel practice, now entirely discontinued.

After a very delightful ride through the forest of Soigny, we reached the village of Waterloo. There we met Lord Uxbridge, about to mount his charger. On recognising us, he remarked, "You're just come in time, for we shall have a smartish affair to-day."

We joined the gallant earl, then in the pride of manly vigour. After some little delay at Waterloo, where we baited our horses, we rode on to the field, and our first visit was to General Maitland. We found him cheerful and calm, as he ever was; yet there was a look about him that told how intensely he felt the loss of his aide-de-camp, and other officers, who had fallen, or been severely wounded.

After passing some time with the General, and the officers of his brigade, all of whom were personally known to my father and myself, we rode towards the spot where the hero of the day was posted. He shook my father by the hand. "William ought not to be here," he added; then continued to occupy himself with the important duties of the day.

Never shall I forget the scene that presented itself, nor the anxiety I felt for Wellington, his personal staff, among whom was my brother George, Lord Apsley, General Alava, and others with whom I had lived upon the most intimate terms of friendship; for young as I was, I could not for a moment doubt that the battle would be an obstinate one, and that many, then and there in the pride of manhood, might shortly be stretched lifeless on the field of glory. The hero of that day gave his orders, and watched the movements and attacks of the enemy. In the midst of danger, bullets whistling close about him, round shot ploughing up the ground he occupied, and men and horses falling upon every side, he sat upon his favourite charger, Copenhagen, as collectedly as if he had been reviewing the household troops in Hyde Park.

At one time the danger to which his Grace was exposed increased so much, that Alava, one of his oldest and best friends, suggested that it would be advisable to move a few yards out of a straggling fire of some French fusiliers; to this the chief at once assented, but, in reining back his charger, never for a moment took his eye off the enemy's line.

While upon the subject of the late General Alava, I may allude to a remarkable circumstance that attended him, and to which the Duke often referred, namely, that this gallant Spaniard was present at two of the greatest victories of this country, by sea and land— Trafalgar and Waterloo. At the former, he was on board the ship of one of his relatives.

Upon leaving the Duke, my father and myself proceeded by the rear to the left of the English line, which at that period had not been attacked; upon our way there, we overtook a brother-officer of mine, the late Sir John Elley, who described the gallant conduct of some of his favourite corps, the Blues, on the previous day, adding that, as some of the horses had been knocked over, he would attend to a previous request I had made, to have a batman allotted to me; the loss this corps sustained in their glorious charge, however, prevented my wishes being attended to.

Our object in visiting the left of the line was to see some of the officers of Picton's division—among them, Colonel Hunter Blair, with whom my father was on the most friendly terms. We found him; and while we were conversing upon the prospects of the day, an officer reported that there was a stir going on in the right line of the enemy opposed to us, and that the moment of attack could not be far distant. With the aid of a glass, I could see, from the number and brilliancy of the staff, that some distinguished general had passed through the French line, and that several guns were advancing to the front.

In less time than I can take to describe it, rapid volleys of artillery were fired into our force, and did deadly havoc. Men who had been ordered to lay down in square were raked by this tremendous fire, and riderless horses were scampering across the plain.

Taking a hasty leave of our friends, we wended our course towards the village of Waterloo; but this was a service of no little danger, for the round shot were flying in every direction, exciting both our horses to such a degree that we were scarcely able to manage them. Feeling assured that our only plan was to proceed cautiously, so as not to place ourselves between two fires, we jogged on at a quiet trot, and finally gained the village.

How different was our return from our setting forth. At every step we encountered dead, dying, or wounded officers and men. Many a familiar acquaintance gave us a ghastly recognition, as the wretched sufferer was being carried to the rear, shot or pierced through the body by bullet or lance; many a brave comrade opened his eyes for a moment, as the clattering of our horses' feet attracted his attention, to close them again in death; and many a gay, thoughtless stripling, who, within four short days, had been a guest at my mother's ball at Brussels, was now stretched in death on the ensanguined turf.

It was a sad and solemn scene, and, as we rode back home, the thought of how many friends and relatives might, before night, be numbered with the dead, completely absorbed our thoughts, until the noise and turmoil of the city reminded us that we were once again in Brussels. On the following day Wellington returned to the city, and then arose the painful duty of announcing to the relatives, the deaths of those of his own staff, who had fallen on the field of victory. Previous to his leaving Brussels to join his army, when it was victoriously marching towards the French capital, I had the good fortune to see him in company with my father. Nothing could exceed his kindness, but oh! how different were his look and voice, as in hurried tones he talked of the severe losses he had met with—of the deaths of those to whom he had been bound by the strongest ties of friendship and companionship in arms.

Of one of these irreparable losses, my fellow-student and worthy comrade, Lord Hay, I must say a few words. The day before the battle of Quatre Bras, Hay, who was in love with a young lady, entrusted his secret to me. He said he felt a presentiment that he should not escape the first action with the enemy, and giving me a gold chain for the object of his affection, and a sword and sash for myself, we parted. We met at my mother's ball on the 15th June. I shook him warmly by the hand; in less than twelve hours he was buried near the spot where he had fallen. Hay was a handsome young man, fond of show and dress, and it was partly attributable to this that he met his death. Mounted on a splendid charger, called Abelard, and decked out in a fancy uniform, he was shot, early in the action, by some straggler belonging to the enemy, who evidently took him for a superior officer. Strange to say, his presentiment came true in two respects. First, he met an early death; and secondly, as he anticipated, no trace of him or his property remained. His servant, a most faithful fellow, lost his baggage; and his family, to whom he was endeared by ties, not alone of consanguinity but of love, did not possess the slightest relic of the departed young hero. I remedied this, as far as lay in my power, by presenting the sword to Hay's brother, the late Lord Erroll, and his sash to his sister. A few months afterwards, I gave into the hands of a young and beautiful girl the chain that had been entrusted to me, and received her thanks and those of her parents for having thus faithfully executed the commission of my old comrade.

Never was there a finer fellow than James Lord Hay. At the time the British army were quartered at and near Brussels, Hay's amusement used to be to "lark" over the fence into the park, and, when chased by the keepers, charge the fence again into the street. Having done the above feat upon more than one occasion, a trap was laid for him by some of the *gensd'armes*, who placed themselves in the different alleys and summer-houses in the enclosure, unarmed, that nothing should interfere with their pedestrian powers in the chase. A signal was also arranged, and every preparation made for catching the intruder. Hay, however, was too canny a Scot, and too good a sportsman to be caught. No sooner, after leaping the barrier, did he hear the yell of the keepers, the shrill noise of the whistle, and the numerous body of his pursuers, than he sought the stiffest part of the enclosure. So impracticable it appeared, that no one except an Englishman would have thought of attempting it, and, in consequence, it was left unguarded. Away went Hay in rapid flight, pretending to be approaching a gap, where he must inevitably have been taken, then, turning short round, made for the stiff part, charged, cleared it, and was safe from his pursuers. A complaint to the Duke, and a hint that such "larks" would not be allowed, put an end to the affair. Poor Hay! Peace to his manes!

The scene at Brussels surpassed all that imagination could conjure up. Upwards of 40,000 wounded—French, Belgians, Prussians, and English—were brought into the town. The wounded were laid indiscriminately on straw throughout the city. Destitute of surgical assistance, the Belgian ladies and females were employed in their humane and indefatigable exertions, bandaging their wounds, serving out nourishment, and soothing and alleviating the pangs of the dying sufferers. Beautiful as woman is in all the charities of life, never does she appear so pre-eminently beautiful as in the chamber of sickness or death, administering to the wants of departing souls. And who were these "ministering angels?"

"When pain and anguish wring the brow."

I would fain ennoble my pages with their names, but

that I know they were those who "did good by stealth," and would "blush to find it fame."

The evil effects of my fall were gradually subsiding; and although the sight of my right eye was completely gone, and my arm was so stiff and contracted, that I could not make the slightest use of it, I was told that in a short time I should be in a state in which I might, without danger, join my general.

In an admirable lecture on the Life of Wellington, delivered at Wells, by the talented and philanthropic Montague Gore, occurred the following traits of the Duke's character:—

"I came back from the battle of Waterloo," says Dr. Hume, "with Sir Alexander Gordon, whose leg I was obliged to amputate on the field late in the evening. This distinguished officer died, rather unexpectedly, in my arms, about half-past three o'clock in the morning of the 19th; and as I was anxious to inform the Duke as early as possible of the sad event, and was standing at the door hesitating whether to disturb him or not, Sir Charles Broke Vere came up to me, and asked if I knew whether the Duke was awake or not, as he wished (he being Quarter-master-General) to take his orders relative to the movement of the troops.

"On this I decided to see if he was awake; and going up-stairs to his room, tapped gently at the door. He told me to come in. He had, as usual, taken off all his clothes, but had not washed himself; and as I entered the room he sat up in his bed, his face covered with the dust and sweat of the previous day, and extended his hand to me, which I took and held in mine, whilst I told him of Gordon's death, and related such of the casualties as had come to my knowledge. He was much affected. I felt his tears dropping fast upon my hands, and, looking towards him, saw them chasing one another in furrows over his dusty cheeks.

"He brushed them suddenly away with his left hand, and said to me, in a voice tremulous with emotion, 'Well, thank God! I don't know what it is to lose a battle, but certainly nothing can be more painful than to gain one with the loss of so many of one's friends.'"

Another instance of his goodness of heart occurs, when a vote of thanks to Wellington was moved in the House of Lords, after the battle of Salamanca. Lord Somers said, "He could tell their lordships, that while his great mind seemed to be wholly taken up with the important cares of his situation, he bestowed an attention almost inconceivable upon the comforts and conveniences of those under his command. Whether they were suffering from fatigue, from sickness, or from privations, they were equally the object of his solicitude. For himself, he knew that to a dear relation of his (Major Somers), whose constitution was fast sinking under the severe duties of his station, his parental kindness was such that it preserved a life, which else had been yielded soon after the battle of Salamanca; nor prolonged to that period, when he laid it down for his country, in a manner which gave him a melancholy pride in saying his son had so died. In alluding thus particularly to his own relative, he was far from meaning to intimate that this was a single case; Lord Wellington's kindness extended to all alike."

That Wellington was stern and inflexible in the discharge of duty, cannot be denied, as the following anecdote will prove:—

During the retreat of the British army at Leria, in Portugal, on the 3rd of October, 1810, when the enemy, under Junot, were hard pressing the rear of our forces, then retiring on the lines of Torres Vedras, two soldiers, one an English, the other a Portuguese, belonging to battalions lately arrived in the vicinity of that city, left their colours, and entered the town for the purpose of pillaging. Upon being discovered they were brought before Wellington by the Deputy Adjutant-General, and the Provost Marshal. "Who saw these men commit the act?" inquired the Commander of the forces. The Provost Marshal and another witness replied that they had found the prisoners in the act of plundering a shop, and assaulting a female who was attempting to defend her property; part of the stolen goods was also discovered in the possession of the accused. Having satisfied himself as to the guilt of the soldiers, the Duke turned round to the Provost Marshal, and in that brief expression which ever characterized him, said, "In ten minutes report to me that these two men have been executed."

The order was promptly obeyed, and scarcely had the rear-guard of the English force left Leria, than Junot, at the head of his corps, marched into the town. The first sight that attracted the attention of the French Marshal were the inanimate bodies of the two culprits, still suspended in the air.

An English staff officer, who had remained behind, with a flag of truce, to attend to the wounded, was immediately questioned as to the offence for which the soldiers had suffered.

"Plundering, and violence towards an inhabitant," responded the surgeon.

"Ma foi!" exclaimed Junot, shrugging his shoulders, "la discipline Anglaise est bien sévère."

That the plan of a joint attack on Napoleon, when the Emperor had been drawn into an attack upon the army under the command of the Duke of Wellington had been arranged, is clear from a letter the latter wrote, early on the morning of the battle, to Sir Charles Stuart, then at Brussels. He says:

"The Prussians will be ready again in the morning for anything. Pray, keep the English quiet if you can. Let them all prepare to move, but neither be in a hurry nor in a fright, *as all will yet turn out well.*"*

This was written after the Duke's force had fallen back from Quatre Bras, and when he had become thoroughly acquainted with the inefficiency of a considerable portion of it, and the superiority, in almost all military requisites, of the army of his opponent, whose presence in the field he knew to be equal to an addition of 40,000 men, under any circumstances; under the peculiarly exciting circumstances which had carried them across the frontier, the value of his personal superintendence must have largely increased; yet relying on the endurance of the reliable portion of his troops, and the combination which would enable him to overwhelm an exhausted enemy, the English commander could send confident assurances to his anxious compatriots at Brussels, that "all would yet turn out well."

In the work I have just quoted, there is preserved a memorandum written by the Duke in 1836, for Lord Stanhope's information, in which his Grace ex-

* "Miscellanies collected and edited by Earl Stanhope."

plains, in his own masterly way, the meaning of his statement, that the presence of Napoleon was as an addition of 40,000 men to the force he brought into the field; and he makes in it a suggestive contrast between the position of himself and the Duke of Marlborough, as commanders of continental armies.

My imprudence in venturing upon the Cossack horse, brought other disadvantages besides the materterial one which prevented the performance of my military duties—I lost one of those grand opportunities for distinction which a young soldier covets more than anything. The position to which I had so recently been appointed, would have enabled me to seek "the bubble reputation" with the most favourable chances of finding it. It might, however, have brought a close to my career, as it had done to so many of my brave comrades. So, balancing the chances for and against, I ought perhaps to be content.

But though I was at the eleventh hour shut out of the actual fighting, I was not excluded from the society of the actual fighters, and therefore, partly from being on or near the scene of the battle, during the momentous conflict, partly from associating with many witnesses of the struggle, immediately afterwards, and hearing their reports, I consider myself in a more favourable position for writing about Waterloo than MM. Thiers and Hugo.

I can assure the former, that, to the best of my knowledge, the majority of his statements, historical though they appear, are purely imaginary; and the latter, that, though the incident of the Cuirassiers when sent to attack the English Infantry, being swallowed up in hollow roads, is clearly melo-dramatic, it belongs to the melo-drama of fiction not of fact. I never saw any such gulf as the one described in "Les Misérables," nor did I ever meet with a person who had been in the battle, to whom its existence was known. It might be presumed that the English regiments formed in square so near it, had a tolerably correct knowledge of its whereabouts, but officers, non-commissioned officers, and privates, were ignorant of it at the time, and so have remained, as far as I have been able to learn.

CHAPTER IX.

MARCH OF THE ENGLISH ARMY INTO FRANCE—ATTACK ON PERONNE—LETTER OF THE MARSHAL PRINCE OF ECKMUHL AND GENERAL DAVOUST—DUKE OF WELLINGTON'S AND PRINCE BLUCHER'S REPLIES—MY VISIT TO THE FIELD OF BATTLE—ACCOMPANY COLONEL HUNTER BLAIR TO PARIS—THE DUKE'S GENERAL ORDER—THE DUTCH-BELGIAN TROOPS—A VISIT TO AN ABANDONED VILLAGE—FRENCH SENTRIES—QUARTERS IN THE BOIS DE BOULOGNE—WELLINGTON AND NAPOLEON.

CHAPTER II.

CHAPTER IX.

WELLINGTON was not slow in improving the advantage he had gained. He crossed the French frontier on the 20th, detached a force on the 24th, under Colville, to attack Cambray; and on the 26th, gave orders for a similar one to march upon Peronne. The order given on the latter occasion, was truly characteristic of the Duke. Major-General Sir John Byng, afterwards Lord Strafford, who commanded the 1st corps, having heard, on passing through the village of Vermond, that his Grace was there, waited upon him.

"You are the very person I wish to see;" said the Duke. "I want you to take Peronne; a brigade of Guards, and a Dutch Belgian brigade, are at your disposal. I shall be there almost as soon as yourself."

Byng, having given the necessary orders for Maitland's brigade, and a Dutch Belgian brigade of Chassé's division, attached to his corps, to proceed on this duty, the former was immediately put in motion.

Wellington, on reaching Peronne, just as these troops arrived there, summoned the garrison, then proceeded in person to reconnoitre that fortress; and perceiving the possibility of taking it by storm, gave orders to prepare for an assault. His Grace directed the attack to be made upon the horn-work which covered the suburb on the left of the Somme. Lieut.-Colonel Lord Saltoun, than whom a finer soldier never existed, immediately led on the light troops of Maitland's brigade, stormed, and carried the outwork, with the most trifling loss; on observing which, the Duke being satisfied the place would prove an easy capture, returned to his head-quarters.

On the 25th of June, Blücher received a letter addressed to the allied commanders, by the Commissioners sent from the two Chambers of the French Parliament, in which they communicated the fact of Napoleon's abdication, and of the elevation of his son to the throne. To this the veteran warrior sent a verbal reply, that upon reaching Paris, he would suspend hostilities, provided Bonaparte was given up to him, and certain fortresses delivered as guarantees of good faith, provided always that the Duke of Wellington assented.

The Duke's answer to the letter of the French commissioners, which Blücher had forwarded him, ran as follows:—

"Head-Quarters, 26th of June, 1815.
10 P.M.

"As Field-Marshal, the Duke of Wellington has only at this moment returned to his quarters; he has only now received from Marshal Prince Blücher the letter of their Excellencies, and which their Excellencies had sent to the Prussian outposts.

"When the Field-Marshal last heard from the head-quarters of the allied sovereigns, the 21st instant, their Majesties were at Heidelberg, and they must still be in that direction. It must be obvious to their Excellencies, that the Field-Marshal can neither prevent nor aid their Excellencies in reaching their Majesties; but if he has it in his power, or if their Excellencies think proper to pass through the countries in which the troops are under his command, the Field-Marshal begs that they will let him know in what manner he can facilitate their journey.

"The Field-Marshal was not aware that any officer commanding an advanced post had agreed verbally, or in any other manner, to a suspension of hostilities.

"Since the 15th instant, when Napoleon Buonaparte, at the head of the French armies, invaded the dominions of the King of the Netherlands, and attacked the Prussian army, the Field-Marshal has considered his sovereign, and those powers whose armies he commands, in a state of war with the Government of France; and he does not consider the abdication of Napoleon Buonaparte of his usurped authority, under all the circumstances which have preceded and attended that measure, as the attainment of the object held out in the declaration and treaties of the allies, which should induce them to lay down their arms.

"The Field-Marshal cannot consent, therefore, to any suspension of hostilities, however desirous he is of preventing the further effusion of blood.

"As the only object on which their Excellencies desired to converse with the Field-Marshal was the proposed suspension of hostilities, they will, probably, after the perusal of his sentiments and intentions as above declared, consider any interview with him an useless waste of their time; but if their Excellencies should still do him the honour to desire to have an interview with him, the Field-Marshal will be ready to meet them at the time and place they shall appoint.

"The Field-Marshal begs their Excellencies will receive the assurances of his high consideration.
"WELLINGTON."*

Previous to the attack made by Bulow upon Aubervilliers, on the night of the 29th, Blücher was joined by Wellington, when both commanders agreed not to suspend their operations until Bonaparte was delivered up to them. Another attempt was made to bring about an armistice by Marshal Davoust, Prince of Eckmühl, who addressed the following letter to both Wellington and Blücher:—

"Head-Quarters, La Villette,
"June 30th, 1815.

"MY LORD,—Your hostile movements continue, although, according to the declarations of the allied sovereigns, the motives of the war which they make upon us no longer exist, since the Emperor Napoleon has abdicated.

"At the moment when blood is again on the point of

* Despatches, vol. xii., p. 512.

flowing, I receive from Marshal, the Duke of Albufera, a telegraphic despatch, of which I transmit you a copy. My Lord, I guarantee this armistice on my honour. All the reasons you might have had to continue hostilities are destroyed, because you can have no other instruction from your Government than that which the Austrian generals had from theirs.

"I make the formal demand to your Excellency of ceasing all hostilities, and of our proceeding to agree on an armistice, according to the decision of Congress. I cannot believe, my Lord, that my request will be ineffectual; you will take upon yourself a great responsibility in the eyes of your fellow-countrymen.

"No other motive but that of putting an end to the effusion of blood, and the interests of my country, has dictated this letter.

"If I present myself on the field of battle, with the idea of your talents, I shall carry the conviction of there combating for the most sacred of causes—that of the defence and independence of my country; and, whatever may be the result, I shall merit your esteem. Accept, &c.,

"THE MARSHAL PRINCE OF ECKMUHL,
"Minister at War."

To this the Duke of Wellington replied in the following terms:—

"Head-Quarters, July 1, 1815. 10 A.M.

"MONSIEUR LE MARÉCHAL,—I have just received your Excellency's letter of the 30th June, in which your Excellency communicates to me the intelligence you have received of an armistice having been concluded by General Frimont with Marshal the Duke of Albufera.

"I have already made known, in writing, to the French commissioners, sent to the Allied Powers, and verbally to the commissioners sent to me, the reasons which have prevented me from suspending my operations; which reasons I have cause to believe are fully adopted by the allies of my Sovereign, and of those whose armies I have the honour of commanding.

"I have every wish to prevent the further effusion of the blood of the brave troops under my command; but it must be upon the conditions which shall secure the re-establishment and the stability of the general peace. I have the honour to be, &c.,

"WELLINGTON."

Blücher's answer is truly characteristic, and shows the feeling he entertained for the Marshal, under whose government of Hamburg, the greatest excesses had been committed upon his own countrymen:—

*To the French General Davoust.**

"MARSHAL,—It is not conformable to truth that, because Napoleon has abdicated the throne, there exists no further motive for war between the Allied Powers and France. His abdication is conditional—that is, in favour of his son; but a decree of the Allied Powers excludes not only Napoleon, but every member of his family from the throne.

"If General Frimont has considered himself authorized to conclude an armistice with your General opposed to him, that is no motive for us to do the same. We shall pursue our victory; God has given us strength and resolution to do so. Beware, Marshal, of what you do, and forbear devoting another city to destruction; for you know what liberties the exasperated soldiers would take, should your capital

---

* The original letter was in German.

be carried by storm. Do you solicit the maledictions of Paris in addition to those of Hamburg?

"We shall enter Paris to protect the respectable inhabitants against the mob, by whom they are threatened with pillage. An armistice can be made with security nowhere but in Paris. This, our relative position towards your nation, be pleased, Marshal, not to mistake!

"Let me finally observe to you, Marshal, if you mean to negotiate with us, it is a matter of surprise that, in defiance of the law of nations, you detain our officers despatched with letters and orders.

"In the usual form of conventional civility, I have the honour to be, Marshal,
"Your obedient servant,
"BLUCHER."

I fretted and fumed and found fault with the members of the medical profession for still pronouncing me unfit for duty; on the day but one after the battle I accompanied my father to the field of Waterloo, and never did such a sight present itself to our view; there lay heaped together dead men and horses, for the wounded had either been removed or put out of their misery by the camp-followers and peasantry, who first murdered and then pillaged them. The stench was awful, and a sadder scene I never witnessed; for I thought among those whose mangled corpses lay exposed to the sun, many had left fathers, mothers, wives, sisters, children, and friends to mourn their loss.

At length the happy day arrived when I was

reported well enough to join the army, and within half an hour of the last meeting I had with my surgeon, I was in my saddle ready to make the best of my way to the head-quarters of the brigade of Guards.

Just as I was about to take leave of my father and mother, Colonel Hunter Blair, who had been wounded at Waterloo, drove up to the door in his gig; he, although unable to mount his horse, was eager to join the army, and it was soon arranged that our horses and baggage should be sent off together, under the care of a veteran batman of his, and that I should take a seat in his carriage.

Our journey was delightful, the weather was fine, my companion most agreeable, and our interest was kept alive by now and then falling in with some detachment of the Allied Army, or of meeting small bodies of the wounded or straggling enemy. Colonel Blair fought the battle of Waterloo over again with me, described the death of Picton, told anecdotes of that gallant soldier, and raised my warlike enthusiasm to such a pitch, that I longed to be by the side of my General, then, as we heard, fighting his way to Paris.

By an arrangement made with the Colonel's batman, our horses, mules, and baggage were to rest every night at places he had appointed. As the servant was an old campaigner, we found them snugly settled upon our arrival, and every attention paid them by the villagers. This was owing to a proclamation issued by Wellington previous to his quitting Malplaquet. Translated, it was as follows :—

"Nivelles, 20th June, 1815.

"GENERAL ORDER.—As the army is about to enter the French territory, the troops of the nations which are at present under the command of Field-Marshal the Duke of Wellington, are desired to recollect that their respective Sovereigns are the allies of his Majesty the King of France, and that France ought, therefore, to be treated as a friendly country. It is therefore required that nothing should be taken either by officers or soldiers for which payment be not made.

"WELLINGTON."

How clearly does the above prove the justice and impartiality of Wellington, who makes no difference between the higher and lower grades of his army.

When, at a later period, some highway robberies had been committed by the British troops near Beauvais, the Duke wrote to the officer commanding the brigade of cavalry, holding him responsible that a stop should be put to those disgraceful practices, and ordering, if other means failed, "that guards, and a chain of videttes in sight of each other, should be placed along the high road, through the whole length of the cantonments; the rolls to be called every hour during the day and night, at which officers and men were to be present."

It will thus be seen, that every precaution was taken by the Duke to ensure the orderly conduct of his troops on the march to Paris; and, to the honour of the English nation be it recorded, that in the ranks of the British army, with the exception of the one referred to, scarcely an excess took place.

It was not so among the Dutch and Belgian troops, who committed every species of outrage. Two of the officers who had participated in such breaches of discipline, were reported to his Grace, who immediately put in force the General Order of the 20th of June, by punishing the offenders with the utmost rigour of martial law.

To show that some of the allied forces were not quite as merciful to their enemies as were the British troops, I must mention a circumstance that occurred to me on my way to join the army in company with my gallant friend Blair, father of poor Hunter Blair of the Guards, who fell in the Crimea. One night, when within fifteen leagues of Paris, one of the wheels of the vehicle became so hot, that we found it impossible to reach the next village, which was fortunately close at hand. Descending from the carriage, and fastening the horse by his head to a tree, we made the best of our way to the small hamlet. Upon reaching it, we were challenged by the sentry, who, seeing we were English officers, called the sergeant of the guard, which we discovered to be a Prussian one. We then inquired for the officer commanding the detachment, and found that it was merely a party under the orders of a non-commissioned officer, who shortly made his appearance.

In vain did we attempt to make known to him that all we required was some grease for the wheels.

Finding he could not understand the English or French languages, or make head or tail of my German, we pointed to a cupboard in the temporary guard-room, and, with pantomimic gestures, attempted to explain our wants. The cupboard was opened, a flask of wine, some bread and fruit offered us, but nothing of an oleaginous quality was there to be found.

We were proceeding to another cottage, when an idea seemed to flash across the mind of our conductor, that we were in search of plunder. Calling out a file of men, he made a forcible entry into every tenement in the village, the inhabitants of which, with some few exceptions, had quitted their homes in the morning. Breaking open all the doors and cupboards with the butt end of his musket, the sergeant made signs to us to do as we pleased; but, to his great surprise we rejected even a purse full of money that had been discovered in a drawer of the Curé's house.

In crossing the kitchen, despairing of finding what we were in search of, my companion's eyes were attracted towards a large piece of lard, which, for all we know to the contrary, might have basted the tithe pig, if tithes had been known in France. Rushing to the shelf, we seized the lard and a pat of butter, tendering compensation to the frightened cook, in the shape of a five-franc piece, which, unknown to our guides, we slipped into the peasant's hands. She, an old crone of sixty years of age, must have taken us for genuine Don Cossacks, who at that period were supposed to rob the lamps of their oil, although payment on such occasions was not the habit of that predatory race.

We now hastily joined our vehicle, and proceeded on our journey. At daybreak we witnessed a conflagration in the rear, and heard that the formerly peaceful hamlet, where our adventure on the previous night occurred, had been set on fire by the detachment who had so willingly offered us their assistance in plundering the unoffending inhabitants.

After three days' travelling we approached the army, and Colonel Blair and myself parted, he to seek his brigade, and I to join General Maitland. Mounting my horse, and wishing my companion "God speed," I was shortly gratified at finding myself within range of the sentries of the Guards. Gunthorpe, the brigade-major, happening to be out walking, met and welcomed me cordially; then conducted me to the

General's quarters. There I saw my chief, and congratulated him on his escape during the sanguinary combats of Quatre Bras and Waterloo. Although tolerably cheerful, he still mourned over the loss of many of his brother officers, and the gallant band of soldiers he had led on to victory.

As I had an hour to spare before dinner, having secured my billet in a small farm-house, I strolled with Gunthorpe about our cantonments.

"Take my advice," said he, in that quaint manner for which he was famed, "and don't go within fire of that line of sentries," pointing to some French infantry; "they are much too near to be pleasant. Yesterday, by way of keeping their hands in, I suppose, they blazed away at one of our young fellows. It was fortunate he was not hit; for after going through the campaign, and having still some toughish work on hand, it would have been a sad inglorious death, to have been potted by one of those chasseurs."

I thanked him for his advice, and then inquired as to the probability of the war being carried on.

"Johnny Crapeau," replied he, "won't let us enter Paris without some trouble; and I own for one, I don't much care how many Frenchmen I meet in the open field; but town fighting, against an infuriated populace and soldiery, is not quite to my taste."

Nor was it, I own, to mine, and I was not sorry

on the following morning to be told by Gunthorpe, "that there was no chance of any more 'scrimmages,'" as peace was about to be concluded, and such proved to be the case. The last days of the imperial government had faded away; Fouché had surrendered the capital to the invaders; and the gallant French soldiers, dispirited and crest-fallen, had marched out of the city, to retire behind the Loire. The brave troops that had assembled at Vilette, under the command of Davoust, and who would rather have died on the field than have turned their backs upon their opponents, were compelled to join their comrades, and to consummate, in temporary exile, the downfall of their beloved Emperor.

After a few days, we took possession of Vilette, and from thence proceeded to the Bois de Boulogne, where we bivouacked. A beautiful villa in the neighbourhood, furnished a most comfortable residence for Maitland and his personal staff—I, as the youngest member of it, occupying a very picturesque summer-house in the garden.

It was an interesting sight, on the first Sunday after our tents were pitched in the above wood, to see a square formed of those who had escaped death in the recent short but terrible campaign, and to hear from the eloquent lips of the respected chaplain to the brigade, the Reverend Mr. Stonehouse, words of consolation to the friends and relatives of the fallen, and appeals to the hearts of those present to devote their lives to the service of Him who in the hour of danger had protected and preserved them. Not a few tears trickled down the sun-burnt and weather-beaten visages of many a warrior, as he listened with grateful acknowledgment to the sound doctrine so ably promulgated by the minister of religion.

Within a few days of the triumphal entry of the victors into Paris, I was appointed an extra aide-de-camp to my former chief, Wellington, who, never failing in his word, gave me one of the vacancies caused by the deaths of poor Gordon and Canning.

Thanking Maitland for all his kindness to me, I joined head-quarters, and shortly afterwards had the gratification of marching into the capital as one of the Duke's personal staff. Previous to this period, Napoleon had issued the following declaration to the people of France, of which we give a translation:—

"Frenchmen!

"In commencing the war to uphold the national independence I relied on the union of all efforts, of all wills, and the co-operation of all the national authorities. I was justified therefrom in hoping for success, and I braved all the declarations of the Powers against me.

"Circumstances now appear to me to be changed. I offer myself as a sacrifice to the hatred of the enemies of

France. Would that they were sincere in their declarations, and intended really no ill but against myself! My political life is closed, and I proclaim my son, under the title of Napoleon II., Emperor of the French.

"The present ministry will provisionally form the council of government. The interest which I feel in my son prompts me to call upon the Chambers to organize, without delay, the Regency by a law.

"Let all unite for the public safety, and to remain an independent nation.

"NAPOLEON."

A few days after the above declaration was issued, a "foul transaction" was proposed to Wellington, respecting the murder of his late opponent. This is the Duke's answer, and it is worthy of him:—

Field-Marshal the Duke of Wellington to Sir Charles Stuart, G.C.B.

"Orville, June 28, 1815.

"MY DEAR STUART,—I send you my despatches, which will make you acquainted with the state of affairs. You may show them to Talleyrand if you choose. General —— has been here this day, to negotiate for Napoleon's passing to America, on which proposition I have answered, that I have no authority. The Russians think the Jacobins wish to give him over to me, believing that I will save his life. B——* wishes to kill him; that I shall remonstrate against, and shall insist of his being disposed of by common accord. I have likewise said, that, as a

---

* Blücher.

private friend, I advised him to have nothing to do with so foul a transaction; that he and I had acted too distinguished parts in those transactions to become executioners; and that I was determined, if the Sovereigns wished to put him to death, they should appoint another executioner, who should not be me.

"WELLINGTON."

CHAPTER X.

BOURBONISTS AND BONAPARTISTS—THE ALLIED ARMIES ENTER PARIS—THE DUKE OF WELLINGTON AND THE ASSASSIN CANTILLON—FRENCH JOKES—THE ENGLISH IN FRANCE—WALTER SCOTT—CATALANI—BANQUETS BY THE KING OF FRANCE IN HONOUR OF THE DUKE—FRENCH COOKERY—CELEBRATED RESTAURATEURS—THE PARISIAN THEATRE—THE HORSE-DEALER HUNTED—ENGLISH SPORTS AT NEUILLY—MARSHAL NEY—SIR CHARLES AND LADY MORGAN IN PARIS—THE MARQUIS DE LA FAYETTE—MRS. PATTERSON AND JEROME BONAPARTE—THE BALTIMORE BEAUTY IN FRANCE—HER LOVE OF SCANDAL—SHE SLANDERS THE DUKE OF WELLINGTON—MADAME GRASSINI'S OPINIONS OF NAPOLEON AND WELLINGTON—THOMAS MOORE AT PARIS—THE IRISH PHYSICIAN—THE FUDGE FAMILY—KENNEY, THE DRAMATIST—THOMAS HOLCROFT AND HIS FRENCH WARD—A NERVOUS MAN.

CHAPTER X.

IT was amusing to one who, like myself, had heard the shouts of the Bourbonites during the preceding year, and who had seen the white flag and the royal banners floating from every battlement and tower, to witness the transformations that had taken place within a few months. The tri-coloured standard and the eagle were to be met with in every town and village upon our road to Paris, and in another month, by the magic wand of Wellington, they were again changed to the emblems of the royalists.

Upon a fine bright sunny day in the month of July, the Allied Army entered the city. The Emperor of Russia, the King of Prussia, Prince Schwartzenberg, the Hetman Platoff, the veteran Blücher, clad in gorgeous uniforms, and mounted on their fiery war steeds, attracted much attention; and the moment they appeared, the crowd raised the shout of "Vivent les Alliés! Vivent nos libérateurs! Vivent les Bourbons!" There was *one*, however, in the pageant decked out in no gaudy apparel, wearing few honours, mounted on a noble creature of muscular power, whose full bright chestnut coat was unadorned by trappings of gold and silver. Every eye was turned upon the rider of that faithful enduring animal, who had carried his master throughout the longest battle-day. Unquestionably Wellington and "Copenhagen," upon the occasion I refer to, proved the greatest objects of attention to the assembled populace.

The Grand Duke Constantine separated himself from the *cortége*, and took his station on one side of the Boulevards, to inspect the army of forty thousand men, as they marched passed him. The Sovereigns then retired to their quarters—the Czar to the Hôtel of Prince Talleyrand, in the Rue St. Florentin; the King of Prussia to the Palace of Eugène Beauharnois in the Rue de Lille.

So great was the enthusiasm of the fickle Parisians, that they gathered in the Rue Castiglione to greet their liberators, while one or two infatuated royalists attempted to beat down the statue of Napoleon in the Place Vendôme. In the meantime, the Duke had communicated the result of the campaign and triumphal entry into Paris to the English Secretary at

War, in the following brief and unostentatious lines:—

"Paris, July 8th, 1815.

"My Lord,—In consequence of the convention with the enemy, of which I transmitted your lordship the copy in my despatch of the 24th, the troops under my command, and that of Field-Marshal Prince Blücher, occupied the barriers of Paris on the 6th, and entered the city yesterday, which has ever since been perfectly quiet.

"The King of France entered Paris this day.

"I have the honour to be, &c., &c.,
"Wellington.
"Earl Bathurst, &c."

The Duke of Wellington now took possession of the Hôtel that had been assigned to him near the Place Louis XV., and the staff were billeted about the town. I was fortunate enough to get excellent quarters in the Rue St. Honoré, with a very good stable for my two chargers, close at hand.

Although foreigners of every nation were congregated in Paris, little occurred worthy of notice, until the 24th of July, when the British, Hanoverian, and Belgian troops were reviewed in the Champs Elysées, by the Emperors of Russia and Austria, and King of Prussia. The crowned heads and general officers occupied the centre of the Place Louis XV., near the spot where the ill-fated King Louis XVI. was beheaded. The light-hearted Parisians, not in the slightest degree dejected by the late disastrous events of the campaign, walked, danced, chatted, smoked, and jested, as if nothing had occurred; they laughed at the *sans culotte* costume of the Highlanders; nicknamed the Cossacks, " Les Cupidons du Nord !" and from their light green uniform gave the *sobriquet* of " *Les Cornichons,*" to the Russian infantry.

One man, a vendor of gingerbread-nuts, created much merriment by his roulette-table. I will attempt partly to Anglicise his witticisms :—

"Whoever wishes for a prize, must first *put down a Louis.* He then proceeded—"Numbers from one to twenty are vacant. *Dix huit est le bon numero, il est sorti une fois ; il est sorti deux fois, et je crois bien qu'il sortera encore une troisième !*"

This allusion to the *Prefet D'Angleterre,* as the newly-restored monarch was contemptuously termed, was received with shouts by the Bonapartists, and afforded some merriment even to the Bourbons.

Among other witty sayings, the furniture of the Tuileries gave rise to the following: The curtains and hangings being still decorated with the Imperial N., some one remarked :—" *Ah! le pauvre Empereur, il a des N. mis,* (enemies) *partout;*" nor did the triumphal car, stripped of its steeds, escape jocose observation; for upon one occasion, when " *L'Inevitable Louis* " appeared at the window, a man in the crowd, seeing the horseless car, pointedly exclaimed

—" *Oh, voilà, le Char l'attend!* (*Le Charlatan.*)"

A political squib was shortly afterwards placarded over Paris, and ran as follows—no translation could do justice to it:—

" Les Royalistes visitant les travaux de Montmartre.

"Monsieur, malgré ces preparatifs, on dit que notre bon roi va revenir avec sa famille par la Plaine des Vertus."

" Non, monsieur, j'ai l'ordre de la marche dans ma poche. Le Roi entrera *en fauteuil,* par la Barriére *du Roule*; le Comte D'Artois par la Barriere *des Bonnes Hommes;* Le Duc et la Duchesse D'Angoulême, par la Barriére *des Martyrs;* le Duc de Berri, par la Barriére du Gros Caillou ; Messrs. du Blacas, Château Brilliant, et tout le Ministere par la Barriére D'Enfer et enfin les Allies par la Barrière *de Pantin,* parceque la Barriére *du Trône* sera trop bien gardées."

The city was now all gaiety. On the 31st of July, the Duke gave a dinner of forty—at which all his personal staff were present—followed by a ball and supper.

About the middle of August, a gloom was thrown over French society, by the announcement that Labédoyere had been sentenced to death. Every exertion was made to save his life, but without avail. Nothing could exceed his bravery in his last moments; without waiting to have his eyes bandaged, he uncovered his breast to the veterans who were to shoot him, and exclaimed, in a calm, firm voice, "Be sure not to miss me." In a second afterwards he was a corpse.

Within a few months another sanguinary act threw a dark hue over the Restoration—the execution of Ney. Neither the indomitable courage nor the gallant exploits of this brave warrior, could soften the heart of Louis XVIII.

On the 16th of August, Wellington gave a superb banquet and ball. Among the guests were the Emperor of Russia, the Archdukes, the King of Prussia, his two sons, the Prince of Orange, "Mein leiber Fürst" Blucher, as the Duke was wont to call the veteran, and all the English nobility congregated in Paris. At the above period, Walter Scott, Tom Moore, John Kemble, Talma, Catalani, and Grassini were at Paris, and were constant guests at the hôtel of my chief; they often, too, joined in picnics, got up by Wellington, to witness the beauties of the environs.

Never shall I forget a party to Versailles, which was arranged by his Grace, and attended by some of the loveliest of England's daughters, and by talent scarcely to be excelled. These gardens were laid out in the most exquisite taste by Le Notre, who, Aladin-like, converted rivers into lakes, fountains, and waterfalls; and the banks were peopled with nymphs, tritons, satyrs, mermaids, bacchantes, and marine monsters from the classical studio of Pierre Puget, Coisevox, and Girardon.

It was a treat of the highest intellectual order to listen to the great Scotch novellist, as he brought, with the greatest simplicity of manner, to the "mind's eye," the deeds of Bayard, Du Guesclin, Turenne and Condé; and to hear from the lips of Erin's poet, anecdotes of the lovely La Vallière, her ambitious rival Madame de Montespan, the proud de Maintenon, the far-famed Ninon de l'Enclos, Madame Pompadour, and Henrietta of England. Scarcely less so was it to attend to the two greatest actors of their day, as they expatiated upon the respective merits of Shakspeare, Corneille, Racine, Farquhar, Molière, and other men of dramatic genius, of England and France.

Nor was the feast of reason confined to the above; for, after an *al fresco* luncheon, in some sequestered shady spot, it was most delightful to have one's ears ravished with the enchanting notes of the Queen of Song, the Italian Nightingale, Catalani, the deep-toned voice of the beauteous Grassini, or the pathetic strains of "Anacreon Moore," as he warbled some of his own native melodies.

Wellington was devoted to music, and upon all occasions got together the best private and professional talent that could be found in Paris; indeed, there was scarcely an evening that we had not a concert or dance, so desirous was the Duke to gratify those around him.

Conspicuous among the strangers in Paris was the Sydney Owenson of my holiday trips to Dublin, now altered from the jigging, romping, flirting, singing, harping, "Wild Irish Girl," to the fashionable *belle esprit*, "Lady Morgan." Her husband and herself had taken advantage of the continent being thrown open to English visitors, to see as much as they could of French society; and as they made it known far and wide that they intended to improve the occasion by writing a book, the susceptible Parisians of both sexes were almost frantic in their eagerness to do honour to my Lady and Sir Charles. Bourbons and Bonapartists contended for the distinction of being favourably noticed by the Irish *femme-philosophe*; and it became quite the rage to quote the ambiguous passages of her worst productions, "Ida of Athens," and "The Missionary," as reflecting the strong-minded womanism of the nineteenth century. In return for these compliments, her Ladyship put as much French spirituality as she could upon her Hibernian vivacity, and paid her new friends back in coin of at least equal value.

Her manners, however, were not generally admired.

Indeed, Madame de Genlis, in one of her works, mentions Lady Morgan's excessive gesticulation and loud talking, as disapproved in Parisian circles.

In the metropolis of gallantry it could not be expected that she should entirely give up her habit of flirting, but she did so with such intense discretion, as to excite the admiration of some of the most experienced of her feminine acquaintances. The conquest on which she seemed to pride herself most, was the Marquis de la Fayette—the republican patrician whose efforts in the American Revolution had been mainly instrumental in producing those spasmodic disorders in his own country, which resulted in the Republic, the Consulate, and the Empire. La Fayette was old at this time, but he lived to help in producing other troubles, and to show how weak an instrument may sometimes be selected by Providence for effecting great purposes.

Lady Morgan formed an acquaintance, at the same time, with a lady to whom France was opened by the downfall of the Bonapartes. I remember her very well, both then and subsequently. A younger brother of Napoleon had visited the United States of America, and had been captivated by a handsome girl, whom he had met at Baltimore. She contrived to get him to marry her, but as soon as his family heard of the *mésalliance* they repudiated the connection. They learned that Miss Patterson's father had kept a store, and, as they all were desirous of being elevated by the rising power of their illustrious relative, the ruler of France, they could not endure that a daughter of a tradesman should share in their regal pretensions. Measures were speedily taken to annul the marriage; and, as Jerome was almost as soon tired of the charming Yankee as he had grown enamoured of her, he easily broke his matrimonial bonds, and placed himself at his imperial brother's disposal. He was rewarded with a kingdom and a princess.

The Baltimore beauty, finding herself not only a divorced wife, but a mother, did everything in her power to obtain what she considered her rights; but the truant husband ignored her existence, and the inexorable Emperor would not allow her to enter France. When the Allies had sent him to Elba, Miss Patterson came to Paris, and strove to interest the Bourbons in her behalf, but without success. She had a sufficient income, and liked gay society, and was under the impression that she was entitled to the honours of a royal princess; consequently, her friends of the mercantile class at Baltimore had become distasteful to her.

Madame Patterson, as she now styled herself, found in Lady Morgan a congenial spirit, and she strove to make her sympathise in her wrongs, by treating her with the grossest adulation. Her new friend, however, had been too accustomed to flattery to be particularly sensible to its effect. In vain did she fill sheet after sheet of correspondence with the strongest possible mixture of "soft-sawder," and scandalous gossip; all the return she obtained from her Irish friend took the shape of civil expressions of good-will, that cost nothing.

The lady nevertheless continued to write, and while she assured her correspondent that the latter was infinitely superior either to a De Staël or a De Genlis, she poured out a tide of regrets for her state of desolation. Melancholy as may have been her mood, Madame Patterson had always a keen appreciation for scandal, and there were very few of her communications that did not contain notices of her fair contemporaries, tinged with a feeling that looks very like feminine spite.

The friends were in perfect harmony respecting the great man whom they found enjoying in Paris the fame a great career had procured for him. Madame Patterson, though she had no reason to love the Bonapartes, entertained a Yankee prejudice against the "Britisher," who had helped to hurl them from the high places they had attained, and Lady Morgan was too ultra-Hibernian not to detest anything that brought glory and prosperity to England.

These fair adventuresses, therefore, were bitterly hostile to the Duke of Wellington, and slandered him to their heart's content whenever they got a chance.

In particular, they made themselves very busy in communicating reports respecting the Duke's alleged gallantries—the fact being, that he was the object of hero-worship to several of the most beautiful women then in Paris. I had abundant opportunities for observing the real state of the case, and profited by them as far as I was able. Conspicuous among these belles was a fascinating *cantatrice*, named in a preceding page. The Emperor Napoleon had been enamoured of her, but she always spoke with a marked contrast between the conduct of the English and that of the French hero. The fact is, that the Duke's manner towards ladies was marked by the most deferential courtesy, while that of the Emperor was singularly brusque and unloverlike. The Duke did not particularly admire either the Irish novelist or the American *divorcée*—an unpardonable affront in the eyes of both. Of course they abused his taste. There was a namesake and kinswoman of the latter, to whom his Grace paid some attention, and straightway the heroine of a hundred flirtations, and the discarded of the Bonapartes, did their little possible to ridicule the insensible Duke and the favoured lady.

From a letter written at the time, and but recently

published, the public may learn how spiteful these women could be. "You would be surprised," writes the Baltimore belle of a dozen years before, "if you knew how great a fool she is, at the power she exercises over the Duke; but I believe that he has no taste *pour les femmes d'esprit* [such as herself and her correspondent]; this is, however, no reason for going into extremes, as in this case. He gave her an introduction to the Prince-Regent, and to every one of consequence in London and Paris [his Grace had done nothing of the kind]. She had, however, no success in France, where her not speaking the language of the country was a considerable advantage to her, since it prevented her nonsense from being heard. [The result of the writer's visit to France was a failure, and such advantages as she possessed in speaking and writing indifferent French, have not prevented her nonsense from being published]. Do not tell what I have written to you of this affair, since I should pass for malicious and unfriendly towards my compatriot and relation."* [The only passage in her letter about which there can be no dispute.]

Thomas Moore was here enjoying himself as usual, and looking for materials to work up into satire. He was on intimate terms with the two gossips, and they

* "Lady Morgan's Memoirs, Autobiography, Diaries, and Correspondence." Vol. ii., p. 62.

furnished him with all the scandal they could collect or invent. With Lady Morgan he remained very friendly, till his popularity during a visit to Dublin threatened to eclipse her own, and then the little woman took to quizzing the little man. In point of literary talent there could be no comparison between the two.

With Sir Charles, Moore was on equally familiar terms. The good taste of the physician was exemplified during a professional visit he subsequently paid the poet and wit, when the latter was detained by a bad leg at Florence. Moore was a conscientious Catholic, and Sir Charles Morgan an avowed infidel, very fond of entering upon atheistical arguments. In the midst of a discussion, the former exclaimed, with considerable excitement—" Oh! Morgan, talk no more—consider my immortal soul!"

"D—— your soul!" said Sir Charles, impatiently, "attend to my argument!"*

Lady Morgan often related this to her free-thinking friends, with whom it passed as an excellent joke, at the expense of the poor Christian.

"The Fudge Family," as is well known, was one of the fruits of the poet's visit to France at this period; but the entries in his diary, published by Earl Russell, will convey to the reader a much more faithful account of his French experience. He seems to have

* Lady Morgan's "Memoirs," &c. Vól. ii., p. 87.

been almost as communicative in his daily entries as Mr. Samuel Pepys, and with about as little discretion. Nothing can be more characteristic than his accounts of his nightly triflings with ladies of fashion, while his " Dearest Bessie," who made him a most excellent wife, though she had been a ballet-dancer, was left at home to draw upon her own sources of amusement.

Among the Englishmen who figured in the same circle was James Kenney, the author of numerous plays, chiefly translated from the French, and the once popular farce, "Raising the Wind." He was a banker's clerk, and with only a very small and uncertain income from his writings, he had married the widow of a brother-dramatist—Thomas Holcroft, author of "The Road to Ruin," and numerous plays, novels, and other productions long since forgotten, but more celebrated for his extreme political opinions, and as an active member of the revolutionary Corresponding Society.

He had received into his house the daughter of a Parisian Republican, as his ward—rather a pretty girl, after the French type of feminine beauty; and though he was himself well advanced in years, and had children older than the young lady, when he became a widower, Mademoiselle Mercier became Mrs. Holcroft. The disparity of years was as evident as the disparity in personal appearance, and observations were made of a character similar to those which elicited the famous caricature of Mr. and Mrs. Hope.

In due course the republican dramatist was gathered to his fathers, and his widow, still with lustrous black eyes, and a piquant French nose, found herself but poorly provided for, with a bequest of unfinished MSS., and equally unfinished children. Though of small stature, little Kenney was regarded as a rising man, and the Widow Holcroft thought him worth captivating—did captivate him, in a style known only to Frenchwomen, when they are determined to succeed; and, in due course, the author of "Raising the Wind" found himself proprietor of the lustrous eyes, the piquant nose, the unfinished MSS., and the unfinished children.

Some provision was made for the latter, and they disappeared as juvenile Kenneys took their place. Whether the MSS. were turned to any account has not transpired. The little man adapted plays from the French with remarkable assiduity, and being a pleasant, harmless humourist, became a favourite in the green-room of the principal London theatres, as well as at Holland House, at Mr. Rogers's in St. James's Place, and a few other first-class literary "houses of call."

He was of an exceedingly nervous temperament—

his frail delicate figure, clad in a long loose coat, was often seen in the principal thoroughfares, standing irresolute on the curb-stone, first putting one foot forward towards the road, then replacing it by the other; and when he had drawn upon himself the observation of all the vagabonds in the neighbourhood, he would make a desperate spring forward, and rush across the road as if fleeing for his life.

When entering a house, in going up-stairs he would cross a mat in the passage very much in the same style.

Nor could he bear any trifling noise—such as cutting the leaves of a book, the ticking of a clock, writing on rough paper, a loud footstep, or a creaking door. The postman's knock sent him into a state of most violent excitement, and the dustman's bell used nearly to drive him out of his senses. Whether the Frenchwoman's tongue went too loud or too fast for him, I cannot say—I only know that he frequently absented himself from home, in some quiet lodging, where he remained unknown to his family till Mrs. Kenney discovered his retirement.

On one of these occasions he engaged an apartment in a distant suburb, and was discovered by the landlord about daybreak the next morning, at the open window in his bed-gown and night-cap, pelting his fowls, from a box of mould on the window-sill, whenever the cock began to crow or the hens to chuck. He persevered for a long time to stop the noise the small stock of poultry were making, but without success, and at last appeared convinced that they would be less irritating if he let them alone.

In the latter years of his life poor Kenney's condition became more and more pitiable, and at last he took to his bed in a thoroughly hopeless state. His case was made known to the numerous admirers of his dramatic talent, and a benefit got up for him at one of the theatres. But assistance came too late. He died on the day of the performance, and the funds thus procured had to be applied to his funeral. His widow did not long survive him. She was allowed a small pension from the Government Fund, and returned to France, where she died.

I often met Kenney at the Garrick Club, as well as at other places; but this was subsequent to his residence in Paris contemporary with my stay in the French capital, after the second restoration of the Bourbons.

In the course of the summer, a subaltern officer, named Cantillon, attempted the life of Wellington, by firing a pistol at the hero, which happily missed its aim. It would have been a lamentable end to the career of this great man, after escaping the dangers of so many hard-fought battles, to have fallen by the hand of an assassin. The ball, fortunately, was directed too high, and gave rise to the following epigram—a futile attempt at satire, which, doubtless, the French Peter Pindar thought sublime :—

> " Mal ajuster est un défaut,
> Il le manqua, voilá comme,
> L'Imbecille visa trop haut,
> Il l'avoit pris pour *un grand homme.*"

Who the writer was I never heard, but Alfred D'Orsay was repeating it in the aide-de-camp's waiting-room, denouncing it as a *mauvais plaisanterie,* when I asked him to copy it into my common-place book, and there it is still.

Wellington could well afford to treat this effusion with contempt; and I should not have alluded to it, had it not furnished the topic of much conversation at the time.

Early in September, an English gentleman, of the name of Keen, was assassinated by a Frenchman on the Boulevards, near the Rue Taitbout. The Duke offered a considerable reward for the discovery of the murderer, but without effect, as the dastard who had thus unprovokedly attacked an unoffending person with a sword-stick, took advantage of the confusion to make his escape.

Towards the end of the month, the States-General at Brussels unanimously voted a dotation to the Duke, as Prince of Waterloo, of an estate on the scene of his most successful triumph.

Although hostilities had ceased, France was still far from being in a state of internal tranquillity. Two royal ordinances had been issued; the first declaring that a number of members of the former Chamber of Peers, who had accepted seats in that summoned by Bonaparte, had abdicated their rank, and could no longer form part of that chamber. The second published a list of those generals and officers who had betrayed the King before the 23rd of March, or who had attacked France or the government by force of arms—all of whom were to be arrested and brought before courts-martial.

The freedom of the press, too, had been assailed; and, by a royal decree, all the licences hitherto granted to public journals of every description, were revoked. A new army was to be organized in lieu of that about to be disbanded. But the cause of the greatest anxiety to Wellington, must have been the bitter animosity that existed between the Prussians and the French, independent of the important and all-absorbing question, as to whether the Museum of the Louvre, enriched by Bonaparte's conquests, should be respected. At the capitulation of Paris, in 1814, the principal works of art contained in it remained untouched; and upon a similar demand being made at the time I refer to, the Allied Generals, feeling that the day of retribution had arrived, declined to grant it. Prussia was the first in the field, as Blücher, on his entrance into Paris, peremptorily demanded from the director, M. Denon, the spoils of Berlin, Potsdam, Cologne, and Aix la Chapelle. The Belgian government, aided by our troops, insisted upon a restoration of the rich plunder derived from their cathedrals and churches; while Austria made reclamation for Venice, and the celebrated Corinthian horses were carried off from the Tuileries amidst the execrations of the Parisians.

The inveterate hatred that existed between the Prussians and French, already referred to, displayed itself upon many occasions; and this feeling was greatly aggravated by the name previously given to one of the bridges over the Seine, Le pont D'Jena. Blücher, enraged at the allusion, at once determined to demolish this triumphal monument, and the troops under his command had already commenced operations, by making excavations and filling them with gunpowder, when an order was issued to put an end to this work of retribution. Wellington had exerted his entire influence with the veteran warrior to relinquish his design; and, although the abandonment of the project was attributed to the interference of the Emperor of Russia, I cannot bring myself to believe that the Duke's sage counsel was totally unheeded.

No sooner had the month of September set in, than many of the English officers prepared their guns; but a strict order from the Commander-in-Chief against poaching, put an end to the hopes of many an aspiring sportsman. The royal hunt had commenced its operations, and Wellington was again in the field. An English pack of foxhounds had been got together near Paris, but at that period they furnished little sport, as foxes were scarce in those parts.

Early in this month, Louis le Desiré, or L'Inévitable, as the restored monarch was called, gave a splendid banquet to the potentates, and distinguished military and civil officers. I had the good fortune to accompany Wellington to the Tuileries. Nothing could exceed the magnificence of the entertainment, or the excellence of the cooking; for the royal Bourbon, who was himself a *bon vivant* of the first quality, had given especial instructions to his *chef de cuisine*, to produce upon this occasion a feast worthy of his epicurean reign; and, being ably supported by a host of culinary artists brought together from every kitchen of note in Paris, who looked upon the affair in a national point of view, the dinner served was one that would have gratified the heart of the great Vatel.

At this period the art of good living was brought

to the greatest state of perfection in Paris. The breakfasts at Tortoni's were unequalled, while the *rognons à la brochette*, at Riche's, and the *coquilles* at Hardi's, attracted all the English officers at their morning repast. For dinners, these celebrated artists were not so famed; the Parisians quaintly said, *"qu'il fallait être bien* Riche, *pour dîner chez* Hardi ; *et bien* Hardi, *pour dîner chez* Riche."

Among the most celebrated restaurateurs, who had earned the *cordon bleu*, may be mentioned Beauvillier, Very, Borel, Robert, et Hennevue. The former, like Beaulieu, in his *art poétique*, united precept and example, by publishing a work upon cookery. He was extremely attentive to his guests, running about the room to ascertain if the dinner was to their liking; and whenever a complaint was made, he would shrug up his shoulders, descend to the kitchen, and, after lecturing the cook, would return with a dish dressed under his immediate superintendence. After the restoration of the Bourbons, Beauvillier was the object of much ridicule, from the fact of his doing the honours of his table, decked out in a bagwig, full-dress coat, and sword. Of him, in the words of Plautus, it might be said:

"Hic coquus scite ac munditer condit cibos."

There was another restaurant, kept by Rô Méot et

Juliette, which gave rise to the calembourg—Romeo et Juliette.

In those days each house was famed for some particular dish. Robert excelled in dressing beef in every form, and in private dinners. " Le veau qui tette," an epicurean temple of the Parisian cits, shone prominently forth in *les pieds de mouton*, and *gras double sur le gril*—*Anglicé*, sheep's trotters and tripe. Many a squeamish lady and gentleman who would be horrified at the mere mention of the above dishes in England, would be delighted to partake of them under a foreign name.

"Les trois fréres Provencaux" prided themselves upon Morue à l'ail, a most artistical dish for those who did not object to garlic. Here the cellar was faultless. The Rocher de Cancale had a world-wide reputation for its fish ; there the *gourmet* would commence with half-a-dozen Marenne oysters, and a glass of Chablis, followed by as many small tablespoons of soup as would neutralise the cold sensation of the former ; the finest turbot that the coast of France could produce then appeared, with sauces of the most varied and exquisite flavour.

A story was told and believed, that a turbot did duty for more than one party ; the affair being arranged in this way: the fish was first placed on the table, to show the company how superb it was.

It was then removed to a sideboard behind a screen, where a fish, less fine, was ready to be helped; by this plan the turbot went from room to room; and happy were the party to whom this denizen of the deep paid the last visit, as, upon that occasion, it was helped on the table.

Le Café de Milles Colonnes, with its golden saloons, magnificent looking-glasses, and admirably-appointed kitchen, gratified the eye as well as the palate, by the presence of *la belle* Limonadiére, who, Hebe-like, presided at the bar, dispensing smiles and *sorbets*, ogles and *orgeat*, *œillades* and *eau de vie*, glances and *glaces*, coquetry and *café*, tender looks and *liqueurs*. In short, to adopt a phrase of the famous lexicographer, Dr. Johnson, "one of the arts that aggrandise human life, cooking," was cultivated in a manner that would have gladdened the hearts of Heliogabalus, Dr. Kitchener, Louis *des huitres*, as the ventri-potent monarch was called; and *la Science de gueule* was discussed with as much gravity as the more abstruse sciences of grammar, logic, arithmetic, rhetoric, geometry, astronomy, or metaphysics.

Among the most popular books that emanated from the press was "L'Almanach des Gourmets." The Parisian epicure had not descended to the glutton; his taste was more refined, and he seemed to pride himself upon the character of one of Beaumont and

Fletcher's gastronomers. "He is none of those same ordinary caters, that will devour three breakfasts, and as many bevers and dinners, without any prejudice to their drinkings or suppers, but he hath a more courtly kind of hunger, and doth hunt more after novelty than plenty." Throughout the city almost everyone acted upon the above refined principle.

Among other profound researches upon the subject, it has been remarked by a French author, that "dinner to man, while it fills the stomach, makes void the heart;" and, in confirmation of this doctrine, the writer asserts that a poor man sat for thirty years upon the steps of a celebrated restaurateur's at Paris, and that, although he universally received some charitable gratuity from those ascending, he never received a farthing from those descending. Let us hope this is an exaggerated statement.

The theatres at this period were flourishing. Talma in tragedy; Mademoiselle Mars in genteel comedy; Brunet and Potier in farce; the Gosselins and Fanny Bias in ballet—they formed a dramatic phalanx never surpassed. Tivoli was open to the lovers of *al fresco* amusements; Garnerin ascended in his balloon amidst a blaze of fire-works; Margat took as his aërial companion a stag trained by him. The French capital outshone itself in fun for the million. We had the celebrated learned dog Munito, playing at dominoes and loto. And the sight-seeing English were bitten (we mean figuratively) by the industrious fleas, whose wonderful performance was first introduced in those days.

The disposition to carry out the field sports of Old England abroad, has shown itself in almost every quarter of the globe. We constantly read of racing and steeple-chasing in France, Germany, Italy, Belgium, and Holland; upon the plains of Abraham, near Quebec, at the rock of Gibraltar, in the Ionian Islands, in the wild steppes of the Crimea, at the Cape of Good Hope, in Australia, in New South Wales, and in the East and West Indies; cricket matches, pigeon shooting, fox hunting, yachting, have also been introduced in every place where John Bull has sojourned for any length of time. No wonder then, during the occupation of Paris by the allies, that English racing was introduced. Great, indeed, was the sensation in the metropolis of France when, in October, 1815, the *Paris and London Chronicle* contained the following advertisement :—

"Saturday, October the 21st, a Ladies' Cup (given by the English Ladies in Paris) will be run for on the flat of Neuilly, free for all horses; gentlemen riders, two mile heats. Same day, a Subscription Purse for the beaten horses."

The late Lords Kinnaird and Charles Manners, and that gallant ninety-fifth rifleman, the late Sir Andrew

Barnard, officiated as stewards. The Duc de Berri, Wellington, Lord Castlereagh, and all the distinguished visitors then assembled in the capital, attended this meeting.

Independent of a variety of matches, there was a grand sweepstakes, gentlemen riders, open to all horses—English, French, Austrian, Prussian, Russian, German, Dutch, and Belgian; many "foreigners" were entered, but few came to the post; and this All the World Stakes was won by an English mare, "La Belle Anglaise."

Two events occurred during the day's racing, one of which was attended with fatal consequences, the other was happily not so serious. A foreign horse-dealer, who had made himself very conspicuous on the course by riding in with the leading horses, wrangling, refusing to pay his bets, and setting the stewards and Jockey Club laws at open defiance, continued so refractory, that we felt it necessary to take the case into our own hands; so, cracking our whips, and giving a view halloo, we regularly chased him from the course. Like all bullies, he was a great coward, and the moment he got, as he thought, out of distance, he began to anathematize us and our country in no measured terms. This raised our "dander," as the Yankees call it, and away galloped one officer to whom he had personally alluded, to inflict chastisement upon the scampering hero; others, anxious to be in at the finish, followed the leader, and a regular hunt was got up.

The dealer was well mounted on a thorough-bred English hunter, and for some minutes kept ahead. Just as he was quitting the plains, the noise of our halloos reached a German picket stationed at the entrance of a road to Paris. Seeing a mass of horsemen galloping towards their post, the sentry fancied some outbreak had taken place, and acting up to his orders, turned out the guard.

As the runaway hero approached, the commanding officer could not, from the clouds of dust, distinguish who he was or what were the party that followed; but, determining to defend his post against what appeared to him to be an overwhelming force of the enemy, or fall in the attempt, the gallant German gave the word, "Prepare to receive cavalry," and, the front rank kneeling, met the foremost of the charge—the unlucky dealer's horse—at the bayonets' point. The order, "Rear rank, fire!" was about to be given, when, fortunately for us, the cloud of dust having been carried away, the astonished guard saw that the supposed foe were no others than some of their own allies, the liege subjects of his Britannic Majesty, who had now quietly drawn up to see the catastrophe.

We all regretted the fate of the noble steed, which we would have given much to have averted—but a good ducking in a horse-pond was a punishment that his ignoble rider richly deserved, and one that he would inevitably have met with, for his roguery and impertinence, had he not been already so seriously afflicted.

The other event happened to Blücher, who, galloping down the course, and not being aware that a rope was placed across it, fell, and was much stunned. Fortunately, the gallant veteran soon recovered from the effects of the accident, and remained to enjoy the day's sport.

The races, which afforded much sport, were succeeded by a sparring match between two English pugilists—Fuller and Harmer. A purse was handed about for them by that well-known character, the late Joe Kelly, and more than sixty Napoleons were collected. A regular school was shortly afterwards established for the sons of the fancy, near the Oratoire, and was greatly patronized by the French, English, Russians, Prussians, and Germans then assembled in and near Paris. The following is the manner in which they are described in one of the French papers:—

"Two English boxers have already given several representations in the Rue Neuve des Petit Champs. Persons of the most delicate sensibility may be present, for these boxers do not strike so hard as to do each other any injury. In England, after every battle, one or two of the assailants must be declared *hors de combat*, and when they are obliged to carry him off the field in a wheelbarrow or on a shutter, the pleasure is complete. At Paris we are not so greedy, we content ourselves with a few blows, and the demonstration of them is enough."

I must here remark, that at this particular period pugilism flourished, and was supported by men of the highest honour and character; so much so, that during the visit of the allied potentates to the Prince Regent in the previous year, a grand national fistic tournament was got up for their special entertainment.

The King of Prussia, the Prince Royal, Prince William and Frederick of Prussia, Prince of Mecklenburg, General York, the Hetman Platoff, and several of the illustrious visitors, attended a *déjeûner à la fourchette*, at Lord Lowther's, the present Earl of Lonsdale. The most celebrated pugilists of the day were in waiting; Byron's instructor, Jackson, Cribb, Belcher, Richmond the black, Oliver, Painter, and others. After breakfast the men put on the gloves, and showed some excellent sparring; and at the particular desire of several persons of distinction, as the playbills say, Jackson wound up the day's play by setting to with Cribb and Belcher; his quickness, dexterity, and great muscular powers were particularly noticed.

Among other sights that attracted the attention of those resident in Paris, may be mentioned Les Montagnes Russes, an amusement then recently imported from the country of the Czar—one in which the partaker of it ran the risk of breaking his limbs; for the small charge of half a franc. In addition to the original Russian ones, à la barriere des Thermes, we had les Montagnes Françaises at Beaujon, the Egyptiennes in the Jardin du Delta Faubourg Poissoniere; les Suisses, Jardin de la Chaumière in the aristrocratic quarter du Luxembourg; and le Saut de Niagara, at the Jardin Ruggieri, Rue St. Lazare.

Anxious to carry out that spirit of vigour which the French ministry had determined to exercise with respect to state criminals, the issue of Marshal Ney's trial was looked forward to on all sides with the deepest interest. An opinion had long been prevalent, that there was some reluctance on the part of the Government to proceed to extremities against a man of such high reputation in the army. The decision had at first been committed to a military tribunal, who seemed averse to pass judgment upon one of their own body; and, after a second sitting, the court pronounced, by a majority of five to two, that it was not competent for them to bring Ney to trial. Upon this result being known, the King published a decree, enjoining the chamber of peers to proceed without delay to the trial of the Marshal, accused of high treason. The peers came to a unanimous resolution that there were grounds for an indictment.

Ney's trial commenced on the 4th of December, and continued until the 6th, when he was capitally convicted of high treason by 139 out of 160, and was sentenced to the full punishment of death, without appeal. Seventeen peers recorded their opinions in favour of banishment, and four abstained from voting. During the trial, the advocate for the accused having been interdicted from making use of the convention of July in his plea, urged that the Marshal, though French in heart, was no longer a Frenchman, as, by the treaty of the 20th of November, the Government, in tracing a new line round France, had left Sarrebruck, the district from which the Marshal came, out of it.

The brave soldier, despising any quirk or quibble of the law, rose, much affected, and with vehemence exclaimed—" Yes! I am a Frenchman, and I will die a Frenchman! I am accused against the faith of treaties, and they will not allow me to justify myself. I will act like Moreau—I appeal to Europe and posterity."

At a little after nine o'clock, on the morning of the

7th of December, the Marshal was conveyed to a spot near the garden of the Luxembourg. After descending from the carriage, and embracing his confessor, he proceeded with a quick step and firm manner within a few paces of the wall, when, turning round and facing the firing party, he exclaimed, in a calm voice, "Comrades, direct to the heart—fire!"

While delivering these words, he took off his hat with his left hand, placing his right upon his heart. The signal was given, and Ney instantly fell dead, twelve balls having taken effect, three of them in the head.

Conformably to military regulations, the body remained exposed for a quarter of an hour, and was then carried by veterans to the Foundling Hospital.

At half-past six on the following morning, the remains of the great warrior were buried in the cemetery of Père la Chaise.

A variety of rumours were spread abroad in Paris with reference to the execution of Ney. Many, however, were unfounded; but the following anecdote was generally believed. It was confidently stated, that so doubtful were the Government as to the reliance that could be placed upon the military, if called upon to take away the life of one of their bravest generals, that civilians of the lowest grades and debased conduct were selected from the prisons, dressed in the uniform of the regiment supposed to furnish the firing party, who were marshalled and fell in near the Garden of the Luxembourg, to act as military executioners.

Another event occurred, most painful to the feelings of the principal actor in it. Madame Ney, whose devotion to her husband was beyond all praise, waited upon the Duc de Grammont, at the Tuileries, to urge him upon her knees to intercede with the King for the pardon of her husband; and at the moment the request was imploringly made, the Duke knew too well (as he afterwards declared to one of his nearest relatives), that the sentence had been carried into effect.

That Ney was legally guilty admits of little doubt; but under all the circumstances of the case, how much more noble would it have been, if, instead of taking away the life of this brave man, the King had ordered all the troops in and near Paris to assemble in the Champ de Mars, to hear the sentence read; then, appearing in the centre of the congregated soldiers, to have given a free pardon to one who had served France with so much honour and distinction. This act of mercy would have been received by all with but one feeling—that of gratitude.

CHAPTER XI.

MY MISSION TO THE "HAGUE"—MISTAKEN FOR A RUSSIAN GENERAL—FLEMISH ACCOUNT—INTERVIEW WITH THE KING OF HOLLAND—AWKWARD RESULTS OF GETTING A SPEECH BY HEART—A STATE DINNER AT THE PALACE—RETURN TO PARIS—"LES ANGLAISES POUR RIRE"—NEGLECT OF DUTY—THE DUKE'S REPRIMAND—A DREADFUL BORE—THE DUKE'S KINDNESS—HIS GENERAL ORDER—M. DE LAVALETTE AND SIR ROBERT WILSON—THE ENGLISH ARMY RETIRES FROM PARIS—NEWSPAPER ATTACKS ON THE DUKE—HIS VISIT TO THE HAGUE VALENCIENEES—THE DUKE'S PATRONAGE OF FIELD SPORTS—COLONEL FELTON HERVEY—NEGLIGENCE OF THE DUKE'S STAFF—REGULATION UNIFORM—VISIT OF THE DUKE OF KENT AND CAMBRIDGE—REVIEW ON THE PLAINS ON DENAIN—GARRISON RACES—JOE KELLY—THE DUKE'S STATE COACHMAN—FOXHOUNDS.

CHAPTER XI.

SHORTLY after the Allied Army entered Paris, I received orders from the Duke to be the bearer of despatches, containing a copy of the treaty of peace, to the King of Holland, at the Hague. My instructions were to proceed there without delay, to await his Majesty's pleasure, and to lose no time in returning to head-quarters at Paris. In order to make myself very smart and imposing, I paid a visit to the Palais Royal, where I purchased a splendidly silver embroidered waistcoat, and a highly decorated gold-lace foraging cap. Having engaged a carriage for the journey, I received the despatches, and lost no time in quitting Paris.

No adventure occurred on the road, except the vexatious delays at the fortified towns, the bribery of douaniers, the grumbling of postilions, the importunities of beggars, and the usual worries of continental travelling, until I reached the gates of the Hague. The day had been raw, cold, and wet; the mists had risen from the comfortless fields and dykes; and at a little before ten o'clock, I, muffled up in my military cloak, stopped at the outward barrier, or guard-house.

"The bearer of despatches for his Majesty the King of Holland," said I, in my best French. The officer on duty saluted, the sentry carried arms. An orderly entered the guard-room hastily; and in a moment a staff officer, one of his Majesty's aides-de-camp, was on horseback by the side of the carriage.

"Mon Général" (general! brevet rank with a vengeance, thought I), "sa Majesté le Roi, mon maître, m'ordonne de vous informer qu'à votre arrivée en ville il vous recevra à quelle heure que ce soit."

I bowed most graciously—I might say patronisingly.

"Postillon, à l'hôtel de l'Europe—tout est déjà préparé pour vous recevoir, Général."

I had little time for explanation or thanks, for I was whirled rapidly away towards the hotel provided for me. At the entrance two sentries were posted, who received me with military honours. The smiling landlord, with his happy looking comely face, and his wife in the neatest of all gowns and caps, were at the door, attended by a bevy of officious waiters, simpering chambermaids, obsequious cooks, and venerable porters, to greet me on my arrival.

I descended from the carriage, amidst the cheers of a party assembled in the street. In the entrance hall an assemblage of ladies waved their handkerchiefs, presented bouquets to me, crying "Vive le Roi! Vive le Prince d'Orange! Orange Boven!" Knowing, as I did, the admiration the Dutch felt for the gallant conduct of their Prince at Waterloo, I naturally attributed this manifestation to the presence of one who they considered had shared in the glories of that day as aide-de-camp of Wellington; and, "bearing my blushing honours" modestly, I acknowledged the flattering compliment, and entered the room appointed for me.

The landlord appeared, and, after making sundry obeisances, expressed a hope that everything was to the General's satisfaction; then obsequiously adding, "Si Monsieur le Général voulait seulement se montrer au peuple, cette condescendance de sa part serait reçu avec la plus vive reconnaissance par son humble et obéissant serviteur."

Acceding to his request, I appeared at the window, when shouts and exclamations rent the air—never was the enthusiasm of the worthy burghers more vividly excited.

Le Colonel Von R. was now announced, who informed me that his royal master was ready to receive me. I requested a quarter of an hour to make my toilet, which was immediately granted. Just as I had finished my refreshing task, I heard a gentle knock at the door. "Entrez." The landlord made his appearance, with a passport in his hand, which, on presenting to me, I immediately recognised as my own, and which I had left at the gate where I had been received with so much honour.

"Mille pardons, General, est-ce la votre passeport?"

"Assurement."

The landlord left the room rather abruptly, and I could not help imagining that I saw some slight alteration in his manner. On re-entering my former sitting-room, the waiter, after indulging in a very suspicious stare, begged my pardon, and requested I would follow him to another apartment, as that one was engaged.

My surprise and confusion increased; for I evidently saw an ebbing of the previous high tide of respect. Left to myself, I paced the room—the sound of relieving sentries attracted my attention; I threw open the window, and saw them march off without a fresh deposit. I also fancied I heard some expressions which sounded to my ears as rather coming from the north side of favour.

At length, after some little delay, the mystery was

dissolved by the arrival of the royal Aide-de-camp, who most good-humouredly explained to me that his Majesty had for some days been anxiously expecting the arrival of a distinguished Russian officer from St. Petersburg, with the contract of marriage between the sister of the Emperor and the Prince of Orange; that the greatest anxiety had been manifested throughout the country at so important and long-wished-for an event, as the union of the heir to the throne of Holland with a sister of the house of Russia. He explained that the mistake had occurred through the over-zeal of the Captain of the Guard and himself, in not having ascertained the nature of my despatches or the name of their bearer; adding, by way of accounting for his error in taking an English stripling for a Russian general, that many princes have that honour awarded them at a very early age. The passport had first thrown a light upon the subject.

"It now only remains for me," he added, "to assure Le Lieutenant Lord W. Lennox, that his Majesty will grant you an audience on the following morning, at eleven o'clock, and that I feel assured, as an English officer, you will receive every mark of courtesy and attention from those who have so lately fought, side by side with you, on the ensanguined plains of Waterloo."

I made a suitable speech in reply, and retired to

my room, where fatigue and excitement soon gave me sleep.

Upon awaking the following day, and looking to the state of my finances, I found I had what is usually called a very "Flemish account," for, calculating my expenses at the hotel, and my journey back to Paris, I came to the conclusion that the twenty francs I had in my purse, would go but a very short way to meet my outlay. In this dilemma I sent for the landlord, and inquired whether there was any banker in the town who would cash a cheque upon my army agent in London. With a letter of credit, he replied, there would be no difficulty, but without it he feared there might be some trouble—not that any one could suspect a *Mi Lord Anglais* of any dishonourable practice. I then asked the address of the representative of our Sovereign, and having received it, proceeded to find his residence; for in the almost penniless state I was in, I had not heart enough to sit down to breakfast.

"I shall be home at ten o'clock," said I to the waiter; "prepare me some coffee and a cutlet."

"It shall be attended to," responded the attendant.

Following the directions that had been given me, I reached our minister's house, saw the secretary, who presented me to his chief, by whom I was most kindly received, and, after explaining the object of my visit, had the satisfaction of being told that any cheque I might draw upon Messrs. Cox and Greenwood would be honoured.

With a light heart, and a craving appetite, I returned to the hotel; and while breakfast was being got ready, I strolled into the best looking streets, in the hopes of finding some English book, which would wile away the hours of travel. After asking at least at a dozen shops, for the literary food I required, I at last pounced upon a copy of Gil Blas, minus one volume; still, in its mutilated state it was better than half the complete works that I might have got, by writers then living. At this period the printing of English works abroad was unknown; literary piracy had not commenced, and the laws of copyright were respected.

At the appointed hour I presented myself at the Palace. Upon mentioning my name, I was immediately ushered into the presence of the King, who received me most affably.

"Sire, j'ai l'honneur," I commenced, having, previous to my quitting Paris, requested my old friend Galley, to write me out an appropriate speech in the French language, which speech I had got off by heart in the most perfect manner possible.

"Speak your own language," interrupted his Majesty, "I perfectly comprehend it."

This was what the chroniclers of pugilistic encounters, term a regular "floorer," for, although prepared in French, I had not "got up" an oration in my own native tongue, and some of my former master's idioms and compliments to the King would scarcely bear a hasty translation. Still, I made the best of the case, and, in rather a rambling manner, informed the Sovereign of the nature of my mission, feeling very much as a most distinguished ambassador did, who, on presenting himself to Charles X., at the coronation of that monarch, commenced his harangue in the language of the country he was in, and was suddenly "taken aback" by the last of the Bourbons who reigned over France, requesting his Grace to address him in English; thus compelling him to translate extemporaneously a speech that had taken him some time to get perfect.

During my interview the King expressed a hope that I would visit his rural palace, in the environs of the town, and dine with him at four o'clock. Having already seen nearly as much of the Hague as I wished, and preferring the Parisian "city of frivolities" to the stagnant canal town of South Holland, I informed his Majesty that, however happy I should be to extend my visit to the Hague, my duty called me back to the Duke of Wellington, the moment his Majesty entrusted me with an acknowledgment of the receipt of my despatches.

"Under those circumstances," said the King, "and highly approving your motives, you can leave the Hague this evening; my reply to the Duke will be ready before dinner."

Taking my leave, I proceeded to the hotel to order horses to be ready for me, and then, engaging a carriage, drove through the principal street, the Voorhout, the Vyverburgh square, and the park; then through a fine avenue of oak, beeches, and limes, to Scheveling, a small fishing village. As I had still time to spare, and as the driver was a regular "Flying Dutchman," I paid a hasty visit to the castle of Ryswyc, which gave a name to the well-known treaty of 1697.

At four o'clock, punctually, I was at the palace, where I was presented to the Queen, and a large party of ministers and courtiers. The dinner was a stately, though rather a sombre affair. At its conclusion, the King shook me warmly by the hand; and, having received a despatch for my chief, I lost no time in preparing for my journey. At eight o'clock p.m., I drove through the gate which, on my arrival, had been the scene of the adventure I have recorded.

I pass over my journey from the Hague to Paris, which was "flat, stale, and *unprofitable*," for the roads being under water a considerable portion of the way, and extremely heavy the remaining part, I was compelled to take four horses, which I was not permitted to charge for in my small account. Suffice, then, to say, I reached the Duke's residence—where I was then an inmate—about four o'clock in the afternoon, and sought his Grace to report my return, and give the acknowledgment from the Dutch secretary of the receipt of the despatches. Wellington was from home, and I ascertained that he was to attend a grand banquet and ball at the Austrian ambassador's. Then I went to my own room, where I found a pressing invitation to dine early with some young friends, for the purpose of going to the theatre, to see "Les Anglaises pour Rire," which had only lately come out, and to wind up our evening's amusement at the ambassador's ball.

The dinner at Beauvillier's was perfect, the farce truly laughable, the acting of Brunet and Potier inimitable, and the ball most splendid. Whether the champagne had elated me a little, I know not—but all thoughts of the despatches had quite gone out of my head. Suddenly, when standing up for a quadrille, I caught the quick eye of Wellington gazing intently upon me. There was anger in his look. It then for the first time came across my mind that I had reversed the saying, of duty first and pleasure afterwards—and that I had been guilty of gross neglect in not having waited to report myself personally, and the result of my mission, to his Grace.

My anxiety was increased by a brother aide-de-camp telling me that the Duke had not been made aware of my return. As for dancing the quadrille (for in those days men performed certain steps—and did not shuffle through a figure in the slip-shod manner they now do), I found it impossible. I mistook *L'Eté* for *La Poule*—*chasséed* to the right when I ought to have gone to the left—attempted my *pas de Zephyr*, and failed; and offered my hand to my partner, and the lady on my other side, for *la grand ronde*, when I ought to have advanced as a *cavalier seul*.

No sooner had the music ceased than I hastily left my partner, and tried to fall in the way of the great man; but I saw that he avoided me. Disheartened and disappointed, I soon left the festive scene, and returned home to chew the cud of not sweet but bitter fancy. After a restless night, I awoke, and when my servant made his appearance, he handed me an official-looking letter, which I immediately recognised as coming from the Duke's military secretary. It was an order to attend his Grace at ten o'clock, in uniform.

At that hour, with a trembling step and beating heart, I was ushered into his presence, and saw, at once, by his manner, that he was highly displeased.

In a firm yet dignified tone, he pointed out to me my error; told me that his own staff ought to set an example to the rest of the army in the fulfilment of their duties; and that, although, upon this occasion, no evil might arise from my disobedience of general orders, in not having reported myself—that if once officers employed by him were to judge for themselves as to the importance or unimportance of a mission, their utility would be destroyed, and the most serious consequences might ensue. "Obedience to orders is the first duty of a soldier. I hope I shall have no further cause to revert to the subject."

I then took my leave, grateful that an order to join my regiment had not followed the reproof. Still, I felt vexed and annoyed, and my embarrassment was not a little increased by the fact of its being my day's waiting, when, as a matter of course, I should be thrown more in the Duke's way. But Wellington, as I shortly found, was not of a resentful nature—the moment he had spoken, and had seen a disposition on the part of the offender to reform, he treated him as if nothing had occurred.

During the morning, I made a resolution of being particularly attentive to my duties, and when I was released at four o'clock until dinner-time, I was happy to find that there was no longer any mark of displeasure left upon the Duke's countenance. As the aide-de-camp in waiting, my post was at the head of the table; and although somewhat restored to my usual peace of mind, I could not help feeling greatly depressed at having so justly incurred my chief's disapproval.

The party was small, so the conversation was general; and, as a matter of course—when is it otherwise?—my recent visit to the Hague, which was to me a most disagreeable subject, was started by a young man fresh from Oxford, who was not aware of the cause of my late disgrace. In vain did I try to change the subject, not wishing the Duke to know what pursuits had occupied me on my return; but no sooner had I made the attempt than the persevering youth came back to the charge.

"And when did you return?" and "Did I not catch a glimpse of you at Beauvillier's?—and were you not at the Variétes?—and how came you to leave the ball so early?"

"Shall I mount you at the review to-morrow?" said the good-natured Lord Sandys, then Lord Arthur Hill, addressing the talkative mischief-maker, and anxious to give a new direction to his thoughts.

"I shall be greatly obliged," he responded; then turning to me, continued—"I called upon you at four, and your servant told me——"

What this disclosure was about, I never knew; for

the Duke, seeing my perplexity, and unwilling to be made acquainted with more of my sayings and doings, abruptly terminated the dialogue by asking me to drink a glass of wine. He then proceeded to question me as to how the new piece had been received at the theatre. This entirely drove the Hague out of the heads of all the party; and I could not but feel most grateful at the noble conduct of the Duke, who, disdaining upon this, as he did upon all other occasions, to get information in an underhand manner, had kindly come to my rescue, had shown his forgiveness in pledging me in a bumper of claret, and had terminated a conversation which might have led to very unpleasant consequences, through the want of tact of an idle collegian.

It was by such acts of kindness, affability, and consideration, that Wellington won the hearts of his officers. Upon points of military discipline, he was firm and strict; but the instant the duties were performed, he entered fully and freely with his personal staff into all their amusements; promoting, as far as lay in his power, hunting, shooting, fishing, and other manly field-sports.

On the 30th of November, to our great dismay, the Allied Army broke up, when Wellington issued the following order:—

"Paris, November 30, 1815.

"GENERAL ORDER.—Upon breaking up the army which the Field-Marshal has had the honour of commanding, he begs leave again to return thanks to the general officers, and the officers and troops, for their uniform good conduct. In the late short, but memorable campaign, they have given proofs to the world that they possess, in an eminent degree, all the good qualities of soldiers; and the Field-Marshal is happy to be able to applaud their regular good conduct in their camps and cantonments, not less than when engaged with the enemy in the field.

"Whatever may be the future destination of those brave troops, of which the Field-Marshal now takes his leave, he trusts that every individual will believe that he will ever feel the deepest interest in their honour and welfare, and will always be happy to promote either.

"WELLINGTON."

An event occurred on the 20th of December, which created a considerable sensation—the escape of Lavalette from the Prison of the Conciergerie. The following details respecting this event may be relied upon. For several weeks Madame Lavalette, whose health had been greatly impaired, in order to avoid the movement of her carriage, had used a sedan chair; this conveyance was carried into the prison, and deposited in a passage near the under-turnkey's room. At four o'clock on the day of the escape, Madame Lavalette arrived, as usual, dressed in her ordinary costume—a loose cloak, Parisian bonnet, and a large veil—accompanied by her daughter, a young lady of eleven years of age. About half-past five, the prisoner, arrayed in his wife's dress, taking his daughter by the arm, and supported by one of the turnkeys, slowly descended to the chair, when, nothing having occurred to excite suspicion, he passed before the inspectors and guardians, and was soon restored to his friends and liberty.

In the meantime, Madame Lavalette, who had enveloped herself in her husband's cloak, sat breathlessly in her arm-chair, with a book in her hand, and a taper burning on a table before her. At half-past six the jailor entered the room, and soon discovered the successful *ruse* that had been played.

This escape reminds one of a similar act which was practised in England after the Rebellion of 1715, attended with equal success, when Lady Nithsdale assisted her husband to make his escape from the Tower of London in female attire.

On the 22nd, the Duke of Wellington held a grand assembly at the Elysée Bourbon, which was attended by the Ducs de Berri and Feltre, Marmont, and other distinguished English and foreign personages. His Grace was most attentive to his former opponent, and conversed freely with the French Marshal.

On the 4th of January, the English sentries at the gates of the Palais Royal, were relieved by those of the National Guard, and, within two days, a circumstance took place under one of the colonades, which might have been attended with most serious consequences. Colonel Thoroton, of the Guards, happened accidentally to come in contact with Victor, and immediately offered an apology for the unintentional act. The French Marshal, instead, however, of accepting the explanation, indulged in such strong language, that, in the heat of the moment, the Guardsman replied to it by the English process of knocking him down. A court of inquiry was immediately ordered by Wellington, and Thoroton was slightly reprimanded. On the following night he was present at an evening party given by the Duke.

About the middle of the month, the greatest excitement prevailed in Paris by the arrest of three Englishmen—Sir Robert Wilson, Captain Hutchinson, and Mr. Bruce, on the charge of having favoured the escape of Lavalette; and a question was raised how far Captain Hutchinson, who formed one of the effective English army, was liable to a civil process. The Duke at once declined all interference, leaving the affair to be settled by the laws of France.

The trial, however, did not come on in the assize court until the 22nd of April. Madame Lavalette, who was called by some of the accused, replied to an interrogatory of the President, M. Romain de Sage, in the following words:

"I declare that the persons now arraigned, contributed in no respect to the escape of M. Lavalette. No one was in my confidence. I alone did it."

On a subsequent audience, M. Dupin opened his defence for the English gentlemen. The President then concisely, and with great impartiality, summed up the evidence. The jury retired to deliberate, and in about two hours returned a verdict of guilty against Messrs. Wilson, Bruce, and Hutchinson. The President having read the articles of the penal code applicable to the prisoners, in which the punishment prescribed was imprisonment for a term not exceeding two years, nor less than three months, without hesitation, pronounced for the shortest term.

A general order, dated Horse Guards, May 10th, conveyed a severe reprimand to Major-General Sir Robert Wilson, from his Royal Highness the Prince Regent, for having obtained, under false pretences, passports in feigned names from the representatives of his own sovereign, and in having made use of such passports for himself, and a subject of His most Christian Majesty under sentence for High Treason. Captain Hutchinson was also strongly censured for "having been an active instrument in a transaction of so culpable a nature, more especially in a country in amity with his Majesty, where the regiment in which he was serving formed part of the Allied Army."

"Taking into consideration the degree of punishment awarded to these officers by the French authorities, the Prince Regent was unwilling to visit them with the full weight of his displeasure, and was therefore content at the expression of his royal highness's sincere reprehension, which was to be promulgated to the army at large."

At this period some inquietude was shown in Paris, owing to a rumour that an attempt upon the life of the King would be made in the Tuileries; nothing, however, occurred to justify such a report.

Towards the end of the month, Madame Lavalette was restored to liberty, the tribunal declaring that there was no ground for her accusation. The connivance that the French Government were supposed to have had in the escape of her husband gave the caricaturists of Paris an opportunity of showing their wit. One of the best, represented the hero escaping in a female dress, palpably too short to conceal him, and followed by a dog holding a stick in his mouth, with a lanthorn at both ends. The animal was called *un Chien Barbé*, and was meant to represent Monsieur Barbé Marbois, Minister of Justice; the lanthorns showing the part the worthy functionary took in lighting the prisoner through the passages of the Conciergerie.

Nor were the epigrammatists less fertile in their

imaginations upon public men and affairs, for the two following "squibs" shortly appeared: the King was described as *Louis deux fois neuf;* while the numerous lucrative places held by Messieurs Roger Collard, De Serre, and Pasquier, gave rise to the following couplets:—

CONJUGAISON DU VERBE CUMULO.

" Cumulo," dit Roger Collard;
" Cumulabo," responde De Serre;
" Sat cumulavi, pour ma part,"
Ajoute Pasquier, leur compere,
Las de voir cumuler autant,
Amis, délivrons nous sans scrupule,
De tout ce trio cumulant,
Le peuple, que ne rien cumule."

On the 26th, the Duke gave a fancy ball, which was attended by the French royal family, the foreign princes, the corps diplomatique, and other distinguished persons then in Paris. Nothing could exceed the splendour of the costumes, and no one was admitted except in fancy dress or uniform. A quadrille representing the four seasons was the great feature of the evening; it was danced by an equal number of English and French ladies, all exquisitely dressed by Madame le Roi, the leading dressmaker of her day.

Upon the following morning, the whole of the British infantry were withdrawn from Paris and its environs, and the heights of Montmartre were delivered up to the French troops by the late Colonel

Mackinnon, commonly called "Dan," who commanded the rear-guard.

The English cavalry commenced their march on the ensuing Monday.

It is not to be supposed that a man holding the exalted position Wellington did, should have been entirely exempt from a variety of serious and petty annoyances, created by those who were envious of his well-earned honours, or inimically disposed towards him as the greatest conqueror in the world, and who endeavoured by the vilest slander to lower him to their own degraded level. For some years the Duke had been a victim to the scurrility of the foreign press. As early as the year 1813, a most infamous libel appeared in the Cadiz newspapers, founded upon an official representation from the Xefe Politico (political chief) of the province of Guipuz-coa, addressed to the Minister of War, complaining of the allied British and Portuguese army in the storming of St. Sebastian. The principal charge was, "that the town had been ill-treated because its former trade had been exclusively with the French nation, to the disadvantage of Great Britain."

To this Wellington indignantly replied that the accusation brought forward was one that could not be applied to the soldiers, "who could not be supposed to know, or to reflect much upon what had passed before they attacked the place; that, so far from the principal officers having harboured so infamous a wish as to destroy the town from motives of commercial revenge or any other, they had done all in their power to prevent it; and that he individually, against the urgent solicitations of several persons, refused, as in the cases of Cuidad Rodrigo and Badajoz, to allow the town to be bombarded, although it would have been the most certain mode of forcing the enemy to surrender."

In consequence of the above attack, the Duke addressed the following letter to Sir Henry Wellesley, then minister at Cadiz:—

"I do not know how long my temper will last; but I was never so much disgusted with any thing as with this libel; and I do not know whether the conduct of the soldiers in plundering St. Sebastian, or the libels of the Xefe Politico and Daende, made me most angry."

Disgusted as was the hero with the slander of the Portuguese authorities and writers, it remained for a scurrilous portion of the English press to heap even greater obloquy upon the Duke. Happily the example was not followed. Wellington might well have despised such despicable attempts, for he was regarded, not alone as the liberator of Europe, and the greatest commander of any age or country, but was looked up to as a man free from all glaring immoralities. The Duke had treated many attacks against himself with the utmost contempt; but when the name of an innocent and unoffending lady was mercilessly dragged before the public in connexion with his own, with that chivalrous feeling for which he was famed, the Duke at once made up his mind to appeal to the laws of his country. Never shall I forget the day when, being employed in the not very onerous task of writing invitations for a ball, the Duke, accompanied by General Alava, entered the waiting-room in which I was sitting. Seeing that they were in earnest conversation, I rose to avoid being intrusive.

"You can go on," said the Duke, "I have no private communication to make."

I therefore proceeded in my duty.

"Have you the newspaper?" inquired the chief, in a voice that made me feel he was anxious his remark should be heard; "I suppose it's the usual style of attack?"

While Alava was looking over the columns for the offensive article, the Duke (playing with his watch-chain, which he often did when absorbed in thought) continued:—"Oh! that mine enemy would write a book! But, perhaps it would be better to take no notice." The paragraph was then pointed out and read to

Wellington for the first time, for he had hitherto only heard that some libel had been inserted. In a second, a sudden change came over his features, while he hastily uttered—" That's too bad!—the writer's a walking lie—never saw her alone in my life; this must be checked."

Nothing more was said; but shortly afterwards a writ was served upon the proprietor of the *St. James's Chronicle*, for a libel on Lady Wedderburn Webster. The trial came on before Chief Justice Gibbs, in the Court of Common Pleas, the damages being laid at £50,000. The late Lord Campbell, and Sergeant Best, afterwards Lord Wynford, appeared for the plaintiff, and Sergeant Lens for the defendant. The imputation was conveyed in the following terms:—

"It was said at Brussels that when the Duke of Wellington returned from the battle of Waterloo (which, *en passant*, ought to be called the battle of Mont St. Jean), he went to visit the wounded—perhaps the wounded heart was meant. A word to the wise."

In another copy of the same paper, the following lines appeared, purporting to be written at Brussels:—

    BRUSSELS, 1815. FASHIONABLE ALLITERATION.
    " In the letter W. there's a charm full divine,
      War, Wellington, W——, W——, and Wine."

These doggrel verses were followed by more pointed insinuations.

After a trial of some duration, during which Wellington's assertion, that he had never seen the much calumniated lady alone, was proved beyond doubt, the jury found a verdict for the plaintiff. Damages £2,000.

While upon the subject of the press, I may here remark, that during this period the English newspapers were vigorously prohibited in France, the government of the newly-restored monarch highly disapproving of the liberty then evinced by what has since been termed the fourth estate.

On the 16th of March my chief gave another *soirée* and supper. Some apprehensions had been created in the morning, that the party would have to be put off, as his Grace complained of indisposition. It appeared that the Duke had eaten something the previous day which had disagreed with him, and the *gobe mouches* immediately spread a rumour abroad, that an attempt had been made to introduce poison into his food; his appearance, however, at dinner, in comparative good health, gave a satisfactory answer to this idle fabrication.

Again was the Duke subjected to further annoyance, in consequence of some unfounded statements having appeared in the English newspapers, respecting an alleged conversation that had taken place between Count Jules de Polignac and himself. This led to a correspondence between the two distinguished personages; the Count declaring that the visit was one of politeness, and that it was not for the purpose of conferring with his Grace upon the subject of a change of ministry in France. Wellington confirmed this statement, adding, "that he had been no less astonished at the interpretation which the English journals had given of a private visit paid to him by the Count; and that he would be happy to see a disavowal of it."

On the 12th, the Duke left for Cambray; and after remaining a week at his head-quarters, reached Brussels on the 19th, where he remained only a few hours, and then proceeded on to the Hague. The dulness of Cambray as a town, after the gaiety of Paris, was felt by all the staff, and by none more than by myself; there was no theatre, no Tivoli, no public places of amusement, no Palais Royal, no Champs Elysées, no Bois de Boulogne, no excursions to St. Germain, Versailles, or St. Cloud; still, on the principle of making a virtue of necessity, we all set to work to promote amusement during our stay in country quarters.

The Duke's house was a large sized one, close to the principal posting establishment, Le Grand Canard;

but, as it would not accommodate all his staff, I was billeted in a small house near it. Being passionately fond of racing and private theatricals, I lost no time in seeing Sir Andrew Barnard, and urging him to do his best to get up a meeting, and some amateur performances.

"We shall have no difficulty about the former," said he; "for an excellent spot has been found within a few miles, which, with a little alteration, will make a capital race course. Horace Churchill has bought 'Monkey,' a Newmarket horse, and Smith and Stewart have a splendid animal among them, which they call 'Confederate.'"

"I'll soon put my horses in training," I responded; "though I fear in such company 'Little Driver' and 'Corsair' won't have much chance—but what about theatricals?"

"It would be glorious fun," replied the gallant rifleman, "if we could get a theatre, but I hear of none that would suit."

"Would not the loft over the stables at Le Grand Canard do?" I inquired, having already reconnoitred the town to find a temple for the dramatic muse.

"I fear the noise of the post-horses, and the execrations of the postilions, would mar a performance there, though Richard the Third would not in vain offer his 'kingdom for a horse;' but there is a greater objection, which cannot be got over—were we to attempt to remove any of the rafts, the whole roof would fall in—at least, so reports the Engineer officer who went over the building."

This was a death-blow to my hopes. Wellington stayed at the Hague only a very short time, returning to Brussels on the 26th of April; here he remained for three days. He visited the military hospital, where there were still some wounded men of the English, Prussian, and Hanoverian armies. Nothing could exceed the feeling of respect and gratitude which the people evinced towards the hero, as he, in the most unostentatious manner, walked or rode through the city, conversing with those of all degrees who had served with him at the ever-memorable battle. On the 29th the Duke left for Valenciennes, and devoted the following day to examining the fortifications.

Valenciennes, which is a second-rate fortress, contains a citadel built by Vaubun. Among its historical recollections may be mentioned that, in 1793, after a siege of nearly three months, during which a considerable portion of the town was destroyed by the besiegers, it surrendered to the victorious arms of the allies under the Duke of York. Upon the march to Paris in 1815, it was again taken by the British troops under Lord Colville, and I may state that the town is interesting, from having been the birth-place of Froissart and Watteau.

On the 1st of May, Wellington reached head-quarters; and no sooner was he established there, than he looked out for a country residence in the neighbourhood, where he might enjoy, in the sports of the field, a little relaxation from the cares of public life. The Château Mont St. Martin, within sixteen miles of the garrison, was selected, and the Duke shortly afterwards took possession of it. It was a large, old-fashioned, French country house, situated in rather a bleak, open district, near the source of the river Escaut. Cambray is a town of considerable importance, famed for its fine manufacture of muslin; it can also boast of having been the episcopal see of Fénélon, who was buried within its walls, but whose coffin was afterwards desecrated by the revolutionists in 1793, when the cathedral was razed to the ground.

Nothing could exceed the hospitality of the Duke, or his desire to promote the amusement of all who came within the circle of his acquaintance; and strangers, paying a passing visit to the Château, or villegiatura, who witnessed the simple habits of the host, could scarcely imagine that they were in the presence of that man, who, according to the authority of a reverend divine, " eclipsed the splendour of Hannibal, and dimmed the glory of Cæsar."

The Duke was ever a great supporter of field sports, and had also during the Peninsular campaign kept a pack of fox-hounds. The object of his Grace was not merely to enliven the leisure hours of himself and officers, during the monotony of winter-quarters, but to encourage a manly and invigorating amusement, tending greatly to promote health, activity, and courage. A gallant brother-in-arms, the late Lord Vivian, during a debate upon the Game Laws, said, " I own I am proud of sporting, and the greatest commander the world ever saw has declared, ' that he found the men who followed the hounds brave and valiant soldiers.'"

The Duke often quoted cases to prove the advantage to be derived from field sports, remarking, "that if fox-hunting was put an end to, the breed of horses would greatly degenerate." One anecdote mentioned by his Grace will fully confirm the justice of this opinion:

During the campaign in the Peninsula, the late Colonel Felton Hervey, of the "fighting Fourteenth" Light Dragoons, who had lost an arm, rode up, by mistake, to a small detachment of the enemy's cavalry. Fortunately, for the British officer, the men happened to be dismounted, and busily employed in cooking their rations. But no sooner was the Colonel discovered, and his rank recognised, than the word "à cheval!" was given.

Hervey, with his orderly, were both mounted on first-rate English hunters, belonging to the former, and finding the odds were greatly against them, immediately started off at a tremendous pace to reach their own lines.

The French dragoons were quickly in their saddles, for their prize was worth gaining, and amidst wild shouts and loud halloes, gave chase to their flying foes; but failed to gain upon them. The noise attracted the attention of some of the enemy's lancers, who, being posted nearer the English forces, were enabled to cut off the retreat of the fugitives. The clattering of the horses' hoofs who had lately joined in the pursuit sounded like a death-knell to the two gallant soldiers.

"Your only chance, Colonel," exclaimed the faithful orderly, " is to make for that ravine!"

Hervey followed the suggestion; the ravine was a confined space, with only room for one horse to enter. No sooner had he gained it, than, on looking round, a terrible sight presented itself—the devoted trooper, knowing that the life of his commanding officer could alone be saved by the sacrifice of his own, had placed himself across the narrow opening, and was literally pierced and cut to pieces. The delay thus occasioned enabled the survivor to pursue his flight, and upon reaching the open, he gallantly charged a stiff fence, and was shortly out of sight of his pursuers.

Once or twice a week a fox or boar-hunt was got up, which was attended by the Duke and his party.

Almost all the young staff officers thought it necessary to assume certain airs; voting the regulation uniform unbecoming, they decked themselves out in fancy costume, with hussar sashes, gold embroidered waistcoats, elaborately-braided frock-coats, richly-laced trousers, and highly-ornamented forage-caps. Independently of this inattention to general orders, they pronounced "*home* service" (as it was termed) a bore! The result was, that the two aides-de-camp in daily waiting were very slovenly in the performance of their duties, which consisted of taking in the names of any persons anxious to see the Duke, writing invitations, and occupying the posts of honour at the dinner-table.

For some time Wellington had noticed these derelictions, and only waited for a favourable opportunity of lecturing his staff upon the subject. An opening soon occurred.

A large party were staying at the château; and, during the evening, the Duke, anxious to have an uninterrupted conversation with one of his oldest friends, about to return to England, and not wishing to be uncourteous to the rest of his guests, proposed that two rubbers of whist and a round game should be made up. The steadiest of his staff at once very properly assented; while others who, like myself, were dead beat with the fatigues of a long day's shooting, and who were to be at the cover's side at an early hour the next morning, preferred their downy pillows to a hand at long whist, or a pool of sixpenny commerce. The result was, that one by one, we stealthily absented ourselves, leaving our host to entertain a somewhat voluble old lady, and a prosy elderly gentleman.

I had just gone off into a profound slumber, when I was awakened by a brother aide-de-camp, the late Honourable Harry Percy, who conveyed to me the unpleasant tidings that the entire staff were to attend the Duke in uniform, at ten o'clock the following morning.

Precisely at that hour, Wellington made his appearance, his looks denoting the strongest displeasure.

"I have sent for you," he said, in his usual quick tone, addressing the culprits by name, "to say that I am not at all satisfied with the way in which you carry on the duties. You are very inattentive when in waiting; often absent when wanted; occasionally late for dinner; sometimes uncourteous to my friends; and seldom or ever dressed according to his Majesty's regulations—thus setting a bad example to the rest of the army; and you, Lord William," addressing himself to me, "have not yet provided yourself with the proper staff uniform. I trust I shall have no further occasion to speak to any of you upon the subject. You are dismissed."

After this mild and just rebuke, need I say that we all determined to do our best to regain the confidence of our chief. The greatest difficulty I had to contend against, was the question of uniform, for unfortunately I had not provided myself with a full-dress coat: and as their royal Highnesses the late Dukes of Kent and Cambridge were in a few days to honour Wellington with a visit, I felt that I might be laid open to fresh censure if I appeared improperly dressed in the presence of such scrutinising judges. Had I lived in these days when a message may be conveyed by electric telegraph to a London tailor to forward a uniform by rail to France, my perplexity would have been removed; but as, at this time, intercourse with the metropolis was very tedious, the thought of procuring habiliments from it was at once abandoned. Cathcart, whose success in the Caffre war fully justified the opinion Wellington ever entertained of him, and whose death at Inkerman was so deeply felt by all— agreed to ride over with me to Cambray, to ascertain whether, among the officers of the staff quartered there, I could procure what I required.

We left the château with strict injunctions from the kind-hearted Colin Campbell, to be back in time for dinner, especially after the manner the Duke had commented upon the unpunctuality of some of his staff. Upon reaching head-quarters, I was fortunate enough to find a friend who possessed two full-dress coats, and I at once concluded a bargain for the best.

All I now required to make my costume complete, was a pair of Hessian boots. To have them finished in time was next to impossible; so I sallied forth in hopes of finding a pair ready made. No sooner had I entered the principal street than my attention was attracted to the window of a French boot-maker's shop, in which appeared a highly-polished, deeply-wrinkled pair, with red heels and gold lace and tassels, evidently placed there for show and not for sale. I do not believe that the proprietor of the original Chelsea bun-house, whose grim-visaged sign stands so conspicuously forth—or any of the numerous tobacconists, hatters, tea-dealers, and mercers, who court notoriety by their wooden Highlanders, tin cocked hats, silver canisters, or golden balls—would express more surprise, if a chance customer were to propose to purchase one of the above devices, than did the worthy *bottier*, when I asked the price of that identical pair of Hessian boots.

At first he assured me that no sum would induce him to part with them, but that, in the course of a week, he would make or procure for me from Paris an equally good pair. Eventually, by the offer of fifty francs, I became their possessor. I at once took them to an English boot-maker, and gave orders that the heels should be made black, the wrinkles got rid of, and the gold lace and tassels removed for those of the regulation pattern.

At the hour named for our departure, I found my comrade waiting for me in the yard of Le Grand Canard, where our horses had been put up, and mounting them we were soon on our way back to Mont St. Martin. In order to save some little distance, we had diverged from the main road, and were quietly cantering across the country, when, all of a sudden, we found ourselves enveloped in a dense fog.

"How truly unfortunate!" I exclaimed; "we shall lose our way, and be too late for dinner."

"Follow me," said George Cathcart, than whom a finer fellow never existed. "Keep as close as you can—I'll pilot you safe."

Increasing the pace, we traversed the open plains and hills, skirted the small plantation, crossed the ploughed land, and at the expiration of an hour were gladdened by the welcome sight of the lights at the Château.

"Why, you came as straight as a bird could fly," I remarked.

"This accounts for it," he responded, showing me a mariner's compass, so arranged in a small lanthern, that, when lit, the index became visible. "Take my advice," he continued, "never be without one—it has often saved me from passing many a night in the open air."

We reached Mont St. Martin in excellent time, and, when assembled before dinner, found no trace of anger upon the Duke's countenance.

Upon the following morning, his Grace, having received an intimation that his Royal visitors would arrive at Cambray in the course of the next day, left for that garrison, and great was his Grace's astonishment, when the staff were assembled, to find one and all dressed according to regulation. He look pleased, expressed his satisfaction, and delicately communicated to me, through Colin Campbell, that he did not insist upon every officer possessing a full-dress coat, so long as he did not indulge in fancies of his own. This was said in consideration of the state of my finances, which were not in an over-flourishing condition; Wellington knowing full well that so expensive a uniform would form a large item, when deducted from the pay of a lieutenant and extra aide-de-camp.

The Duke, who was proverbial for punctuality, and who often remarked that exactness as to time was as necessary in objects of pleasure as in matters of business, was ready at five o'clock in the afternoon to receive his illustrious visitors, and his personal staff were all drawn up to attend upon their chief. Every one has heard the anecdote of the inquisitive personage who inquired of the Duke whether it was true that he had been *surprised* at Waterloo, and his quaint reply, "I never was till now." I am not bold enough to assert that the warrior ever was surprised; but if he were, it was upon the occasion I refer to, when he saw the writer of these pages decked out in a gorgeous full-dress uniform, a pair of white net pantaloons, the brilliant pair of French Hessians, sword, sash, belt, hat, spurs, and feather, all according to strict regulation.

A smile came over his countenance as he looked me over from head to foot; and his playful remark, that he feared my *pas de Zephyr* would suffer from the stiffness of my boots, proved how gratified he was at the attention paid to his former lecture.

At dinner I happened to be one of the aides-de-camp in waiting, and occupied the bottom of the table, when, to show that I had obtained full forgiveness, he took an early opportunity, as was then his custom, of saying, from the centre of a large table, occupied by the illustrious guests, and all the leading military authorities at head-quarters, "William, a glass of wine."

Here let me for a moment digress, and say how deeply I regret that the good old custom of health-drinking during dinner has entirely passed away. Such a friendly recognition often did away with a slight coldness; often cheered a man whom grief had overtaken; often gratified the heart of some veteran, who might otherwise have fancied himself forgotten; and, as was the case in the one I have alluded to, gave me an unmistakable assurance that every angry feeling had vanished away.

The Duke was extremely attached to those of his personal staff who had gone through the deprivations, the difficulties, and dangers of the Peninsular campaign (I select this period, from a desire not to appear egotistical); and certainly those who composed it were, generally speaking, young men of active habits and good constitutions, possessing courage, judgment, quickness, and decision.

The staff consisted of the late Lord Fitzroy Somerset, afterwards Lord Raglan; another gallant Plantagenet, his nephew, the late Duke of Beaufort, then Marquis of Worcester; the late Duke of Richmond, then Earl of March; Lords George Lennox, and William Russell; the Hons. Fitzroy Stanhope, Harry Percy, Alexander Gordon, Colin Campbell, John Fremantle, Canning, and last not least, the Prince of Orange.

The hunting-field in England had made most of the staff fully competent for a not very unimportant part of their duty—that of conveying orders to distant posts, which, in a wild mountainous country, with an enemy on the look-out, was no easy task.

It was a surprise that the French officers could not get over, when they saw the striplings that attended the British Commander-in-Chief; for in their army, few under the rank of full colonels were attached to the Emperor, or his generals. Yet these young soldiers did their duty in the most meritorious manner, so as to gain the thanks and confidence of their chief.

Never shall I forget the look of astonishment the Emperor of Russia gave me, when, at a review of his troops, I addressed myself to his Majesty, on the part of my General, Wellington. I was afterwards told, at dinner, by a Russian officer, who sat next to me, that his Imperial master could scarcely believe his senses, when he heard that a youth in his sixteenth year held so distinguished and responsible a situation as extra aide-de-camp to the Commander-in-Chief.

On the 22nd of October a grand review took place on the Plains of Denain. Their Royal Highnesses the Dukes of Kent and Cambridge were received by Wellington at the head of his army, the bands playing the National Anthem. The troops were then put through a variety of manœuvres, which were in some little degree marred by the state of the ground, a continued rain of eight and forty hours having completely inundated the country. The Duke, however, was no fine weather soldier, and continued his evolutions until nearly five o'clock in the afternoon.

After a splendid dinner, given by his Grace to his royal visitors at Valenciennes, there was a ball, which was attended by their Royal Highnesses, and all the officers of the garrisons of Cambray and Valenciennes, that could be spared from their duties.

Every exertion was made by the late Lord Keane, Sir Charles Colville, and the officers under their command, to render agreeable the sejour of the Royal Dukes and Wellington in the garrison. Dinners, balls, suppers, and amateur performances took place; and the illustrious visitors expressed their admiration at the efficient manner in which the theatricals were got up, under the able direction of Commissioner Fonblanque, late of the Court of Bankruptcy, then an officer in the 21st Fusiliers. Never shall I forget the shout of laughter, that Wellington indulged in, at the performance of the highly-talented author of "Highways and Byways," or the attention with which he listened to the singing of Messrs Meade,

Fairfield, and Kelly—the latter an especial favourite at head-quarters.

Out of the above Corps Dramatique, four of the members afterwards resigned their commissions, and made the stage their profession. Coles, the Calcraft of the Dublin Theatre, a first-rate scholar and writer, Prescott, Yates, and Benson Hill.

Garrison races took place twice a year in the neighbourhood of head-quarters. A company of French comedians had erected and opened a temporary theatre in Cambray, and private theatricals were shortly established at the château, under the immediate patronage of Wellington. The following play-bill was duly issued :

THEATRE MONT ST. MARTIN.
This evening will be performed the favourite farce of
ALL THE WORLD'S A STAGE.

Sir Gilbert Pumpkin . . .	Sir Andrew Barnard.
Charles Stanley	The Hon. Seymour Bathurst.
Harry Stukely	Mr. Stewart.
Diggory	Colonel Egerton.
Cymon	Mr. St. John.
Miss Bridget Pumpkin . .	Lord Arthur Hill, (the late Lord Sandys).
Miss Katty Sprightly . .	Mr. Cradock (the present Lord Howden).

A new Melodrama will shortly be brought out, with entirely new music, scenery, dresses, machinery, and decorations.

In other bills we find the popular farces of the

"Beehive," the "Mayor of Garrett," "Who's the Dupe?" with the announcement that Lord George Lennox would shortly make his *debût* in the character of *Joe* in the "Beehive," and that Mr. Henry Barnard (the late General) would appear, for the first time on any stage, as *Emily* in the same play.

During these amateur performances, the late Messrs. Mathews and Yates visited the Duke, and gave an entertainment, which was most successful.

In the summer of 1816, the Duke inspected the Russian and Prussian armies. Nothing could exceed the brilliancy of these reviews. Sham fights, mimic representations of sieges, "faint images of war," took place; towns were attacked, rivers forded, woods defended, and enemies dislodged. To such an extent was the *esprit de corps* of the contending forces carried, that upon one occasion, when sent by Wellington to order a regiment to retire, as the combatants were getting too much in earnest, I had the greatest difficulty in checking their ardour, although armed with the authority of the Commander-in-chief.

A practical joke was played one night upon poor Joe Kelly, which caused a great laugh at his expense. He had been dining with some convivial friends in the guard-room, and, to the surprise of all, showed the greatest anxiety to get away at ten o'clock, pleading an engagement to escort some ladies to a suburban masquerade. The rest of the party, who had anticipated a musical treat, among them myself, were loud in our wailings; but Kelly was inflexible. The ladies, dressed *en costume,* had called for him, and had sent in a pilgrim's garb, in which their chaperon was to disguise himself—not the only *disguise,* for the wine had passed freely, and all were more or less under the influence of the jolly god.

Kelly was now called upon to sing the "Irish Dragoon," but he resolutely refused, and rose to attend his fair friends, who were impatient to get to the masquerade.

The officer of the guard ordered the sergeant to allow the carriage to pass inside the gates, and the pilgrim got in.

"Drive to the *Temple de Flore,*" shouted Kelly, "*Faubourg St. Louis.*"

The coachman drove on, and, arriving at the outer gate of the fortress, found it locked.

I must here explain that the guard-room, which had been the scene of festivity, was the inner gate near the town.

"What's to be done ?" exclaimed the disappointed masqueraders. Kelly alighted; spoke to the sergeant, found the keys had been sent to the commandant's office, and, greatly crest-fallen, ordered the coachman to return. They had not got many yards, during which the ladies were loud in their lamentations, when they came to a sudden stop—the drawbridge was up, and there was no possibility of proceeding farther. A sentry was on the opposite side, and the guard-room where the poor victim of the hoax had dined, was within hail. In vain did Kelly call for the officer on duty—a deaf ear was turned to his entreaties.

Nothing then was to be done but to bivouac for the night in the glass-coach; and upon the gates being opened in the morning, a few of my boon companions of the preceding evening and myself amused ourselves by strolling within the fortifications to see the coach pass, which it shortly did, containing our hero, dressed in a coarse camlet cloak, ornamented with scallop shells, two ladies in the costume of Swiss peasants, and one in the sober garb of a nun of St. Olave's, all looking jaded, and thoroughly ashamed of their day-light appearance.

Kelly vowed vengeance against the perpetrator of this practical joke, who, fortunately, was never discovered.

There was a celebrated character attached to his Grace, no less a personage than the late Mr. Turnham, his state coachman. Nothing could convince him that the glory of his master had not in some degree descended upon himself, for in conversation he always referred in the plural number to what *we* had done at Waterloo, how well *we* turned out in Paris, and how triumphal *our* entry was into the capital of France. Turnham was a first-rate man on the box, an excellent judge of horse-flesh, and a good sportsman; and considering his heavy weight—sixteen stone at least—rode very well to hounds. When taunted with his Falstaff-like appearance, which caused his horse literally to groan under this mountain of flesh, the rider would good-humouredly respond— "Ah, it's very well for Fremantle, and Felton Harvey, William Lennox, and other light weights, to laugh at me, but at sixteen stone each, I'd show them the way over the country."

With all this familiarity in the hunting-field, Turnham was a most civil, obliging, and trustworthy servant. He generally had a clever horse to sell, and in all his dealings was most honest and honourable; few men were more respected.

Turnham, after quitting the service of the Duke, kept a livery stable in Carrington Mews, May Fair; and, to the day of his death, was most liberally patronised by his former master, and his old friends.

I add here a memorial of one of my sporting acquaintances, of this time and place:—

"Died on the 9th of February, 1830, at Cupar, N.B.,

Mr. Thomas Crane, nine years huntsman to the Fifeshire Fox-hounds, sincerely regretted, as he was in his life respected by his employers. Crane, before his last situation, hunted the Duke of Wellington's hounds on the Continent until the conclusion of the war; and previous to his coming to the Fifeshire, managed Lord Stewart's, now the Marquis of Londonderry's, establishment at Vienna. Crane was no common soul, either with respect to his head or his heart; he was an enthusiast, and thorough master of his profession, both in and out of the kennel, and it did one's heart good, in riding with him over a country, to observe 'his quick eye glisten,' and 'his merry peal' play.

"With much proper feeling did Captain Wemyss, M.P. for the county, and the other gentlemen of the hunt, pay the last tribute to his memory. Crane was himself a native of Shropshire, a rare example to his equals, and to many moving in a higher grade; and the foxes alone in Fife will rejoice that poor Tom is no more."

To show that the sports of the field were not confined to head-quarters, I add a notice of a pack of fox-hounds kept by the late Sir Hussey Vivian, and the officers of the 18th Hussars.

The fox-hounds kept by the late Sir Hussey Vivian and the officers of the 18th Hussars, furnished capital sport. They were hunted by Abbey, formerly huntsman to the celebrated John Ward, and a better man never rode across a country. The foxes in the department Pas de Calais, between Montreuil and Boulogne, must have been considerably surprised at the English invasion; and the tally-ho's of the "Rosbifs," as we were there denominated in *la belle France*, must have been most unpleasing to their vulpine ears. On the 9th of December, we had a splendid run of seven and thirty minutes, finding Monsieur Renard at home in Lefaux wood, from which he immediately broke in gallant style, so gallant that we were almost inclined to take him for one of our own countrymen in his travels. Away he made for the earths in the Etaples sand hills, but being closely pressed by the hounds, who now "snuffed the tainted gale" breast high, he (as we say in the army) brought his left shoulder forward, and took to the "briny," where, not wishing to meet with a watery grave, he ran along the shingles, in the direction of Neufchatel. Near this place he was headed, and after making a few circuitous dodgings, he made for the wood in which we found him, but when within a few yards of it, the hounds ran gallantly into him in view.

Out of a field of sixteen, only five saw the end of the run. The pace was awful.

END OF VOL. I.

LONDON: PRINTED BY MACDONALD AND TUGWEL

www.ingramcontent.com/pod-product-compliance
Lightning Source LLC
Chambersburg PA
CBHW032043220426
43664CB00008B/833